THE TRIAL OF
MADAME CAILLAUX

THE TRIAL OF
MADAME CAILLAUX

Edward Berenson

University of California Press
Berkeley · Los Angeles · London

University of California Press
Berkeley and Los Angeles, California

University of California Press, Ltd.
London, England

© 1992 by
The Regents of the University of California

First Paperback Printing 1993

Library of Congress Cataloging-in-Publication Data

Berenson, Edward, 1949–
    The trial of Madame Caillaux / Edward Berenson.
        p.   cm.
    Includes bibliographical references (p.   ) and index.
    ISBN 0-520-08428-4
    1. Caillaux, Henriette.   2. Caillaux, Joseph, 1863–
1944.   3. Calmette, Gaston, 1858–1914—
Assassination.   4. Statesmen's wives—France—
Biography.   5. Sex discrimination—France—History—
20th century.   6. Press and politics—France—History—
20th century.   7. Political culture—France—History—20th
century.   8. France—Politics and government—1870–
1940.   I. Title.
DC373.C25B47   1992
364.1'523'092—dc20
[B]   91-2689
                                                                         CIP

Printed in the United States of America

9   8   7   6   5   4   3

The paper used in this publication meets the minimum
requirements of American National Standard for
Information Sciences—Permanence of Paper for Printed
Library Materials, ANSI Z39.48–1984. ⊚

For Catherine

Contents

Illustrations

Acknowledgments

A great many individuals and institutions have helped me in the preparation of this book. A National Endowment for the Humanities Fellowship for Independent Study and Research enabled me to indulge in a solid year of research and writing in 1986–87. I am grateful for the endowment's support and for the interest Kay Voyatzis, Mayben Herring, and Mary T. Chunko showed in my work. Later on, a President's Research Fellowship in the Humanities from the University of California provided the additional leave time that permitted me to complete the book. I also benefited from several grants of funds for travel and research assistance from UCLA's Academic Senate.

I did most of the research for this work in the Bibliothèque nationale in Paris, and despite the occasional frustrations of working in that mammoth institution, a historian, and especially a foreign historian, can only be grateful for access to the unparalleled collection preserved there. During my frequent trips to Paris my family and I enjoyed the extraordinary hospitality of our friends Marie-Laurence and Jean Netter. Their generosity made possible much of our stay in Paris, and their friendship made that time all the more rewarding. I am grateful as well to Marie-Laurence for helping polish my French prose and for sharing her exciting work on contemporary French politics.

On the publishing and editorial side of things, it is difficult to imagine how one could have a better editor than Sheila Levine of the University of California Press, an editor whose commitment to history makes working with her a pleasure. I thank Sheila for giving my book a very early home in Berkeley. I am grateful as well to Rose Vekony for shepherding my manuscript through the publication process and to Edith Gladstone for superb copyediting. Special thanks are due to Geri Thoma of the Elaine Markson Literary Agency; her advice and support have helped me all along the way.

Numerous friends and colleagues have read parts or all of the book in manuscript and their contributions have helped this work considerably. My thanks to Elinor Accampo, Judith Coffin, Nancy Fitch, Carlo Ginzburg, Ruth Harris, Steven Hause, Ted Margadant, Patricia O'Brien, Karen Offen, Hans Rogger, and Debora Silverman. I have relied extensively on the work of numerous other historians as well, and I hope my notes and textual references will do some justice to the intellectual debts I have incurred.

By far my greatest debt is to my wife, Catherine, whose brilliance as a writer, editor, and reader has helped me in more ways than I can express. She read every word of every chapter, often several times, and to say that her criticism was invaluable would be to understate the case. I am grateful for the way she pushed me to write better and think harder. Catherine's work and thought, more-over, in the fields of psychology and male-female relations have educated and inspired me, as has the example of her prose. Our intellectual companionship is just one part of a life together and with our son Jimmy that makes me feel fortunate indeed. This book is dedicated to her.

Prologue

On 16 March 1914 at six o'clock in the evening Henriette Caillaux was ushered into the office of Gaston Calmette, editor of *Le Figaro*. Calmette's last visitor, the novelist Paul Bourget, had advised him not to receive her; the impromptu call was strange, to say the least. During the preceding three months Calmette's conservative newspaper had subjected Henriette's husband, Joseph Caillaux, a former prime minister and head of the left-leaning Radical party, to a campaign of libel and character assassination that was ignoble even by the decidedly lax standards of the Third Republic. This campaign had reached its low point on 13 March 1914, when Calmette violated the one canon taken more or less seriously by Parisian pundits: the stricture against publishing a politician's private correspondence. The front page of *Le Figaro*'s 13 March issue featured the facsimile of an intimate letter Joseph Caillaux had written some thirteen years earlier to the mistress who would later become his first wife (Henriette was his second). The letter contained evidence of political double-dealing on Joseph's part and ended with an embarrassingly amorous signature, "Ton Jo" (Your Joey). By reproducing this document the editor Calmette added ridicule to his overwrought outrage against Caillaux. Even more important, the letter touched Joseph and Henriette where the moral climate of 1914 made them most vulnerable: their checkered personal pasts.

The violence of Calmette's campaign notwithstanding, the editor, as Bourget would later testify, received Madame Caillaux with consummate grace. Calmette was noted for a good-natured gallantry in Parisian literary circles, where he wielded considerable influence.[1] And though he was about to divorce his wife of twelve years, he could not but treat the spouse of his enemy with the consideration due a woman of standing. "I cannot refuse to receive a woman," Calmette had told Bourget minutes before admitting the elegantly dressed visitor.[2]

1

Madame Caillaux wore a fur coat over a gown strangely formal for a late afternoon business call. Her hat was modest, and a large furry muff linked the two sleeves of her coat. Henriette's hands were hidden inside the muff. Before Calmette could speak she asked, "You know why I have come?" "Not at all, Madame," responded the editor, charming to the end. Without another word, Henriette pulled her right hand from the mass of fur protecting it. In her fist was a small weapon, a Browning automatic. Six shots went off in rapid succession, and Calmette fell to the floor clutching his abdomen. *Figaro* workers from the surrounding offices rushed in and seized Madame Caillaux. Little could be done for their *patron* but there was no question in their minds as to what had occurred. They had apprehended a murderess, smoking gun in hand. Henriette Caillaux did not, however, agree to be treated as a common criminal. "Do not touch me," she ordered her captors. "*Je suis une dame!*"[3]

Instinctively, the office workers released their grip as Henriette attempted an explanation for what she had just done: "Because there is no longer any justice in France . . ." But before she could finish, an anonymous voice cut her off with an impatient "Shut up." A local doctor examined Calmette hastily, and as the wounded man was loaded onto a stretcher the police prepared to take Henriette away. She would have no part, however, of a police wagon and announced to the gendarmes present that her car and driver were downstairs and that she would go to the police station in her own vehicle. Madame Caillaux may have been a murderess, but she was a society lady as well; the officers agreed to her demands. With the police close behind, Madame Caillaux was chauffeured to headquarters where the *commissaire* formally charged her with murder.

Four months later, after a lengthy pretrial investigation and relentless publicity, Madame Caillaux's trial opened to an overflowing chamber of the Paris *Cour d'assises*.[4] The date was 20 July 1914, just two weeks before all Europe exploded into war. The diplomatic situation already appeared ominous to those who dared to consider it; unbeknownst to most Europeans, it became far worse as the case proceeded. By the midpoint of the trial, high Serbian officials had been given a diplomatic note from Austria that made the beginning of armed hostilities in the Balkans only a matter of time. At Germany's urging, Austria had prepared an ultimatum whose conditions were so harsh as to force Serbia into a Balkan war that the Austrian and German high commands were ready, even eager, to fight.[5]

Meanwhile French President Raymond Poincaré, unaware of the ultimatum Austria had been planning for weeks, had gone to St. Petersburg to shore up his alliance with a Russian government that was itself allied to Serbia. The Austrians knew that Poincaré intended to leave Kronstadt en route to Norway late in the afternoon of 23 July, and they purposely delayed issuing their ultimatum until just after the French president had left Russian soil. Austria and Germany wanted Poincaré—and Prime Minister René Viviani, who was traveling with him—isolated at sea and therefore diplomatically impotent for the duration of the six-day voyage back to France. Deprived of French leadership, the Triple Entente (England, France, and Russia) would find it difficult, the Austrians and Germans presumed, to respond effectively to a situation Berlin hoped to control.[6]

Thus, in this moment of international peril, the French leaders were as isolated from the escalating crisis as the Parisians were oblivious to it. For with Poincaré and Viviani alone at sea and inaccessible to the daily press, French journalists were free to neglect the mounting international crisis—a crisis from which most of their readers wanted to be shielded in any event. Instead of giving the diplomatic situation the attention it required, newspapers focused so intensely upon the Caillaux Affair as to create the illusion that virtually nothing else existed. So single-minded was the French press in its fascination with the Caillaux that Roger Martin du Gard made this fixation the subject of an important episode in his historical novel *Les Thibault. L'été 1914* (1936). In it, Martin du Gard depicted the frustration of his politicized hero Jacques Thibault, who finds himself unable to discover a satisfactory account of the diplomatic situation in any major French newspaper. "The story of the Caillaux trial," explains the narrator, "filled the entire front page of nearly all the daily papers."[7] During this crucial final week of July 1914, therefore, the French public was preoccupied not with the growing likelihood of war but with the trial of Madame Caillaux.

Parisians avidly followed the case in the city's numerous mass-circulation dailies, papers that not only reproduced the trial transcript verbatim but commented extensively on an event whose dramatic possibilities escaped none of the editors in question. The Caillaux case was the first trial in the history of France to feature depositions from a president of the Republic, and many of its other participants ranked among the most powerful and noteworthy members of French society. They included two former prime ministers, cabinet ministers, members of parliament, directors of the leading newspapers, medical experts, literary celebrities, and intellectual luminaries. The courtroom contest was conducted, moreover, by two of the Dreyfus affair's most celebrated lawyers. Fernand Labori, having defended Emile Zola as well as Dreyfus himself, now represented Madame Caillaux, while the distinguished old nationalist Charles Chenu pleaded for the Calmette family. He did so in accordance with the French judicial code, which provided not simply for a government prosecutor to press the state's murder charge but gave the victim's family (the *partie civile*) the right to courtroom representation as well.

At the opening of the trial, the central fact of Calmette's assassination was not a matter of dispute. Henriette Caillaux did not deny the shooting, and several witnesses confirmed that she indeed had done it. But throughout the eight-day proceedings she steadfastly professed her innocence nonetheless.

From the assassination itself to the beginning of World War I, the Parisian press relentlessly stoked the fires of this unusual trial. Journalists called it the "trial of the century," and its headlines commanded the attention not just of Parisians but of people the world over. Germans reveled in what to them was an almost incredible example of French frivolity at a moment of international crisis. And the British press was only too happy to narrate the details of yet another Parisian scandal, maintaining throughout the bemused tone of the morally superior. American correspondents, for their part, adopted a sober prose of disapproval tinged with hostility toward the Caillaux.

In Paris, the trial was narrated by the capital's finest *chroniqueurs*, drawn by an army of artists, photographed for the growing number of picture weeklies. Not until 27 July, a day when a trial recess produced no news, did the diplomatic crisis begin to rival Madame Caillaux for front-page attention. And as late as 29 July, three days before France mobilized for war, journals as important as *Le Petit parisien*, *L'Echo de Paris*, and *Le Temps* devoted more front-page space to the affair than to the hostilities abroad.[8]

The conduct of the *Cour d'assises* itself created a theatrical atmosphere that helped make press accounts even more compelling. Defendants, attorneys, witnesses, and even the presiding judge himself were allowed long soliloquies that enabled them to appeal beyond the jury to public opinion at large.[9] And in making their appeals, they were hindered by few legal or procedural restraints. Not only did French defendants have the opportunity to explain themselves at great length—Madame Caillaux's initial deposition lasted an entire afternoon—but they possessed the right to respond to the testimony of any other witness. Moreover, the defense lawyer, the public prosecutor, as well as the attorney for the aggrieved individuals enjoyed, in the words of the legal theorist Eugène Sice, "the most absolute latitude," "the broadest rights" to introduce evidence and question witnesses in any way they deemed necessary, short of outright defamation of character. Attorneys were not required to alert opposing counsel, or even the presiding judge, before introducing new evidence in a trial; lawyers for the defense commonly highlighted their closing statements with documents and exhibits unknown to the other side. Since the defense attorney's statement concluded the trial, the prosecution could not respond to the new evidence, however questionable it might be.[10] As for the presiding judge of the *Cour d'assises*, his powers, according to Sice, were "as vast as possible." The Président possessed the right, which he usually exercised, to interrogate the defendant—or any witness—for as long as he desired. And he seemed able to make whatever comments he wanted to any principal in his courtroom. In a notorious case of 1879, a Président who had gone so far as to accuse one defendant of "adding lies to infamy" was later found by the *Cour de cassation* (a kind of supreme court) not to have overstepped the bounds of his authority. Some twenty-five years later, another Président saw fit to interrogate Marguerite Steinheil, the defendant in a celebrated murder case, for three full days.[11]

Extensive as the Président's powers were, they were far from absolute. He did not possess the right to discipline either counsel unless he could demonstrate that one or the other had created a "tumult" in the courtroom. But because the *Cour d'assises* was regularly in a state of tumult—few settings could be more explosive than a felony court in which defendant, attorneys, witnesses, and judge could say almost anything to almost anyone with impunity—it was impractical for a Président to attempt to discipline a lawyer, no matter how provocative. Mighty though he was, the Président had, therefore, to contend with attorneys who enjoyed powers almost as extensive as his own, a situation that encouraged procedural stalemate and courtroom confrontations that no one had the authority to resolve.[12]

Thus the *Cour d'assises*, with its cacophony of all-powerful voices, its paucity of restraining procedures and rules of evidence, was a far cry from the decorous and controlled chamber of Anglo-American law. The French court seemed almost structured for drama; given a certain kind of case, it could produce a spectacle more compelling than anything the theaters could provide. It presented that spectacle not solely to those assembled in the courtroom, but to a nationwide audience drawn to the event by an unrestrained penny press.

Not only did the Caillaux case produce sensation, it invited judgment. Accordingly, the press did its partisan best to lay blame and assess causes. In general, right-wing and centrist papers charged that the killing had fulfilled Joseph Caillaux's wish to silence his political enemy, while Radical (center-left) and Socialist journals claimed that Calmette's libelous campaign had driven Henriette Caillaux to momentary insanity. Politicized readers, as a result, quickly divided along ideological lines. For the right, Madame Caillaux was a cold-blooded killer acting at her husband's behest; for the left, she was the victim of political machinations beyond her feminine control.

This ideological reading of Madame Caillaux's act made sense in the politically charged context of 1914. Joseph Caillaux was one of France's most powerful—and controversial—politicians whose many enemies hoped to profit from what immediately became known as the *affaire Caillaux*. His friends, for their part, took equal pains to minimize the damage to their cause.

Since 1914, most historical accounts of the Caillaux Affair have followed the original partisan pattern by arguing for one side or the other. Those on the right have continued to find Henriette Caillaux guilty, whereas those on the left have tended to absolve her of responsibility for her act.[13] It is often interesting, and sometimes crucial, to return to the arguments of a notorious trial simply to relive them, or better yet to reevaluate the testimony and the final decision on the basis of new evidence or new techniques. But in the case of Madame Caillaux, to pass judgment and assess blame yet another time would be pointless; no significant new evidence has surfaced to resolve the still ambiguous issues once and for all. What gives the Caillaux Affair its continued importance is the extent to which the documents it produced—the stenographic record of its testimony, the journalistic debates, the archival residues—give us access to spheres of the Belle Epoque's culture and politics that might otherwise be difficult to discern. This "beautiful era," from 1890 to 1914, is crucial to recent history, for beneath its surface of aristocratic elegance and bourgeois prosperity lay the conditions of a cultural and moral crisis that helped make it an overture to the most brutal war Europe had ever known.[14]

The importance of the people and the issues involved made the trial of Madame Caillaux not just a window onto the political and cultural history of the period, as any judicial case might be, but a crucial, even formative, part of that history. In my attempts to interpret the trial's meaning nearly a century after the fact, I consider not just the contents of its testimony and the categories of thought that gave it meaning. I also try to discern the ways in which that testimony helped shape—or at least crystallize—the cultural and political perceptions of those following the case. By reading out from one discrete, but in its own way momentous, event onto a wider field of politics and culture surrounding and encompassing it, I assess the ways in which French men and women perceived some of the most fundamental aspects of their culture: the meaning of crime and criminality; the legitimacy of political leadership; the changing conceptions of masculinity and femininity; the relations between family and nation, fathers and rulers; the differences between moral and immoral, just and unjust, honorable and dishonorable acts.

For some time now historians of medieval and early modern Europe have been using the records of trials, both religious and secular, to explore cultures and societies obscured by the absence of any other written records. This kind of work, made famous by Emmanuel Le Roy Ladurie, Natalie Zemon Davis, and Carlo Ginzburg, formed the vanguard of the shift from an economic and social history miscast as *histoire totale* to what could be called *histoire microscopique*, an approach to the past through one exemplary event or person.[15] The shift from social to anthropological history has not been without its problems, but it has enabled us to glimpse elements of religious belief, family life, sexual practices, and political power that we might otherwise have missed.

Curiously, this new microhistory has been limited almost exclusively to medieval and early modern history. It may be that this work has been so influenced by cultural anthropology—a discipline oriented toward nonmodern societies—that the emerging anthropological history has almost naturally devoted itself to earlier periods. The Caillaux Affair makes it clear, however, that historians of the recent past can also use key trials to consider aspects of culture and politics often obscured in narratives of larger historical processes. Between a *grande histoire* of important public events and a *petite histoire* of private and unimportant ones lies an *histoire microscopique* able, as here, to illuminate crucial links between gender relations and political conflict, between family drama and high politics, between personal honor and patriotic allegiance. Parisian society, moreover, is particularly suitable for microscopic analysis because France's centralization brings together in its capital city the diverse elements of a complex modern society: government, commerce, industry, the high courts, intellectual life, high society, and the press. In this dense urban setting a singular event like the Caillaux Affair, which touched on so many aspects of Paris's intense and interwoven life, can open new insights into the elusive links between politics and culture.

Unlike many trials of the medieval and early modern periods, the case of Henriette Caillaux has bequeathed to us a complete documentary record in verbatim transcripts of the courtroom proceedings. Official court stenographers recorded every word of testimony in the case, and the major Paris newspapers published these transcripts in their entirety. Thus, except for the occasional typographical error or inadvertent omission, newspapers like *Le Figaro* and the quasi-official *Le Temps* provide an exact record of every statement made by the presiding judge, the defendant, the witnesses, and the attorneys for the duration of the trial.[16]

This does not mean, of course, that the transcripts *are* the trial.

The trial itself was an oral and visual event in which tone of voice and facial expression, silences and gestures, helped structure the meaning of what was said. So, too, did audience reactions and the general emotional temperature of the courtroom. The transcripts, it should be noted, do refer to some of these sights and sounds, especially to audience reactions and to certain dramatic gestures such as Madame Caillaux's fainting spells, but transcript comments like "Mouvements dans la salle" hardly convey the tensions and drama that a courtroom incident can evoke. Nor do the countless journalistic commentaries that attempted to describe the atmosphere in and around the *Cour d'assises*, the appearance of the defendant, the attitudes of the judges, the look and style of the witnesses and attorneys. These accounts fill in much of what the transcripts leave out, but we must treat them with extreme care for, inevitably, they painted their verbal portraits from a particular point of view.

The dozens of photographs and drawings of courtroom scenes published in daily newspapers and picture weeklies add to our sense of the visual, largely obscured in the written transcripts. Nonetheless they cannot be taken as transparent representations of the trial itself. Editors determined which pictures would be used and which ignored, and their decisions were based in part upon how the photographer had rendered his subject. If the editor was hostile to Madame Caillaux, he may well have chosen not to publish a photograph that cast her in a sympathetic light. Newspapermen could not, however, completely determine what their readers would see—and how they would see it—because photographs and drawings often provide crucial visual information unintended by either the artist or his editor. In the drawing reproduced here (figure 1), *L'Illustration* may have intended simply to portray Madame Caillaux testifying to the court. But what it reveals, surely without meaning to, is the overwhelmingly male composition of the court. Madame Caillaux stands out starkly as a lone woman speaking to a sea of mustachioed male faces, as a woman subject to their gaze, open to their scrutiny. To viewers of the late twentieth century the picture shows the inescapable importance of gender in this case.

As these comments make clear, the transcripts serve as a *textual* representation of the trial, supplemented by the commentaries that surrounded it and the pictures that illustrated it. Without precisely

1.   Madame Caillaux testifies before an all-male court (Maître Chenu, third from the left on the bottom row, is the Calmette family lawyer; in the center, the white-haired man is Maître Labori, Henriette Caillaux's attorney (*L'Illustration*, 25 July 1914).

reconstituting the trial, the documents provide an excellent means of analyzing the realities revealed—and produced—by this celebrated case.

Given the nature of my sources and their status as a textual version of a trial of considerable historical interest, I structure my own narrative after the structure of the judicial proceeding itself. Each chapter corresponds (with one exception)* to a single day of the trial and to the individual who dominated that day, either through his or her own testimony or through the testimony of others. Each chapter deals as well with the topic or set of topics paramount on each successive day. In its chronological structure, the book echoes the order of the trial, with the important exception that within each chapter I move back—and sometimes forward—in time and space in my efforts to interpret the meanings of issues raised on a given day. This narrative approach results in a "thick description," an effort to examine the case of Madame Caillaux as a

* Chapter 6 corresponds to the sixth and seventh days of the trial.

manifestation of meanings that help explain not only the trial's outcomes but the key ideological and cultural conflicts in which it was embedded.[17]

Those ideological and cultural conflicts, and many other political and cultural phenomena as well, form the context of the trial, the surrounding aspects of life and thought that shaped what occurred in the courtroom and to which the trial itself gives new meaning. Parts of this context I construct from primary sources; the rest I draw from the contributions of numerous historians and other scholars whose work illuminates and informs my own.[18] My history thus necessarily refers to their histories but not merely as texts, as the poststructuralists would have it.[19] If we take history to be, at least in part, the knowledge of the past that results from research accomplished and evaluated according to the standards of a highly developed scholarly discipline, then we can refer to a historical context that exists "outside the text."[20] That context exists as a set of findings about the past—provisional, incomplete, and molded by language as it necessarily is—constituted in the present by a community of scholars and readers.[21]

Because the central character in this trial is a woman, a crucial aspect of its context is the way the (mostly male) writers of the period perceived women, and especially female criminals. Gender, always "a useful category of historical analysis,"[22] is therefore central to the attempt to understand the Caillaux case and the society that shaped its outcome. During the Belle Epoque, concerns over the meaning of masculinity and femininity loomed particularly large as men endeavored to assert the existence of natural and hierarchical differences between the sexes. This French preoccupation with gender—and with marriage, divorce, and the family as well—resulted in large part from fears following the country's defeat by Prussia in 1870 and from a perceived decline in French power that commentators related to moral decay and to changing relations between the sexes. If France was weak, writers commonly asserted, its weakness stemmed from a growing demographic deficit caused by the emancipation of women, the legalization of divorce, and the emasculation of men.

During the Belle Epoque private life and public preoccupation, sexuality and nationality, culture and politics, coalesced around the question of gender. Many of France's most pressing political concerns—especially its fears and obsessions over a potential war with Germany—were regularly expressed as aspects of an intensified war between the sexes. Political history was truly "enacted on the field of gender," as Joan Scott aptly puts it;[23] the *affaire Caillaux* allows part of this gendered history to be told.*

---

* I say *part* of the story of gender because the documentary record reflects the era's masculine bias. Since most writers of this period were more interested in men than in women, in the mostly male sphere of politics and business rather than the mostly female sphere of home and reproduction, we know far more about the principal male figures in this drama than the female ones. As a result, my discussions of Joseph Caillaux and Gaston Calmette are more dense and complete than those of Henriette Caillaux and Berthe Gueydan, Joseph Caillaux's first wife. I try to compensate for this documentary imbalance, but the paucity of information about the childhood and family backgrounds of the two women imposes inescapable limits on my efforts.

Henriette Caillaux and the Crime of Passion

Madame Caillaux was by her own description a "bourgeoise." Her parents lived comfortably not far from Paris in the town of Rueil. And she grew up with the expectation of a proper and early marriage. This Henriette Rainouard accomplished at age nineteen when she moved directly from her parents' home to that of her new husband, Léo Claretie. Twelve years her senior, Claretie wrote for *Le Temps* and possessed a modest reputation as a man of letters. The couple had two children, without whom, Henriette claimed, the marriage would not have lasted as long as it did. In 1908, after fourteen years together, Henriette asked Léo for a divorce. She had become involved with Joseph Caillaux a year earlier, and Léo allowed their union to end at once. There could be no question, however, of a quick marriage to Caillaux; he was still wedded to Berthe Gueydan, his wife of less than two years. Berthe proved more reluctant to give up her spouse than Claretie had been, and she succeeded in delaying Henriette and Joseph's marriage until October 1911.[1]

Once Henriette had realized her dream of marrying Joseph Caillaux, all was well. Or at least everything could have been, she declared on the first day of her trial, "if our lives had not been poisoned by slander."[2] She had found in her marriage to Caillaux "the most complete happiness." She was blessed with a husband who cared for her, a daughter,* and an unusually comfortable domestic life. Together, she and Joseph possessed inherited property and investments worth more than 1.5 million francs, placing them among the nation's wealthiest families. They enjoyed, as she put it, "a large fortune that allowed us to live in great comfort."[3] The photo

---

* Her second child had died in 1908 at the age of nine.

2.   Henriette Caillaux in a simple pose early in her marriage
to Joseph Caillaux (*L'Illustration,* 21 March 1914).

in figure 2, taken long before the Caillaux Affair, depicts that comfort with a look of happiness and serenity.

Unfortunately for the happy couple too many skeletons remained in both closets for their bliss to last. Joseph's political hubris had made him countless enemies, and the couple's adulterous premarital relationship would allow these opponents to cast their political attack in moral terms. As the trial proceeded, the right could condemn Caillaux's political stance, not on its own terms, but as the inevitable product of corrupt values.

Adultery, divorce, wealth, scandal, and high politics—here were the ingredients of a real-life melodrama that would unfold in late July 1914 from one judicial session to the next. For Parisians, with their love of spectacle, their addiction to the feuilleton, it was not to be missed. And because the French legal system placed virtually no restraints on the press, editors and columnists felt free to comment extensively on every aspect of Madame Caillaux's trial. Newspapermen seldom waited for a jury's decision before declaring a defendant guilty or innocent, and in the case of Madame Caillaux they made their judgments long before the trial even began. During the pretrial *instruction,* a procedure similar to our own highly secret grand jury investigation, the press published nearly all the evidence presented even though to do so was, strictly speaking, illegal. Thus, well before the trial opened on 20 July 1914 in the Paris *Cour d'assises,* Henriette Caillaux's case had already been elaborately tried in the court of public opinion.

In this atmosphere of journalistic license, the French press possessed more power to shape the outcome of trials—especially trials involving sex and politics and defendants like Madame Caillaux— than did the press of many other countries. "The English would never allow the press to comment so extensively on a matter before the courts," declared the conservative *Mercure de France* in an article on the *affaire Caillaux.* They would never permit journalists "to prejudice the verdict and publish the key documents of the trial. All this would constitute for them the crime of 'contempt of court,' which is severely punished."[4]

Once the trial actually began, journalists were all the more eager to narrate and comment because its cast of characters represented practically the whole of the Third Republic's social and political elite. And because the press focused so much attention on the Caillaux trial, the principals in the case took what advantage they could of the almost unprecedented publicity. The Caillaux and their opponents knew that what they said and did in the courtroom would shape the press's presentation of the case and thus the public's perception of their respective claims. Perhaps they realized as well that press accounts would affect the jury too, whose members were not prevented from discussing their case with family and friends or from reading about it themselves.[5] In effect, France's citizen magistrates, men drawn largely from the literate but far from independent-minded ranks of the lower and middling middle class, witnessed each case twice.[6] They heard it first inside the courtroom as members of the *Cour d'assises* and then outside it as part of a reading public influenced by the emphases and interpretations of mass journalism. By reading the papers, they could relive—and revise—the impressions they had formed in court the day before.

Thus when Judge Albanel asked Madame Caillaux to tell the jury "everything that seems useful to you," she knew she would have an unfettered opportunity to speak not just to the court but to the nation at large.[7] As can be imagined, Henriette Caillaux had much to say, and she proceeded to testify for several hours, interrupted only by the judge's occasional queries. A skillful speaker could take handsome advantage of such oratorical freedom, and Henriette more than held her own.

Because Madame Caillaux admitted to having shot and killed Gaston Calmette, her defense had to turn on extenuating circumstances, on the insistence that she should not be held responsible for her crime. The stakes were high, for if the jury were to find Henriette Caillaux responsible she could be subject to life imprisonment at hard labor or even to the penalty of death. If, however, she could convince the twelve citizen magistrates that her own emotions or the actions of other people had rendered her less than fully accountable, then under French law the jurors would have the option of returning a verdict of "guilty with extenuating circumstances." Such a verdict would save her from capital punishment or life imprisonment but would mean a minimum sentence of five years' imprisonment at hard labor. The only way Henriette Caillaux could avoid punishment altogether was to convince the jury that the circumstances on and around 16 March 1914 had been so extenuating as to require a verdict of "not guilty."[8] Since Henriette admitted having shot Calmette, such a verdict would not be easy to obtain. All her testimony was nonetheless directed toward this end. To achieve it, she portrayed herself as the victim of passions beyond her control, as a woman rendered irresponsible by emotions more powerful than will itself. Uncontrollable impulses, she maintained, had silenced the normal promptings of consciousness, making her lose control over her own actions. Calmette's campaign against her husband—and against herself as well—had upset Henriette to the point of allowing her nerves a brief but free reign. She was not, therefore, responsible for what she had done; hers was a crime of passion.

In explaining herself this way, Madame Caillaux made her appeal on two different, but related, levels. On the one hand she evoked an older romantic discourse, one that indulged, even idealized, women ruled by their passions. And on the other she invoked a newer scientific language that gave a powerful, almost determining, role to the nervous system and the unconscious mind. Thus Madame Caillaux moved back and forth in her testimony between literary and scientific images of the crime of passion, appealing to the jury as a heroine of uncontrollable emotions and to the experts as a victim of deterministic laws. Together, the two discourses heightened her chances of acquittal. Literature made the woman of ungovernable passions familiar and sympathetic, while criminal psychology placed her beyond the law.[9]

French editors and journalists understood the defendant's effort to portray herself as a passionate heroine, as the tragic author of a *crime passionnel*, for even as they described her manner and her appearance they did their best to undermine or to endorse the image she had endeavored to create. Conservative papers read guilt in her appearance, while those to the left of center generally noted suffering, pathos, and passion. In its opening portrait of Madame Caillaux, the rightist and anti-Caillaux *Illustration* asked its readers to imagine not a wronged victim or a female ruled by emotion but a careful player who measured her every word. For *L'Illustration's chroniqueur*, Henriette's dress itself betrayed an emotionless banality of character, a character that could command no sympathy:

> Her silhouette, soberly draped in black lightened only a bit by the blonde hairs beneath her simple plumed hat, is that of a young woman, discreetly elegant. It is the silhouette of a "bourgeoise," to use Madame Caillaux's expression, but of a bourgeoisie without character or distinction. She is almost neuter with her expressionless eyes, her thin nose, her thin lips, her heavy profile . . . the slightly cracked timbre of her voice. Though a bit harsh at times, jerky, staccato, measured, her voice reveals none of those sudden irruptions that betray emotion, passion, pain. No spontaneity, but much deliberation behind her exposition.[10]

Thus for *L'Illustration* Madame Caillaux's aura, youthful and elegant at first glance, was stolidly bourgeois upon closer inspection. The sober black suit topped by a simple feathered hat aimed for elegance but highlighted instead the ordinariness of her looks, the dullness of her character (see *L'Illustration*'s sketch, figure 3). The thin nose and lips, the cracked but measured voice gave away her lack of passion. She was so plain as to be unfeminine, even "neuter." This was no romantic heroine capable of great crimes of passion. Unspontaneous, methodical, she planned her every move. The passage's meaning could hardly be more clear: Madame Caillaux's crime had to be premeditated; she bore full responsibility for her act.

The daily *Le Matin*, somewhat more sympathetic to the Caillaux, drew its portrait with different strokes: Madame Caillaux's entrance was "studied perhaps, but full of mastery and self-possession." Her "modest black suit, barely brightened by the mauve of her blouse, is perfect for the occasion!" And appearing in this "discreet outfit," continued the *chroniqueur*, "with her eyes lowered, her pale coloring, her blonde hair, Madame Caillaux was a woman who seemed genuinely mired in unhappiness."[11] *Le Matin*'s description was far more nuanced than *L'Illustration*'s had been, for on the one hand Caillaux seemed to exude a kind of confident self-control, but on the other she betrayed a modesty and lack of pretention in the ensemble she wore. Absent from *Le Matin*'s account were all intimations of ordinariness and banality of character, and its writer took pains to affirm her vulnerability—and therefore her femininity—as well.

No one expected sympathy for Henriette from *Le Figaro*, and throughout the trial the deceased editor's colleagues prosecuted her on nearly every page. Their description resembled *L'Illustration*'s: a superficial elegance that failed to mask her essential ordinariness. She had a "physiognomy that hinted vaguely at a kind of Parisian elegance, but without distinctiveness and without charm." Overall, her look gave her "the banality of a shopgirl," the banality, that is, of the female commonly seen during this period as representing the vanity and superficiality of women at their worst.[12] But despite this blandness of appearance, "in her testimony she was harsh, dry, and without any emotion whatever."[13] *Le Petit Journal* went even further, suggesting that her features themselves revealed pride and premeditation. "Physically . . . she produces the impression of a con-

3. Henriette Caillaux addresses the court (*L'Illustration*, 25 July 1914).

ceited and willful woman. Her eagle's beak of a nose . . . gives to her profile a daring and haughty character exaggerated by the pale thin lips."[14] Finally, the right-wing *Echo de Paris* claimed that her black suit and feathered black hat conferred on Madame Caillaux "the physiognomy of a funereal Valkyrie."[15] She was a death rider from the depths of Wagner's imagination.

No doubt such descriptions did much to sway newspaper readers for or against Henriette Caillaux. Even more important were the psychological and sociological theories of crime and criminal behavior they had popularized since the 1890s and exhibited extensively during the trial itself. These theories tended to assign responsibility for crime not to the conscious will but to forces over which individuals had no control: inherited traits, environments conducive to crime, and impulses emanating from the unconscious or "suggestions" acting upon it. People committed crimes, the experts increasingly maintained, not by choice but because heredity, environment, and psychology drove them, often against their will, to violent and evil deeds.[16]

The crimes for which France's leading criminologists considered all individuals, and women in particular, least responsible were crimes of passion. Such crimes occurred, so the experts argued, when violent emotions triggered motor impulses arising from the unconscious—seen not as a Freudian repository of repressed wishes and unknowable desires but as a physiological switchboard that transmitted nervous charges to the rest of the body. These impulses could quickly and easily overwhelm an individual's rational faculties. As a result, a normal person could temporarily become an emotional automaton. Because such a transformation could theoretically happen to anyone, the experts claimed, it was difficult to hold the authors of certain "passionate" crimes responsible for their actions.[17]

With these deterministic theories widely disseminated in the press, where true-crime stories and popular installment novels had done much to arouse sympathy for heroines of the *crime passionnel,* Madame Caillaux benefited from both positivistic science and romantic literature. Both had made French men and women of the Belle Epoque reluctant to punish individuals caught in the grip of passion, emprisoned in an irrational state that science itself now deemed capable of engulfing almost anyone.

When Madame Caillaux took the stand on 20 July 1914, she began by describing the emotional effects of *Le Figaro*'s campaign against her husband. She knew he was honest and honorable, but the newspapers and the politicians were saying he had committed the most incredible crimes. According to them, he had given the Congo to Germany's emperor in exchange for privileged financial information that led to a fortune on the Berlin stock exchange. And with that illicit money Joseph was said to have bought Henriette a jeweled crown worth 750,000 francs. Joseph Caillaux, in other words, had shorn the nation of a prized colony in order to shower his wife with diamonds. Had this kind of reportage been confined to Paris's lowbrow scandal sheets, Madame Caillaux told the court, she might have been able to dismiss it. But what was so distressing about the sordid affair is how widely these lies were spread and believed. Calmette's *Le Figaro* was enormously influential, and the editor's good name gave credence to what he said. Everywhere Henriette went people seemed to mock her, to subject her to insult and derision. "Everyone greeted me with ironic smiles. . . . [And] I felt that they all were making fun of me and that I was slightly ridiculous."[18]

One day while sitting in the visitors' gallery of the National Assembly, Henriette found herself in the midst of a hostile crowd. When her husband mounted the tribune, people began to shout: "Caillaux, Congo; Caillaux, Congo. Go back to Berlin! Go back to Berlin!" The whole gallery seemed to erupt against her. "I was forced to steal away in shame. I didn't want to say anything; I was like a crazy person . . . I was overwhelmed with emotion."[19]

Never before had she felt such hatred directed against the man she loved. And it grew worse. At teas and parties she regularly heard her husband called "that thief Caillaux." And not without a malicious glee, her servants and tradesmen kept her apprised of all that was said against the Caillaux. The whole country, or so it seemed to Henriette, believed she and Joseph owed a lavish style of life to the Congo sale, to stock fraud worth six million francs, and to one deceitful business arrangement after the other. Joseph Caillaux was said to have enriched himself and his wife at the expense of ordinary citizens and shareholders.[20]

Above all, Henriette maintained, she loved her quiet life at home, but at the same time she valued her standing in society. By threatening both, *Le Figaro*'s campaign had made her miserable. Polite society had expelled her, while the newspaper on her doorstep had brought slander and hatred into the sanctum of her cushioned interior. She became distraught, nervous, anxious. She could not sleep. One of Caillaux's aides testified that he "was struck by the transformation that had come over Madame Caillaux . . . she seemed to me depressed, older even. She had about her the aura of a hunted animal." Likewise, Isidore de Lara noticed in his friend Henriette "a certain exaltation followed by moments of depression and discouragement."[21]

This, Henriette testified, was her state of mind in the days leading up to 13 March when Calmette published the facsimile of a letter

that would forever be known by its affectionate closing, "Ton Jo."
Caillaux had written the note in 1901 to Berthe Gueydan, then his
mistress and later his first wife. At the time, Gueydan was married
to the aide of one of Joseph's colleagues on the Council of Ministers,
or French cabinet, where Caillaux held the portfolio of minister of
finance. There could be no denying the authenticity of the document, for Calmette reproduced one of Caillaux's signatures beneath
the one on the letter. In it Caillaux, long the champion of France's
proposed new income tax, had written: "Today I crushed the income tax bill while seeming to defend it."[22] Calmette claimed he
had printed the letter purely for political reasons, intending simply
to demonstrate the finance minister's hypocrisy. But he did not fully
convince, for the telltale "Ton Jo" was not excised. By leaving it in,
the editor gave the document not just a personal flavor but an illicit
one. It stood as evidence of Caillaux's adulterous liaison and thus of
his questionable morality.

The Caillaux believed that the "Ton Jo" letter had found its way
from Gueydan to Calmette and that the editor most likely possessed
copies of other personal letters as well. This other correspondence
affected Henriette directly, as it included love letters Caillaux had
written to her while married to Berthe. Henriette and Joseph believed, or so they testified, that by publishing "Ton Jo" Calmette
had signaled his intention to print the letters to Henriette as well.

What made them feel certain of this intention was the means by
which Calmette had prepared his readers for "Ton Jo." Shortly
before the letter appeared, *Le Figaro* had announced a forthcoming
"intermède comique" in the anti-Caillaux campaign followed by a
somewhat guilty disclaimer written by Calmette: "We are at the
decisive moment when we must not back away from any procedure
no matter how much it violates our customs or how inimical it is to
our standards and tastes."[23] For the Caillaux the word "intermède"
necessarily meant that something would follow, and the disclaimer
indicated that, like the "Ton Jo" letter, what followed would violate journalism's unwritten rule against bringing private correspondence into the public realm.

The Caillaux' claims about these letters were crucial to their case.
Not surprisingly there was considerable debate at the trial over
these issues. Charles Chenu, who pleaded for the Calmette family,
argued that the "intermède comique" was just that, an interlude.

The "Ton Jo" letter was to provide some tragicomic relief before *Le Figaro* moved on to other more properly political matters. Calmette possessed no other letters, claimed several of Chenu's witnesses; even if he did, he was too much the gentleman to print them. No, Chenu told the court, the shooting of Calmette had nothing to do with letters, for no evidence existed that the editor planned to publish anything beyond "Ton Jo." The shooting, he maintained, was purely political, designed to silence a campaign of *political* revelations that showed Caillaux for what he really was.[24]

Henriette and Joseph's response to Chenu's position was clear and plausible. Whether or not Calmette actually intended to publish other personal letters, they believed he did; in their enervated state nothing else mattered. Raymond Poincaré, president of the Republic and a political enemy of Joseph Caillaux, lent support to the Caillaux' argument. In a sworn deposition Poincaré confirmed that just after "Ton Jo" had appeared, a distraught Caillaux told him of his fear that Calmette would publish letters harmful to Henriette. Caillaux had added, according to the president's deposition, that the prospect of seeing the letters in print had horrified his wife.[25]

So upset, in fact, was Henriette that she claimed to have contemplated suicide. "I thought about killing myself that day [when "Ton Jo" appeared]. . . . If you only knew what I would have given that day—if someone had asked me, I would have gladly given my life in exchange for the promise that these letters would not see print."[26] Why so extreme a response? Even before "Ton Jo" appeared she had felt depressed and humiliated; the letter made her lose control. "I had lost my good sense, my reason itself."[27] In her already anxious state, the fear that her past immorality would be exposed for all to see pushed her to the brink. "To publish these letters or any part of them would have been to lay out all that was most intimate to me, my most intimate secrets, the secrets I hold most dear and keep most hidden. It would have been to strip me of my honor as a woman. I had always been told that for a woman to have honor meant to live a life completely aboveboard, without liaisons, without adventures." Her father, a rich bourgeois with old-fashioned values, had always said to her: "A woman who has had a lover is a woman without honor." Were her father alive, Henriette concluded, he would disown her.[28]

By the middle of March Henriette had become so distraught that

her husband, oblivious until then, finally became aware of her anguish.[29] And probably without realizing it he made matters worse
by telling her he was going to "bash Calmette's face in" (*casser la
gueule à Calmette*).[30] He did not know exactly when he would do it,
but when the time was right he would. This reckless statement,
Henriette testified, convinced her that Joseph intended to commit
an act of violence against Calmette, perhaps even to kill him.
"At that moment a cinematographic film . . . flashed before my
eyes . . . I saw my husband, skillful shooter that he was, killing M.
Calmette. I saw him arrested, dragged before the criminal court." It
was at this point that "little by little the idea of substituting myself
for him . . . took over my mind."[31] Henriette had composed in her
brain the film script of a duel that could only end tragically for her
husband. The only way to prevent the scenario from being played
out was for Henriette, as she put it, "to go myself to demand
satisfaction from the editor in chief of *Le Figaro*."[32] As a woman she
could not challenge Calmette to a duel, but no code of honor could
prevent her from employing more feminine means. She had expressed a desire to "demand satisfaction" only at the *instruction*. At
the trial she explained herself somewhat differently: "My husband
would have protected me if I had been attacked; if he hadn't done it
he would have been a coward. But I, I wanted to defend him, just as
he would have defended me."[33]

Henriette's claim in this part of her testimony was to have acted
in her husband's defense, to have endeavored to protect him from a
duel that would have ruined his political career. But as we will see,
nothing could have benefited Joseph's career more than a duel with
Calmette, given the Belle Epoque's virtual obsession with dueling
and the belief, widespread among the male elite, that by fighting a
duel a man righted an affront to his honor and demonstrated virtuous masculinity. It may be, therefore, that by her attack Henriette
unconsciously sought not to defend her husband but to harm him,
not to strengthen his career but to undermine it. For the effect of
her action was to impugn his masculinity and associate him with
serious crime. In shooting Calmette, she may have sought not just
to silence her attacker but to end a political career that had caused
her so much pain and had made her, as she would explain to the
juge d'instruction, "tired and angry to have been the object for two
long months of insults and defamation."[34] Such, at least, was the

speculation of one prominent journalist, Guy de Cassagnac: "The pistol shot that has just killed Gaston Calmette has also killed, by ricochet, Joseph Caillaux: is this perhaps what the murderess had in mind?"[35]

Perhaps it was. There is evidence that Caillaux's political career had caused his wife considerable unhappiness not just in the wake of Calmette's press campaign but almost from the beginning of their relationship. In 1909, involved with Joseph in an extramarital affair, the then Henriette Rainouard condemned her lover for refusing to end his first marriage before being safely reelected to parliament: "With your miserable politics," she wrote in a letter seized by Berthe Gueydan and later submitted to the court, "you trample on both our hearts. You seem to find in that dirty beast [i.e., in politics] so much pleasure that it means more to you than anything else."[36]

Even after their marriage in October 1911 Henriette continued to be upset over—even jealous of—Joseph's political career. When he was asked to return to the cabinet as minister of finance in December 1913, she begged him not to accept, fearing "that something terrible will happen to us."[37] It is impossible to know precisely what she meant by this statement, but she may well have thought that something terrible would happen to their marriage. Perhaps the union was already troubled; according to the journalist Georges Suarez, rumors in circulation at the time held that "the marriage was in serious difficulty."[38] Some suggested that Joseph was involved with another woman. Even if untrue, the gossip alone would have been extremely upsetting, especially after the appearance of "Ton Jo," a letter Joseph had written to an earlier love. Its publication may have reminded Henriette that her husband had a history of ephemeral commitments and that he had not hesitated to leave one wife for another.[39] Joseph himself suggested as much in his testimony on the second day. "What could have disturbed [Henriette] more," he asked the court, "than a letter written by her husband to another woman? and what could have been more hurtful than the passage in [Calmette's editorial] commentary in which he said that the end of my first wife's marriage had marked the death of her illusions, her dreams, and her faith?"[40] Given Joseph's apparent inattention to Henriette's needs, and with all the rumors in circulation, the second Madame Caillaux may well have feared for the impending collapse of her own illusions, dreams, and faith.

Thus by March 1914, having endured week after endless week of political and personal attacks and of rumors concerning an extramarital affair, Henriette may have found her jealousy over Joseph's political life transformed into hatred of it, into a desire, however unconscious, to commit an act that would accomplish two purposes: silence Calmette and drive her husband from political life. It may be that Henriette's crime of passion, if such it was, took not just Gaston Calmette for its object but Joseph Caillaux as well. In committing her act, she perhaps imagined that she could restore Joseph exclusively to her. In a sense she did, for the assassination of Calmette not only required Joseph to resign from the government he dominated; it ensured his commitment to her defense. Joseph was deeply implicated in Henriette's crime by virtue of the newspaper campaign that had led up to it, and her trial provided the opportunity to vindicate himself as he endeavored to defend his wife. As part of that defense he had to commit himself anew to their marriage, for he needed now to appear proper and upstanding in the face of a conservative attack that condemned his political positions on moral grounds.[41] Commenting on the assassination's effect on the Caillaux marriage, Louise Weiss, the couple's longtime friend and confidante, would write years later: "These pistol shots welded together two beings who would soon come to hate each other. Their marriage was their true punishment . . . [for] the trial had rendered it indissoluble. The decision of the jury achieved the status of a sacrament."[42]

Henriette's assassination of Calmette may indeed have brought Joseph back to her but too late, it seems, to revive their love. Toward the end of Henriette's life Weiss asked what her initial feeling had been as she watched Calmette collapse to the ground in front of her. After a moment's hesitation Henriette responded, "that I did not love the president* [Joseph Caillaux]."[43]

It is likely that Henriette's statement—assuming Weiss's report is accurate—represented a retrospective transformation to conscious expression of what, decades earlier, had been largely an unconscious feeling. There is no evidence, in 1914, that Madame Caillaux

---

* After World War I, Caillaux insisted on being addressed as "le Président" or "Monsieur le Président" in recognition of his tenure as *Président du Conseil* or prime minister in 1911.

overtly questioned her love for her husband or that she manifestly wished harm to come to his career. To do so would have been to violate the very premise of their marriage: Joseph was, after all, prime minister at the time they took their vows. What seems to have reached Henriette's consciousness instead was the reversal of her unconscious wish—the feeling of love, not its absence; the desire to defend her husband, not to reduce his career to ruin.

Whatever her true motivations on the afternoon of 16 March 1914, and these we can never entirely know, she left the following note for her husband, just hours before her fatal visit to *Le Figaro:* "I realized that your decision [to fight Calmette] was irrevocable. And so I decided to take my own steps; I am the one who will do justice. France and the Republic need you; I am the one who will commit the act."[44] Henriette hastened to add in the courtroom that she had intended not actually to kill Calmette but to scare him: "I wanted to give him a shock."

These declarations may sound like evidence of premeditation on Henriette's part. But by drawing on contemporary beliefs concerning psychology and the unconscious she claimed otherwise. Over and over again Madame Caillaux explained her deed by saying she had momentarily lost control over her thoughts and her actions. "I was driven by a will that had taken the place of my own." And this substitute will had robbed her of all rationality. "I lost my good sense, my reason. . . . It was crazy [to go see Calmette], I know it. It was crazy!"[45] Earlier, during the *instruction,* she had gone into somewhat more detail, describing her body as the theater of a struggle between two opposing wills in which the violent irrational one simply proved too strong: "It was like having two separate beings inside myself, like two separate wills. On the one hand I wanted to go to an afternoon tea a friend had invited me to, and I put on a dressy dress; if I had been [she meant, if I had planned to go] to *Le Figaro* to accomplish the deed that I accomplished, I wouldn't have dressed up. On the other hand I felt a greater force take hold of me and it was the one that drove me."[46] It is noteworthy that she said "if I *had been* to *Le Figaro*" as if somehow her true self had not gone there at all. Perhaps she genuinely believed what she hoped to convince the jury: that the real Henriette Caillaux had committed no crime. An alien will had momentarily transformed her into someone else.

Virtually everyone who argued on her behalf, from her husband, to the sympathetic press, to Maître Labori, laid great emphasis on the psychology of her captive will. Hers was not, they claimed, an ordinary shooting; it was a crime of passion. Such crimes had to be judged differently, for people who committed them were not fully responsible for their acts. As one pro-Caillaux journalist put it, Madame Caillaux had begun by mid-March 1914 "to behave as if in a dream." She "acted without realizing what she was doing, as if driven by an unseen force that, nonetheless, was inside her."[47] The Radical *Lanterne* called the assassination "an act of unreasoned passion" to which "no will could oppose itself."[48] And her lawyer concluded that his client "was unconscious of her actions and must have been suffering from a mental disturbance."[49] Labori's conclusion was prompted, he told the court, by an unnamed but highly reputed specialist in mental illness who wrote that Madame Caillaux had obeyed "a subconscious impulse that resulted in a split personality." She had become "an automaton without will" for whom "the automatism of her weapon [the Browning] corresponded to the automatism [i.e., the unconscious operation] of her mental state."[50]

In making these arguments, Henriette's supporters echoed France's prevailing psychological wisdom on the crime of passion. And such wisdom abounded. France of the Belle Epoque was fascinated, even obsessed, by the *crime passionnel*, by murder involving jealousy, anger, and frustrated love. Psychologists, criminologists, and lawyers produced a steady stream of doctoral theses on the subject, while journalists and novelists turned the *fait divers*, or true-crime story, into a popular art. Nearly everyone, it seems, sought titillation or perhaps illumination from tales of passion-driven murder— of jealous husbands who stabbed their wives' lovers, of young women seduced and abandoned who poisoned the men who had betrayed them.

For the most part the French treated these crimes with indulgence, especially when women committed them.[51] Novels and newspapers romanticized individuals whose rage and jealousy exploded into violence, while juries regularly acquitted those, male and female, accused of "passionate" crimes. Significantly, the era's professional literature tended to encourage leniency on this issue.

Experts from all the relevant fields constructed a weighty intellectual justification for the people's tolerance of the crime of passion. It stands to reason, then, that Madame Caillaux and her supporters would hope to tap this reservoir of indulgence for murder. After all, whether friend or foe of the accused, virtually everyone connected with the case accepted the principle of a crime of passion defense. Save for the extremist *Action française*, the parties involved would leave unquestioned the notion that crimes of passion deserved special consideration. The argument in court would turn solely on whether or not Henriette's act ought to be considered such a crime. As the Caillaux' friend at *La Guerre sociale* put it, "I have no worries about the outcome of the trial as long as the jurors judge it as a crime of passion."[52]

Although no one cited precise statistics, those concerned with crime and the psychology of criminality believed that *crimes passionnels* were on the rise.[53] According to Louis Proal, one of the era's leading jurists, "such crimes [of passion] . . . are no novelty; what is new is their frequency."[54] Sensationalist reportage certainly made it seem that way, and Ruth Harris's recent research confirms, at least for Paris, the accuracy of these perceptions. Harris finds that murderous *crimes passionnels*—along with murders in general—increased steadily during the Belle Epoque. In 1880, five of the thirty murders committed in Paris were listed as crimes of passion, whereas by 1910 *crimes passionnels* accounted for thirty-five of one hundred murders. Men committed more crimes of passion than did women, but only because men committed far more murders overall. Virtually all the murders for which Parisian women stood trial— six in 1881, eleven in 1905, fourteen in 1910—were considered *crimes passionnels*, and only a third of all murders by men enjoyed the same appellation. As for the results of these murder trials, women were almost always acquitted, whereas men were acquitted less than a third of the time, suggesting that most of those who could plausibly defend themselves on grounds of passion were likely to be set free—although men were slightly less likely to be absolved than women. The criminologist Louis Holtz claimed at the time that most of those accused of crimes of passion remained unpunished; Harris's findings substantiate his view.[55]

These statistics were responsible, at least in part, for the Belle Epoque's professional interest in the crime of passion. Almost without fail the authors of learned books on the subject deplored the juries' laxity toward the authors of such crimes. But this jeremiad was usually reserved for the opening chapter. The substantive parts of these works tended to explain the psychological processes that produced crimes of passion in ways that in fact absolved killers of responsibility for their actions. For example, a well received medical thesis* by Hélie Courtis (1910) began by announcing that "nowadays, the crime of passion has become a crime without personal responsibility" and that "it is time to react against a disastrous tendency that portrays the murderer as a kind of persecuted martyr." But by the end of his book, after examining the psychology behind the crime, he concluded that "even if we cannot justify impunity for criminals of passion, they do merit indulgence from the judges."[56] Likewise, one of Poitiers's legal notables announced in a major speech before the local bar that the "sentimentalism à la Rousseau" currently in vogue had created an "unhealthy pity toward criminals." The result was a "state of anarchy" in which murder increasingly went unpunished. This harsh rhetoric did not, however, prevent him from concluding that "love is an essentially dominating power" and that "confronted with that power . . . it would be absurd to speak of full personal responsibility and unjust to withhold our pity and our indulgence."[57]

The period's commentaries on the crime of passion owed contradictions such as these to a pair of theoretical positions in the new field of criminal psychology that made personal responsibility difficult to establish. The first turned on a new belief in the power of the unconscious mind, in the ability of this most primitive realm of the psyche—its other realms being the subconscious and the conscious—to release nervous charges so powerful they could threaten consciousness itself, momentarily seizing absolute control over an individual's behavior. The second position concerned the lack of any absolute distinction between sanity and insanity: no one, psychologists had come to believe, was perfectly sane, and "normal" people often exhibited pathological behavior.

Related to these psychological theories was a social psychology

---

* Doctoral theses (especially ones published) are excellent indicators of the range of a given period's accepted professional opinion; dissertations that fell outside that range tended to be rejected. Rejection meant no degree, no professional credential, and usually no publication.

developed late in the nineteenth century that blamed the era's nervous disorders, believed to be widespread, on the tensions of modern urban society. "Neurasthenia" became the commanding diagnosis of fin-de-siècle French men and women overwrought and enervated by the claustrophobic intensity of their citified world. Noise, congestion, advertising, theater, social conflict, all overloaded the nervous system, creating a population of emotional time bombs. And for the working class, poverty and the perilous boredom of industrial labor magnified their effects. In the words of Louis Proal, city life, the "preoccupations of the struggle for existence, and the anxiety of poverty" have all "shatter[ed] the nervous system" as have "excessive indulgence in pleasure, worldly preoccupations, long evenings in theaters and drawing rooms."[58] How else, argued Proal and his colleagues in the social sciences, could one explain the era's high rates of suicide, divorce, crime, and alcoholism as well as its incessant revolutionary propaganda? Fin-de-siècle France had developed a culture of neurasthenia, one of whose by-products was the crime of passion.[59]

So urban society overloaded a nervous system that, for psychologists, was fragile enough by itself. According to Joseph Maxwell, a doctor who doubled as an assistant attorney general in Paris, a husband who found his wife in bed with another man could easily lose all rational control as the impulses of his nervous system took over.[60] Or as Courtis put it, the passionate criminal was characterized by "psychic troubles that suppress all control by the intellectual faculties over the muscular reflex that constitutes the murderous deed." He acted not out of premeditated cruelty but under the influence of "a succession of muscular jolts originating in a pure motor impulse." When a violent emotion like jealousy, or rage, or frustrated love took hold of an individual it "distort[ed] the functioning of the nervous system," producing "an explosion of simple reflexes, a succession of violent mechanical acts." The subject descended into "un état passionnel," a transitory state that could overtake a sane individual just as easily as a pathological one. This state resulted from "a momentary modification of the cerebral circulation . . . caused most often by a burst of emotion." In other words, a normal individual overpowered by emotion could become subject to the automatic mechanisms of his nervous system. Even those with "the most peaceful dispositions" could be overcome by

nervous impulses that produced "the muscular reflex that con-
stitut[ed] the murderous act."[61]

The message of this discussion is clear: normal people could
commit crimes of passion without ceasing to be normal. They simply were jolted into "a transitory pathological state . . . [that made]
normal individuals sick for one tragic moment." That is why, the
psychologists argued, the criminal of passion had to be distinguished from the real malefactor, who in the emerging French view
was the recidivist. The latter had been programmed by society and
heredity for a life of crime and operated out of a "cold cruelty . . .
and delight[ed] in the . . . satisfaction of vengeance." Unlike the
passionate individual who displayed profound remorse for an act of
violence, the recidivist* showed "physical and moral insensitivity to
the suffering of others."[62] The former acted out of love; the latter—
whether as burglar, assassin, or thief—acted from egotism. He
sought "to gain personal profit and material pleasure from his
crime." The passionate criminal, by contrast, was "essentially 'disinterested,' impelled by the violence of his love or his hate." He
derived no material benefit from his crime and afterward reverted
to his normal self.[63]

These arguments found their way into the press, and journals
sympathetic to the Caillaux would use them to plead for Henriette's
acquittal. On the trial's opening day *La Lanterne* asked its readers to
consider the state of Madame Caillaux's nerves: "After days and
weeks during which the nerves of this woman were constantly
shattered by polemics, by affronts, and by inexpressible terrors, the
moment arrived when *no conscious will* could work against the lure
of a meeting [with Calmette], and then against the insanity of
murder. The psychology here is simple."[64] The left-wing *Guerre
sociale* borrowed the psychologists' language even more directly:
"For months, her poor nervous machine sustained everything, endured all, but one day her system became overloaded, the machine
was thrown off course, and finally the boiler blew up." By the day of
the crime Madame Caillaux had reached a degree "of exaltation, of
neurosis, that blots out all ability to reason." Hers was "the act of a
lunatic, of an insane person whose reason and good sense could
return only after the nervous détente produced by Calmette's de-

---

* Italy's influential criminologists called the recidivist a "born criminal."

mise." The editor concluded by declaring that none of the women he loved and respected the most—including the most emotionally stable—would be "incapable in certain situations of a similar stroke of madness."[65]

It seems likely that jurors were affected by such arguments; Louis Proal certainly believed they were. In his seven-hundred-page work on passion and criminality, he claimed that since Rousseau, France's popular literature and drama had idealized criminals and created a popular sympathy for those who acted out of emotion. As he put it, "Novels and plays have so extolled the nobility of crimes of passion and so eloquently justified revenge that juries, quite forgetting the duty they have been summoned to fulfill, fail entirely to defend society and pity, not the victims, but the authors of crimes of this nature."[66] No doubt there is hyperbole here, but the statement contains more than a grain of truth. After all, one of the most popular plays of the late nineteenth century, the younger Dumas's *La Femme de Claude*, extolled the virtue of murderous revenge. And even Paul Bourget, the conservative writer and close friend of Calmette, published a sympathetic novel about a woman's crime of passion shortly after the editor's death.[67] Proal might have added that the romantic notions about passionate criminals pervading novels and the theater now appeared to find confirmation in the new science of criminal psychology.

The writer André Gide showed how this psychological theory affected jurors, including himself, in a memoir he wrote after serving in a provincial *Cour d'assises*.[68] In one case, Gide and his fellow jurors were asked to judge a man who had killed his mistress after she had twice refused to sleep with him. The jury, Gide reported, had been hostile to the defendant until a doctor testified that "a psychiatric and biological examination as well as the special impulsive nature of his [the defendant's] crime indicates a mental anomaly that attenuates his responsibility." What the doctor's statement meant to Gide's fellow jurors, the novelist wrote, was that the defendant's sexual frustration had transformed itself into an impulsive energy that extinguished his judgment and his will, causing him to kill the woman he loved against his own conscious intentions. As evidence that the defendant had not really wanted to kill his mistress, the doctor pointed to a series of severe wounds on the killer's own hands, explaining—apparently without irony—that the man had held the knife by its blade, not its handle, to prevent it from penetrating too deeply. That the killer had suffered while inflicting dozens of shallow wounds on his lover seemed to have impressed the jury deeply, for Gide wrote that the doctor's testimony turned several jurors in the defendant's favor. The panel struggled and struggled with its decision but ultimately found him guilty.* Gide dissented, however, finding that this was indeed a *crime passionnel*, which by definition deserved leniency. The novelist may ultimately have convinced wavering jurors of his view, for two days after the trial had ended the twelve members came together and, unanimously, asked the judge to pardon the defendant.[69] Despite this turnabout, it is notable that the jurors had initially responded with a verdict of guilty, suggesting perhaps that they found male authors of crimes of passion somewhat less deserving of leniency than their female counterparts.

Other leading intellectuals were less sympathetic than Gide to the *crime passionnel*, but nearly all those who commented on the jury explained in similar terms its penchant for indulging the perpetrators of such crimes. Summarizing a general perception of the jury, a writer calling himself Dap declared that "everything considered passionate, impulsive, is deemed worthy of indulgence."[70] The prominent individuals surveyed in the period's endless *enquêtes* on the jury system blamed this leniency almost unanimously on the pernicious influence of journalistic and professional opinion as well as on the theater and popular literature.[71] For his part, the eminent philosopher Henri Bergson agreed in an *enquête* sponsored by *L'Opinion* that "there is no doubt juries reveal themselves, in many cases, scandalously indulgent. They are almost always disposed to absolve crimes labeled 'passionate,' " and by passionate they mean "any crime that does not have robbery as its motive." But Bergson blamed not the press or psychologists or even popular literature but the *Cour d'assises* itself. He maintained that juries, especially Parisian juries, tended to excuse crimes of passion because the *Cour d'assises* seemed to them more like a theater than a place where decisions of life and death must be made. With its dramatic oratory, its robed magistrates, its noisy audience, the Paris *Cour d'assises* produced a dramatic spectacle not unlike the drama of the real theater or the

---

* Only a simple majority was needed in a *cour d'assises* to either convict or acquit.

accounts of murder and mayhem reported in the penny press. The *crime passionnel's* dramatized quality, he continued, led jurors to regard it as a kind of deus ex machina injected into real life by some "exterior fatality, as if it were an unreal event, an incident from a dream," that had nothing to do with "the regular work-a-day world of daily life that alone counts as reality." One final reason, according to Bergson, for the jury's indulgence for passionate crimes stemmed from the nature of the French law itself. The criminal code required jurors to rule not according to their reasoned understanding of the law, but solely according to the "impressions" they received from witnessing the case. The law, in other words, required jurors to judge the consequences of the unbridled passions of others on the basis of unreasoned passions of their own. Jurors, Bergson declared, "abandoned themselves to their feelings, to impulses untempered by any rational thought."[72]

Newspapers and other publications seldom solicited the opinions of ordinary jurors, but one such individual did manage to have his views published in *L'Opinion*. Léon Prévost, a milkman who had sat on the assize court jury in 1913, was asked why he had voted to acquit a young woman accused of murdering her lover in a fit of passion. "The man," he responded, "had done miserable things to her, and she took her revenge."[73] Apparently Prévost considered this explanation sufficient in itself, for he made no effort to reveal why murder was the appropriate—and justifiable—form of revenge to take.

Not only jurors but lawyers too deemed criminals of passion worthy of sympathy and indulgence because they could not be considered responsible for their actions, however murderous. Attorney Joseph Sur declared that "love extinguishes reason . . . and the most mild mannered become criminals. . . . The passionate person is no longer his own master."[74] Even Louis Proal himself argued that violent passions could temporarily turn normal people into murderers. "If we observe during their confinement criminals . . . who have found satisfaction in revenge, we note sudden reversals of behavior, changes of ideas and sentiments, which show them to be constituted like other people." It is important to note that Proal, like Henriette Caillaux, intertwined the two discourses—literary and scientific—to explain the crime of passion. For him, literature and the sensationalist press encouraged passionate crimes, but they did so because of their unconscious effect on the human nervous system. Passion, Proal wrote, "strains the nerves and . . . causes positive pain so long as it remains unsatisfied. This pain ceases on the accomplishment of the act of vengeance, for it brings about a discharge of the electricity that had been contained within the nerves."[75]

Given such discussion, much of it aired in the press, jurors and lawyers alike might ask themselves why individuals should face severe punishment for violent acts produced by a nervous system operating on its own. Moreover, jurors might unconsciously suspect that they themselves could fall under the spell of emotions gone awry. Had not the psychologists and their popularizers in the press suggested that no one, not even the calmest and most normal individual, was immune from such passionate responses? Or perhaps some harbored secret hopes that they too could be capable of heroic flights of passion. Popular novels and drama might rouse such hidden hopes even if they did not actually move people to commit tempestuous crimes.

What may have reinforced many of these feelings was the new way in which psychologists mapped the mind. Like Freud, French psychologists in the late nineteenth century had discovered a realm of the psyche inaccessible to the conscious mind.[76] They considered human beings to possess interior forces and inclinations that individuals themselves did not—and probably could not—know to exist. A whole realm of the mind seemed to have a life of its own, a life that could operate independently of the conscious will. For a people unaccustomed to conceiving the mind in this way, the unconscious must have been a profoundly important and disturbing notion. No longer, it now seemed, could individuals claim to exercise full control over their own behavior. Part of the psyche was strange even to itself.

These notions raised more than a few troubling questions for French men and women of the fin de siècle. To what extent were individuals responsible for their actions? Could the concept of free will be reconciled with the existence of an unconscious? And in the light of unconscious motivation how were certain criminal actions to be judged? Such questions seemed particularly relevant to the crime of passion, for many of those who killed out of jealousy or frustrated love had never before committed a single criminal offense, much less an act of murderous violence.[77] Their crime could easily be seen as originating in unknown impulses lodged in the unconscious, impulses that even normal individuals were powerless to stop. As the criminologist Raymond Saleilles put it, "there are acts that occur all by themselves . . . [as] elements of our inner being manifest themselves on the surface . . . without the conscious realization on our part that we could act otherwise."[78]

Meanwhile, criminal psychologists began to chart the psychic trajectory that led from unconscious motivation to uncontrollable act, from passionate impulse to violent crime. It all began, wrote the Italian criminologist Enrico Ferri, "in the obscure atmosphere of the unconscious." Next it traveled into the subconscious where an individual's moral and ethical values came into play. If these were unusually strong, the violent drives might never see the light of day. But, more commonly, the criminal impulse continued on to the conscious part of the mind where it "in most cases encountered no obstacle in the brain, or at least none powerful enough, and, thanks to a propitious environment, it manifested itself in the form of an exterior and muscular impulse."[79]

The amount of time separating the original impulse from the physical act of violence depended on the strength of the unconscious force and the weight of its opposing conscious resources. When the original sensation was enormously powerful and the conscious defenses weak or off guard, the physical reaction occurred immediately. Somewhat stronger defenses resulted in a "delayed reflex" (*réflexe retardé*); an individual with highly developed moral sensibilities might delay the reaction for days or even weeks. According to Maxwell, "the pull of the violent act encounters a resistance in the unconscious of the individual who struggles not to succumb to it." Unfortunately, however, those who succeeded temporarily in inhibiting the violent impulse might only make it worse. For in Krafft-Ebing's words, "within those having passionate natures, passion continues to grow on its own even while it is being combated by the person's own moral and intellectual entreaties." Come an accident or a minor disturbance and "the last germs of reflection and self-possession will be destroyed." This is why crimes of passion sometimes took place long after the original emotional shock. The struggle between impulse and consciousness continued "until the day when, resources of resistance having been exhausted, the impulse wins out." For this reason, said Courtis, "we must be very careful in attempting to assess the extent to which the criminal of passion is responsible. Even the most noble natures can slip up, and in their case more than any other a detailed analysis of the crime must accompany that of the delinquent's mental state."[80]

As this psychological discussion made abundantly clear, the concepts of free will and individual responsibility had become so clouded with ambiguity that even when premeditation could be observed, psychologists hesitated to assess responsibility. What seemed like premeditation on the part of a criminal of passion might instead have been "the struggle going on in the theater of the soul between the moral sense attempting to resist the criminal auto-suggestion and the passionate tempest that ultimately succeeds in demolishing all its obstacles."[81] Days and weeks might have elapsed between the original impulse and the act of violence, but delay did not mean the accused had spent the time planning his crime. He might instead have been trying to prevent it, endeavoring in vain to subdue the emotions surging within himself. Ferri even found such apparent premeditation "altruistic," for it showed a genuine "concern for the victim," an effort, however unsuccessful, to spare his life.[82]

With all of these troubling uncertainties it is no wonder juries found it increasingly difficult to convict defendants accused of murder. Indeed, the more serious the charge, the more reluctant jurors were to convict; individuals hesitated to sentence defendants to death or to a life of hard labor given the apparent possibility that deep psychological forces beyond their control had impelled them to kill or maim. Such reluctance was reinforced by the nature of French criminal law, whose all-embracing code instructed jurors to rule not according to any legal standards of proof or to any legal definition of admissible evidence but purely according "to the facts that constitute" the case at hand.[83] Law and fact were strictly separated, with the magistrates concentrating exclusively on the former, the jurors exclusively on the latter. Thus judges were forbidden from instructing the jury as to how it should evaluate a case's evidence in terms of any relevant law; magistrates were unable to give the jury guidance as to kinds of evidence it was authorized to consider. Jurors, wrote Eugène Sice, were to rely on "no other judge but their conscience alone." And to render their decisions they were permitted, even required, to consider any evidence they as individuals deemed relevant.[84] But in doing so, they were forbidden from taking into account the legal or penal implications of the ruling they were to make. Jurors were forbidden, in other words, from taking possible sentences into consideration in rendering their verdicts.*

France's courtroom code was a product of the French Revolution's effort to create a legal system accessible to the average citizen, of a revolutionary ideology that exalted common sense over professional judgment. This ideology reached its apex during the period of radical Jacobin rule. Robespierre and his fellow Rousseauians considered the ordinary individual, uncorrupted by the prejudice and sophistry of civilized existence, much more likely to render humane justice than the educated man.[85] It followed, therefore, that jurors ought to be guided solely by their own impressions, unencumbered by a priesthood of professional magistrates. To facilitate such personal and impressionistic rulings, the revolutionaries decided to have jurors, most of whom would be unschooled in the law, make their rulings purely on the basis of fact. "The facts," Robespierre declared, "are always the facts; even the most common of men can be the judge of them."[86]

On this question Robespierre revealed great naïveté; however well intentioned his legalistic populism, it made judicial decisions highly arbitrary, for the facts were rarely self-evident. Such was especially the case during the Belle Epoque when the bewildering array of new psychological and sociological theories—all widely disseminated in the press—made it difficult for jurors to know what the facts were, much less how to interpret them. Given the psychological considerations that had been introduced into the problem of guilt and innocence, from the omnipotence of impulse to the frailty of conscious will, the facts hardly spoke for themselves. And jurors, having been influenced by these popularized theories and then buffeted by courtroom emotions, found the facts of a given case relative at best. "As things stand today," wrote Jean Cruppi, the eminent lawyer and future minister of justice, "with the tangle of systems, with vulgarized theories disseminated everywhere—the-

---

* In practice, of course, jurors commonly tailored their rulings to the sentences required by the code. If they considered the prescribed sentence too harsh, they often decided to acquit.

ories of atavistic inevitability, of determinism, of the corrupting influence of certain social milieux—who can confidently declare a man guilty without emotion or any doubt whatever? . . . The school, the barracks, the book, the newspaper—all have acted on people's minds [even the most limited ones], disturbing their straightforward and absolute notions with latent psychological doubts, doubts that the words of the lawyer and the expert will bring to consciousness."[87]

During the trial of Madame Caillaux, it was precisely to these doubts and uncertainties, to the elasticity and ambiguity of the facts in cases of passionate crimes, that Henriette and her supporters appealed. They sought to establish as fact for the jury's eventual deliberation the notion that Henriette's emotional state had rendered her irresponsible, had led to an act for which she should not be held accountable. Having done much to accomplish this goal, the Caillaux and their allies went on to enlist psychological theories designed to undermine certain troubling "facts" established by the other side, especially the one on which they were most vulnerable: her apparent premeditation.

On the day of the shooting Henriette not only purchased and tested an automatic weapon, she wrote her husband a note announcing her intentions: "It is I who will perform justice . . . it is I who will do the deed."[88] This information, Henriette claimed, appeared more damaging than it actually was, for even while she made preparations for her encounter with Calmette she dressed for a late afternoon tea to which she had been invited. In other words, Henriette "didn't know what [she] was doing" and planned all at once for two different eventualities. It was as if a pair of opposing forces were struggling inside her, pulling her in opposite directions. Thus, she changed into a gown appropriate for an "elegant" afternoon tea (figure 4) and then composed a note saying she was off to "perform justice" at *Le Figaro*. "I was a long way from deciding to go to *Le Figaro* and make a scene; but finally, I said to myself, if I make a scene, that will make me late for dinner, and so I wrote [to my husband]." The point of her testimony here was to portray a debilitating indecisiveness, to appear to have been so torn by the two opposing plans—one harmless, the other fraught with danger— that she lost control over her own actions. "I was pushed," she told the court, "by a will that had taken the place of my own."[89]

4.   Henriette Caillaux in the dress she would have worn to the reception at the Italian embassy on 16 March 1914 (Agence Nouvelle, Paris).

Here was testimony that, intentionally or not, conformed to the psychologists' portrait of a criminal of passion. The experts had cautioned that what might seem to a lay person as premeditation could instead be evidence of an intrapsychic struggle between impulse and will. And Henriette denied premeditation on the grounds of precisely such an inner confrontation. She testified that on the day of her crime she sought not to plan her act but to prevent it. She had run errands and prepared for the next day's party. She had dressed for tea and planned to be home for dinner. She had tried in short to be normal. But despite all her efforts, she lost control. Unconsciousness triumphed over consciousness, impulse over will. "The idea of premeditation is absurd," declared *Les Hommes du jour*. "Psychologically, what we have is a poor insane person incapable of controlling herself."[90]

Even with her pistol pointed at Calmette, Henriette Caillaux claimed to have made one final effort to prevent herself from actually harming him, a last desperate attempt to deflect her unconscious impulses from their most potentially grievous result. "At the moment when I fired the first shot I experienced an almost imperceptible flash of consciousness, and that was to shoot down toward the ground."[91] By forcing herself to aim low, she imagined she would do no more than "create a scene"; Calmette would remain unharmed. Unfortunately, the editor instinctively dropped to the floor, placing himself directly in the line of fire. Calmette's reflexive reaction thus foiled the last of Henriette Caillaux's unrelenting efforts to prevent herself from fulfilling the inexorable demands of emotions gone awry.

Throughout her lengthy testimony, then, Madame Caillaux's story of unintended crime and unbridled passion seemed designed to appeal to a popularized psychology that stood a good chance of influencing the jurors' verdict. Perhaps they would not hold her responsible, and perhaps they would even identify with her. Passion, they might find, had transformed Henriette's mundane domesticized existence into a life of romance and heroism. To jurors of modest petty-bourgeois means it could be the stuff of forbidden dreams.

Joseph Caillaux

The Politics of Personality

With the end of Henriette Caillaux's testimony on the first day her trial took on a new aspect. No longer would it be entirely her affair, no longer would she be in charge of her own defense. Attention now shifted to her husband, Joseph, the former premier and leader of the Radical party who was one of France's most powerful and controversial political figures. Presenting his testimony on the afternoon of the trial's second day, Joseph Caillaux seized control of the case, moving it beyond the murder of which his wife was accused. Though Henriette Caillaux's act remained the object of the trial, Joseph Caillaux made himself its subject. He turned the proceedings into an examination of his life and of the politics he represented, defending his wife as he defended himself.

To press his case he deployed all the resources and all the techniques that had made him a master of parliamentary combat. With Joseph Caillaux's testimony, commented the Radical *La Lanterne,* "the courtroom was brusquely transformed into a political meeting hall in which two parties came together to do battle, each with the furious desire to deliver the final blow."[1] He appeared to relish the challenge of undermining not just the charges leveled by Calmette but the widespread perception that he posed a triple threat to French society: as architect of what many considered a revolutionary tax on income, as proponent of an "antinational" accommodation with Germany, and as exemplar of a libertine morality that threatened family life and national unity.

And so during the seven remaining days of the trial Joseph gave no fewer than eleven depositions, intervening at will and setting the pace, rhythm, and emotional intensity of the case. When he needed a break after the first phase of his monologue on the trial's second day, he suspended the session himself, inviting the judge only to confirm his act. Even after his three-hour deposition was over he secured, on subsequent days, the right to respond whenever his name was mentioned. At times Joseph seemed to reduce Henriette's distinguished attorney, Fernand Labori, to the status of junior partner as he spoke to the judge, jury, and witnesses with the authority of a sitting prime minister. Even the editors of *L'Illustration*, utterly hostile to the Caillaux, had to admit that Joseph was "a prodigious fighter" whose testimony was "not without a certain grandeur."[2] *Le Figaro*, the most antagonistic voice of all, only magnified his power and authority by declaring that "he seemed every bit the haughty conqueror. Robespierre or Tallien must have looked this way as they made their entrance into the Jacobin club" (figure 5).[3]

In reality, no one could have been more unlike Maximilien Robespierre—the Incorruptible—than Joseph Caillaux. Where Robespierre was prim, proper, and coldly restrained, Caillaux was flamboyant, unconventional, and irrepressibly emotional. But *Le Figaro's* efforts to identify Caillaux, a proud bourgeois who disdained revolution, with the notorious embodiment of Jacobin terror reflects the extent to which his enemies feared and hated him, the controversy that seemed perpetually to surround him. At the same time it reveals the fascination that Caillaux, like Robespierre, managed to arouse in spite of it all. Ever since Joseph Caillaux had soared to political prominence with his appointment as minister of finance in 1899 at the age of thirty-six, journalists and other observers had taken a sustained, even uncharacteristic, interest in describing, criticizing, and simply trying to understand this most singular of Third Republic politicians. No one else, it seemed, dressed with such flair, flaunted women so openly, or displayed a combination of intellectual power and financial acumen such as his. No one, in short, seemed to neglect his culture's reigning code of politesse and modest comportment as ostentatiously as he.

Joseph Caillaux's ascension to the cabinet came only a year after he had been elected to the Chamber of Deputies for the first time. Such rapid promotion was highly unusual in French politics, and Caillaux owed his early success to the peculiar circumstances of 1899. After a long and bitter struggle between the opponents and sup-

5. Flanked by his loyal allies, Joseph Caillaux enters the courtyard of the Palace of Justice on 20 July 1914, the opening day of the trial (*L'Illustration*, 25 July 1914).

porters of Captain Alfred Dreyfus, the Jewish army officer unjustly convicted of treason, the pro-Dreyfus side had emerged victorious at the beginning of 1899. The ruling conservative republicans, having refused to reopen Dreyfus's case, lost their political majority, and René Waldeck-Rousseau, a humanitarian centrist, was called to form a progressive "government of republican defense."[4] Waldeck's task was to shore up a republican regime that many on the left believed had been severely shaken by the nationalists and anti-Semites, the representatives of the army and the Church, who had sought not just to condemn Dreyfus but to undermine France's fledgling democracy.

To stabilize the republic, the new premier chose a cabinet designed to encompass the whole spectrum of committed republicans, right to left. And because he took the unprecedented and highly controversial step of including the socialist Alexandre Millerand within the republican government, Waldeck needed someone on the right to give it conservative ballast. Joseph Caillaux seemed the perfect choice. He had been elected to parliament as a republican, but everything else about him smacked of conservatism and the social elite. He came from a family of millionaires, albeit of middle-class origins, and as local notables in the largely rural Department of the Sarthe his parents lived the life of the landed aristocracy.[5] His father, Eugène, director of a major railroad company late in his career, had been minister of finance in 1877 under the conservative government of "moral order."*

As a boy Joseph had been brought up in the aristocratic tradition with English nurses and English governesses and had received his primary education from tutors at home. Later on he studied law and economics, and at age twenty-seven he became a member of France's elite corps of *inspecteurs de finance*, high civil servants usually of impeccable social standing and established fortune, whose job was to audit the state's financial affairs.[6] In this capacity Caillaux wrote the definitive work on France's complex system of taxation and won a teaching position at the conservative Ecole libre des sciences politiques, an expensive private institution that attracted well-to-do students who found the Sorbonne too middle class and too republican.[7] Thus, to his background of social conservatism— reassuring in itself to France's most timid republicans—Caillaux added considerable expertise in the realm of finance and taxation. This too was reassuring because his economic views conformed to the reigning laissez-faire orthodoxy. During his first year in parliament he was careful to limit his interventions to technical matters, thereby maintaining his aura of conservatism while doing nothing to alienate those to his political left.[8] Caillaux may have been young and politically inexperienced, but he provided crucial political balance to a cabinet that Waldeck-Rousseau hoped would be broadly representative.

From the beginning of his political career Caillaux had sought to exude a similar restrained republicanism in his home arrondissement of Mamers. He represented himself as the updated version of his father, as a fiscal conservative who understood peasant frugality but who had embraced the republic as France's modern form of government. Though his first electoral effort, a contest for a town council seat, had ended in defeat in 1896, the experience gave Caillaux an enduring taste for political life. Two years later he set his sights on the Chamber of Deputies, France's lower house of parliament.[9] The seat Caillaux coveted had belonged since 1871 to the

---

* In a famous incident in 1877 known as the *seize mai*, the government of moral order tried to undermine the young Third Republic by dissolving a legislature composed in its majority of dedicated republicans. The effort did not succeed, and the new republic was safe—at least until the Dreyfus affair reached its height in the late 1890s.

duc de Doudeauville, a wealthy septuagenarian landowner who claimed titles of nobility dating back to the eleventh century. The venerable duke was one of France's leading monarchists, a position that by the late 1890s put him in restricted political company; nevertheless, his local prestige and economic power had enabled him to stave off republican challengers for more than two decades.

Before deciding to run against Doudeauville Caillaux took the interesting step of offering himself to the duke as his successor in parliament. Joseph's father had been a deputy from the Sarthe, an ally of the duke's; the younger Caillaux perhaps felt it only natural that he should inherit a parliamentary seat. Joseph's social and political background was so aristocratic in style and method that his impulse was to seek an investiture, not to campaign democratically for office. The duke, however, had no interest in ceding his place to the less wellborn likes of Joseph Caillaux, and the aspirant was politely but firmly told that the duke would succeed himself.[10] Only then, with the possibility of aristocratic investiture closed to him, did Joseph look to the left for his political opening; he resolved to run as a republican.

Alfred Fabre-Luce, one of Caillaux's early biographers, wrote that this incident alone had determined the leftward orientation of Caillaux's political career.[11] But his is too narrow a view. As a student and then as a high civil servant Caillaux had already committed himself to the republican regime, solidly in place by the late 1890s for more than twenty years.[12] The decision to consult the duke betrayed neither opportunism nor a lack of commitment to republican politics but a belief that his wealth and standing entitled him to a parliamentary seat whatever his affiliation.

The duke's rejection may have convinced Caillaux to join the republican camp; doing so did not move him to renounce his family's aristocratic pretensions. In his campaign Caillaux blended his social standing and republican politics into an image of aristocratic modernism that promised gradual change within a republic overseen by natural leaders like himself. "Order and Progress in the Republic" became his slogan, the bicycle his symbol. He toured the countryside on the newfangled vehicle, emblem of technological progress and forward movement. But to remind voters of his reassuring ties to the land and the past, he looked and spoke like a gentleman.[13]

Thus, in his challenge to the real seigneur he made himself a republican seigneur. Caillaux, wrote Fabre-Luce, "presented himself to the crowd as an aristocrat and the crowd accepted him in this guise." He completed this princely persona with dandyish clothes and a haughty manner designed to impress a provincial populace that already saw him as a "Monsieur."[14] To many peasants of Mamers, he seemed little different from the real nobleman whose parliamentary place he hoped to win. "I don't see any difference between Monsieur Eugène Caillaux's boy and Monsieur le duc de La Rochefoucauld [also known as Doudeauville]," explained a peasant voter who ultimately defected from the duke to Caillaux and helped the young republican win the election.[15] On 8 May 1898 Joseph Caillaux was proclaimed deputy from the Sarthe with 52 percent of the vote.[16]

It would not be long before Joseph Caillaux, echoing the noblemen of yore, began referring to his constituents as "my peasants" and to his district as "my fief."[17] And as the years went by he would do everything he could to reinforce this image. During a visit to the Sarthois commune of Saint-Aubin-de-Locquenay in September 1901, a cannon salute greeted Caillaux as he entered the village. Church bells rang in his honor, and a local brass and reed band serenaded his dinner with the mayor. After the meal, a torchlight procession of more than five hundred people accompanied him to the next town on his itinerary.[18] It is likely that Caillaux himself had something to do with arranging this reception, for such political and personal showmanship would become a hallmark of his career, the aristocratic demeanor a staple of his personality.

As Joseph Caillaux's political career soared from obscure backbencher in 1898 to minister of finance (1899–1902, 1906–1909, December 1913–March 1914), to prime minister in 1911, he stood out in the grey world of Belle Epoque politics as virtually no one else did. The leaders of the French Republic were, in general, a staid lot. They seemed to raise middle-class ordinariness to a principle, and even those who advanced radical ideas took pains not to call attention to themselves in any other way. Their dress was conventional, their manner restrained, their private life always respectable on the surface.[19] In a critique of Léon Gambetta early in the regime, Henri Brisson laid down the rules for cabinet ministers. "We must choose men whose honorability is incontestable and whose private life

cannot be the object of ridicule or contempt for our political opponents."[20] Even Jean Jaurès, the Socialist leader who longed for
the transformation of bourgeois society, led a private life that was
strictly middle class. His wife, like the wives of most other political
leaders, remained at home and out of sight. Few spouses worked
outside the home or sparkled at dinner parties, nor were they
expected to. On the contrary; Joseph Caillaux's first wife, Berthe
Gueydan, provoked social condemnation for hosting a series of
highly visible soirées at the minister's residence. It was bad enough,
people felt, that she entertained like a *mondaine*, but to do so as a
remarried divorcée violated polite society's most basic rule, namely
that the irregularities of one's life had to be carefully hidden away.[21]
In the words of Jean Estèbe, author of an exhaustive study of the
Republic's political elite, "The case of Caillaux seemed . . . shock-
ing. To marry a former mistress after her own divorce was hardly
acceptable to the public opinion of 1906."[22] To exhibit his marriage
in public completely crossed the line. Both transgressions so of-
fended the father of Berthe Gueydan's adolescent niece Isabelle that
he refused to allow her to attend either the wedding or the ministerial parties, despite her close relationship with her aunt. Berthe's
uncle, Isabelle later wrote, was shamed by the marriage to the
degree that his health deteriorated and he died shortly thereafter.[23]

As for the way Caillaux's marriage affected his political career,
Roger de Fleurieu, Caillaux's lifelong opponent from the Sarthe,
wrote that Joseph emerged from the legislative election of 1906
"diminished" not just because his majority had been reduced but
because he had "married a divorced *mère de famille*."[24] Perhaps
Caillaux believed that he need not play by the cultural and moral
rules of his day. As a self-styled aristocrat, as someone proud of his
high birth and intellectual talent, he considered himself exempt
from these norms. He thought, as the journalist Louise Weiss put it,
"that no rule was made for him."[25] But what Caillaux may not have
realized was that the rules were made precisely for people like him,
people whose personalities almost compelled them to violate what
the political culture of the Belle Epoque valued most of all: the
preservation of an unruffled surface of cultural and moral order.
The greater the pressures for change, the louder the clamor for
workers' rights, women's rights, artists' rights, the more the Belle
Epoque's social and political elites endeavored to maintain at least

the appearance of what was familiar, stable, and proper. It was as if the elites believed they could be unorthodox only when the masses were orderly. With society in ferment, as it seemed to be during the years before 1914, those at the top buried their own cultural and moral transgressions to set an example of order and moderation.[26] Hence the difficulties facing Joseph Caillaux, who, as a member of this elite, refused to obey its increasingly rigid code of conduct.

As Henriette Caillaux's trial would show, Joseph's inability to accept the cultural codes of his society, much less to embody them, ultimately gave his enemies the means to overthrow him, means that Caillaux's command of parliamentary and party politics would otherwise have denied them. Only by making Caillaux's private life public, by making his cultural nonconformity a political issue, could his opponents remove him from a political world of which he was a master. Caillaux's ideological positions on foreign and domestic policy threatened large sectors of France's elite, but because much of the country supported those positions his opponents could unseat him only by making certain cultural issues—issues having to do with family, morality, fidelity—explicit political.

Sadly for Caillaux, his own troubled personality eased their task. Others less flamboyant than Joseph Caillaux, men like Raymond Poincaré who became prime minister in 1912 and president of the Republic from 1913 to 1920, remained unscathed by the kinds of transgressions that ultimately brought Caillaux down.[27] The difference between the two men was that Poincaré observed the conventions of hypocrisy embedded in the culture of the Belle Epoque and Caillaux did not. According to the era's unwritten code, a political leader could have a mistress, even was expected to have one, on the condition that he did not appear with her in public.[28] In *Mes mémoires*, Caillaux tells the story of a vacation he and Poincaré took to Italy with their mistresses: "mine I displayed, his he kept hidden." Caillaux later wrote that this difference of behavior between him and his future rival revealed a fundamental "difference of nature," one that helps to explain why Poincaré could incarnate what were seen as French values on the eve of the Great War and Caillaux could not.[29] As for their marriages, both Caillaux and Poincaré wed divorced women, but there the similarity ended. Unlike Caillaux, the future president of the Republic chose a woman willing to remain in the background, allowing the public to forget about her past.

Not only did Caillaux exhibit his mistresses in public, he went so far as to vaunt his success with women in the midst of parliamentary debate. In a 1905 discussion over whether to raise tariffs to protect certain silk cloths, Caillaux displayed an extraordinary knowledge of women's finery, both outerclothes and undergarments. Opposing the new tariffs, Caillaux argued that it would be fruitless to protect the particular kinds of silk currently suffering from foreign competition because women's tastes were too unpredictable. "Ten, twenty, and especially thirty years ago," he proclaimed from the tribune, "rich fabrics of thick silk, fabrics that hung straight and heavy on the body were essential to the female costume. Today, by contrast, soft and supple silks, mousselines, have taken over, have become the favored materials of dresses as well as undergarments (*applause*, interjected the parliamentary record)."[30] Caillaux, already known for his "liaisons élégantes," made it plain to his envious parliamentary colleagues that women's undergarments were hardly a matter of mystery to him.

Thus, unlike Raymond Poincaré, who seemed to embody the cultural conventions of his age, Joseph Caillaux regularly defied them. "What a man!" wrote Caillaux's first biographer, Paul Vergnet, as early as 1918. "Businessman, ladies' man, political man. He's excessive and rash in everything he does, from finance to love to politics. . . . This bald Don Juan, this great financier, insolent as a tax farmer of the ancien régime, . . . acknowledges the acclamations of Jacobin revolutionaries while counting the votes of his elegant female followers watching from the reserved gallery above."[31] Vergnet's portrait sums up what virtually all commentators saw in Joseph Caillaux: ego, excess, and enormous success— Caillaux as the ultimate demagogue, appealing to the revolutionary crowd while courting the wives of aristocrats with his money and power. This was a cartoon image, of course, but one that even some of his friends upheld, save that they added other crucial components: great intelligence, hard work, the drive for peace abroad and orderly change at home.

Still, given the way he dressed, given his aristocratic airs, given the way he treated those around him, Caillaux kept the cartoonists in his midst supplied with an abundance of material. Most of France's politicians dressed so customarily in the basic bourgeois black that journalists and biographers seldom bothered to describe their clothing. With Caillaux, they almost always focused on it, providing a reportorial attention to appearance usually reserved for women. The Socialist leader Jean Jaurès set the tone for all descriptions of Caillaux's appearance by calling him a "dandy straight out of Balzac."[32] Georges Suarez filled in the details: he wore "gloves the color of fresh butter, his chest swollen under a silk vest and between the lapels of a frock coat with the word 'seigneur' written all over it."[33] Others remarked on his vests of white satin, his coats so "elegantly cut" (figure 6), shoes of supple leather, spats, cane, and the omnipresent monocle, "attached by a black ribbon and in constant play either in his eye or between his fingers."[34] In dressing this way, Caillaux sought more than the aristocratic distinction of a dandy; he meant to thumb his nose at prevailing standards of behavior, to prove he could live by his own rules and succeed nonetheless. As a young cabinet minister in 1899 he created a scandal by appearing before the Senate one July day in fashionable summer clothes, something never done whatever the temperature. Worse, some thirteen years later, announcing his resignation as prime minister, he went to see the president of the Republic straight from a hunting expedition and still dressed, à l'anglaise, for the chase.[35]

Caillaux's looks received nearly as much attention as his dress. "No one," wrote Fabre-Luce "was as bald as he," and his svelte form sharply distinguished him from the portly patriarchs who surrounded him in government. Bald as an octogenarian but slim as a teenager, Caillaux exuded an agelessness that affirmed his uniqueness. His friend Charles Paix-Séailles supplied perhaps the most complete description: "His face [was] oval, his features regular: straight nose, thin mouth—shadowed by a moustache whose size followed the fashion between 1900 and 1914—and a sharp clean-shaven chin that betrayed a willfulness far from common. His forehead, greatly rounded, seemed larger and higher than most because of an almost total baldness." Caillaux stood unnaturally erect but managed nonetheless "to seem neither distant nor constrained."[36]

Caillaux's memoirs suggest that he was flattered by the references to Balzac. But some found his bizarre persona to lie beyond the imaginative powers of France's greatest writers. Paul Vergnet wrote that "Alphonse Daudet and Emile Zola would have been hard-pressed to create in their fiction the luminous character that

6.   Joseph Caillaux, formally posed and impeccably dressed
(*L'Illustration*, 21 March 1914).

Caillaux plays in the real world. . . . Even the genius of a Shake-
speare could never have captured him." This image preceded Caillaux to the United States where he traveled for financial negotiations in the mid-1920s. T. H. Thomas wrote in 1925 that "it is only
because Caillaux actually does exist that he is possible. No one
would invent him. No writer of historical melodrama would con-
ceive [such] a character."[37]

These portraits of Caillaux's dress, appearance, and demeanor already suggest a widely shared sense of his personality: arrogant, proud, willful, and impudent, yet with an ability to seduce, even fascinate. Virtually no one admitted to liking him. For the editors of the left-wing *Bonnet rouge*, a paper that "support[ed] him . . . even exalt[ed] him," he had a "wonderful mind but [was] an awful person."[38] Jean Montigny, Joseph's disciple and successor as deputy from the Sarthe, was hardly more positive, describing him as "an unclassifiable personality, capable in the same quarter-hour of being breezy, charming, arrogant, angry, and good-humored."[39] Caillaux's enemies were even less flattering. Octave Homberg, a lifelong opponent who knew him from childhood, wrote that Caillaux "astonished me, flabbergasted me with his cheek and his dismissive manner. With his high-pitched voice he executed everyone." Paul Vergnet called him "a cabinet minister with the allure of a dictator," complaining that he "was the most powerful man since Gambetta to be elevated to the political summit."[40] Reporting on an investigation into Caillaux's misconduct, Maurice Barrès seemed aghast and not a little amazed when Caillaux leaned back and lit up a cigarette in a room in which smoking was forbidden, this just days after Calmette's assassination. "What a man!" exclaimed the nationalist sage. "There is in him something of the spoiled child."[41]

Caillaux certainly appeared to think well of himself. The subtitles of his three-volume memoir, which he characterized as "recollections set down in the spirit of elegant reserve so much a part of my character," bristle with a grandiosity worthy of Louis XIV: *The Pride of My Early Years; My Audacity; Clairvoyance and Force of Character in the Face of Adversity.*[42] As early as 1901 a newspaper headline had referred to him as "His Puffed up Majesty, Monsieur Caillaux," and seventeen years later Judge Bouchardon, an examining magistrate, labeled him "His Boastfulness, Monsieur Caillaux." The judge added, however, that in spite of everything Caillaux "was endowed with a real gift of seductiveness."[43]

His enemies may have been willing to admit to his powers of seduction—he did, after all, achieve considerable political success as finance minister, prime minister, and head of the Radical party. But what was more difficult for them to acknowledge, perhaps because it alarmed them so much, was his sharp intelligence and his ability to get things done. Nevertheless, friends and foes alike tended to agree with the journalist Anatole de Monzie that "no one explained a piece of business better than he; no one better understood its details." Octave Homberg judged him "extremely intelligent, someone who grasped an issue even before it was fully presented to him," and the writer Emmanuel Berl considered him "a kind of genius." Even the Germans agreed, for when Caillaux became prime minister in 1911 Berlin's ambassador referred, albeit grudgingly, to Caillaux's "authentic political talent."[44]

Caillaux clearly merited such recognition, for he understood state finance better perhaps than anyone else in government. The problem was that Caillaux used this intellectual superiority to belittle those around him. He displayed contempt for individuals who seemed slow to understand, and he condescended to almost everyone.[45] As a result he sometimes found it difficult to translate his intellectual talent into political power, especially when he proposed reforms that threatened established interests. Caillaux might have won more support for his controversial proposal to place a tax on income had he not insulted the intelligence of some of those who raised questions about its merits. By doing so, he made it too easy for conservatives to oppose the new tax by opposing its author.

Caillaux's biographers have tended to explain his magisterial personality, his dismissive authoritarianism, his grandiose exaltation of the self, as the product of a princely childhood during which he reigned at the center of family attention. Jean-Claude Allain describes Caillaux's mother as giving him a powerful sense of importance by flattering his ego and showering him with praise for his accomplishments. Combined with his aristocratic background, Allain writes, this maternal support gave Caillaux a natural sense of superiority and underlay the proud willfulness, the aristocratic disdain, for which he would become famous.[46] But there was another side to Caillaux, an insecure, fretful, and agitated side that all too often overwhelmed the self-confidence evident to his constituents in the Sarthe. Caillaux seems to have been plagued by a troubled temperament that vacillated between two extremes of mood and behavior, between highs of self-exaltation and lows of nervousness, obsession, and extreme insecurity. In neither state did he appear firmly in control of himself, but during his high phases he demonstrated a remarkable ability to command the allegiance of his audience. There was something of the actor in Joseph Caillaux, for during his periods of buoyant emotional energy he could project an image of self-possession and masterful control that made him seem almost invincible. But when his mood swung back to darkness and despair he could face neither the crowd nor himself.

In his testimony at the trial Caillaux claimed to have been deeply worried about his wife's emotions during Calmette's press campaign against him—"haunted," as he put it, "by the vision of my wife's whole bearing, so visibly depressed."[47] But he very likely had cause to be concerned about his own emotions as well. According to the written deposition of President Raymond Poincaré, Caillaux appeared "extremely upset" during a private meeting the two had held on the morning of the assassination. At one point in their discussion, Caillaux "stood up and exclaimed, 'If Calmette publishes [more] private letters, I'll kill him.'" The president concluded his deposition by noting that he was "so struck by the state M. Caillaux was in" that he felt it necessary to report their conversation to the prime minister.[48] In his own testimony Caillaux confirmed that he had threatened to kill Calmette and did not dispute Poincaré's representation of his tone. Caillaux also acknowledged that he had told his wife at lunch on 16 March that he would "go and smash Calmette's face in."[49] Before the court he tried to explain this immoderate vow as having been designed to calm his wife with the promise of protection, but her act of violence that very afternoon suggests it may have had the opposite effect.

From these accounts Joseph appears to have been quite as distraught as his wife, something not inconsistent with the way he was to describe himself in moments of candor toward the end of his life. In his memoirs (completed in draft around 1930), Caillaux revealed that he had "experienced nervous troubles . . . since [1905]" though never again "so violently as then." He went on to explain that this first nervous episode was "a real crisis," one prolonged by his unusually narrow margin of victory in the legislative election of 1906. As a result, "the natural inquietude of my personality became aggravated." Perhaps Caillaux's first nervous crisis did not occur until 1905, when he was already forty-five years old, but plentiful evidence exists of the long-standing "inquiétude" of his personality. As Joseph's father lay dying in 1898 he warned his son, then thirty-five years old, to "beware at all times of the explosiveness of your temperament."[50] And much later (1925) Joseph explained his ability finally to reconcile with his old rival Aristide Briand by observing that he now "had less nervous fury and less throbbing sensitivity."[51]

Though Caillaux took care to make such admissions only toward the end of his career, the testimony of countless others reveals a man beset throughout his life by nervous agitation. His emotions, it seems, were so close to the surface that the temperature of his feeling could be read in the color of his hairless head. The journalist Louise Weiss remarked that "his bald cranium became redder and redder with each rising wave of his tumultuous blood."[52] Not that one had to inspect Caillaux's scalp to perceive his extreme emotionality. In a parliamentary reportage following the assassination of Calmette, Maurice Barrès wrote that Caillaux "continually banged both palms on the table as if it were a piano, accompanying and supporting his statements with this music. At times he was profoundly agitated, his eyes and his voice reflecting his troubled spirit. He was absolutely feverish."[53] Summarizing all these accounts, a succession of historians and biographers have endowed Caillaux with a set of adjectives reflecting his emotionality and nervous traits: "petulant," "impetuous," "quivering," "fidgety," "sprightly." Never was he seen as simply moving from one place to another; instead he performed a pirouette, he whirled around, he fluttered, he even cascaded. He was a perpetual motion machine, an organism governed by an "impetuous instability."[54]

Despite all this testimony, the descriptions of others suggest that Caillaux tended not to remain, at least visibly, in the grip of nervous fever. He seemed capable of channeling anarchic and dispersed emotional energy into a productive and convincing display of power, control, and unruffled self-confidence. He could appear, one moment, so consumed with fear and loathing as to inspire hostility and mistrust only to rise to such heights of authoritative control as to elicit great confidence and even reverence. Poincaré noted in his memoirs that immediately after his private meeting on 16 March with an almost frantic Caillaux, the finance minister went on to lead the discussion in the Council of Ministers with "a self-control and an impassiveness that contrasted sharply with the nervousness I had just witnessed alone with him in my office. He is capable of restraining himself with an astonishing self-mastery." Several days later, after the assassination of Calmette, Poincaré was again amazed by Caillaux's apparent ability, in the face of tragedy, "to master a temperament agitated in times past by even the mildest troubles."[55] These sharp swings of mood and behavior, of anger and depression followed by a buoyant display of power and control, betray a personality beset by strong emotions, emotions that ranged from despair to exhilaration. When plagued by despair Caillaux seemed unable to govern himself, much less the country as a whole; when suffused with exhilaration he possessed an actor's ability to shape others' perceptions of himself, making him appear firmly in charge and larger than life.

It seems clear, then, from all these observations that Caillaux was much too complex, much too subject to swings of emotion for any one-dimensional view of his personality to explain his moods and his behavior. Joseph Caillaux exuded both power and weakness, serenity and enervation, vacillating as he did between the poles of grandiosity and despair. Such a bi-polar temperament may well have been his from birth, for current research in psychology and in the biochemistry of the brain suggests that certain aspects of an individual's temperament and mood are inherent traits.[56] This is not to say that genes determine behavior, only that individuals are born with certain temperamental propensities that shape the way they respond to patterns of family life, to their social and cultural environment, and to their particular experiences as children, adolescents, and adults. Caillaux's relatively strong and frequent swings of mood make it appear that he suffered from what psychiatrists now call a "bi-polar disorder," something he himself may have vaguely recognized. At Henriette's trial Joseph characterized the ups and downs of his personal and professional life in words that could apply to his personality itself. "In my life . . . I have sometimes been at the summits, but these summits are always so close to the base!"[57]

Individuals plagued with the bi-polar disorder alternate in mood between peaks of energy, creativity, and sexuality—often accompanied by grandiosity, arrogance, and anger—and troughs of despair, nervousness, feelings of persecution, and low self-esteem.[58] A supportive and even-keeled family life can smooth the extremes of the bi-polar temperament, but in Joseph Caillaux's case his parents differed so much in their own personalities and in the way they treated their volatile son that they produced precisely the opposite effect. For Caillaux, childhood circumstances and relations with his parents acted to sharpen the excesses of his temperament, reinforcing rather than softening the disposition he had inherited.

Enough is known about Joseph Caillaux's home life and early years to suspect that his family was as bi-polar as his temperament. Joseph Caillaux was born in 1863, the first of Eugène and Anna Caillaux' two sons. Anna had been widowed from her first husband with whom she had had a son and daughter. From all descriptions, Caillaux's mother and father were as opposite in personality as parents can be. Anna was Protestant and pious, Eugène Catholic and skeptical. Anna was sweet, warm, loving, pliant; her husband harsh, cold, distant, authoritarian.[59] Joseph's memoirs make clear that what affection he received as a child came from his mother; from his father he received orders and instructions. Though Joseph's memoirs treat his relationship with his father with great delicacy, it is apparent that they were in constant conflict. "At home even more than everywhere outside it," Caillaux wrote, "my father allowed no opposition." When Joseph expressed little interest in preparing for Eugène's alma mater, the Ecole polytechnique, his father ordered him to do so. Happily for the younger Caillaux he was not admitted, but still his father remained reluctant to let him do anything else. Thanks, however, "to the support my mother gave me I secured [my father's] authorization to study law and to prepare to become an *inspecteur des finances.*" This concession did not prevent Eugène from exercising strict control over Joseph's course of study, for his father "specified the rules of order and work whose austere design I would be required to follow." Joseph responded with "a bit of grumbling," but he "complied nonetheless." Later on, when Joseph had reached his thirties, the issue of his bachelorhood created not a little difficulty within his family. But while his mother "invited him tenderly" to find a wife, his father "berated [him] hostilely" on the subject. Father and son "clashed" as a result and exchanged "bittersweet words."[60]

In all of Joseph's descriptions Anna appears loving and supportive, Eugène distant and critical. His mother regularly intervened on Joseph's behalf and gave him to believe that he was her "preferred child."[61] Shortly after Eugène's death, Anna wrote to her closest friend, the countess of Beausacq, that Joseph was her "sole ray of sunshine; but he is that so profoundly, it makes me rejoice with all my heart." This letter prompted a note from the countess to Joseph who wanted him to know "how much [Anna] adores you, how happy you make her, and how your successes give her the greatest joy."[62] Joseph apparently felt similarly about his mother and idealized her to the point of worship, calling her "my venerated mother." Anna's portrait, Joseph wrote in his memoirs, "fills up the room where I work." And as he labored his mother's gaze seemed "alive on the canvas, enveloping [me] to this day."[63]

It seems clear from these descriptions that Joseph Caillaux's parents were as polarized as he was, creating a family life so contradictory as to reinforce the extremes of his temperament. His mother saw him as perfect, as a prince of a child, while his father defined him as inadequate and disobedient. Anna validated the majestic pole of his temperament, Eugène the depressive. Divided within himself, Joseph would have benefited from parents capable of providing a unified vision of himself, a vision that fortified neither of his extremes and enabled him to act more securely and even-handedly in the world. Instead, the Caillaux family's emotional contradictions intensified the discord within Joseph's temperament, profoundly complicating his later responses to the demands and requirements of professional and personal life.

Emerging from the contradictions of Caillaux's temperamental and familial complexity was a tangle of fluctuating identities that ranged from spoiled child to sexual predator to consummate actor-politician. Each aspect of his personality would plague his adult relationships, but he himself recognized only one: his comportment as a "spoiled child," abundantly confirmed by contemporaries (Barrès, Vergnet, Fleurieu) and historians (Allain, Bredin, Fabre-Luce) alike.

Anna Caillaux's reinforcement of the exalted part of Joseph's temperament had instilled in him a fantasy of omnipotence and invulnerability in which he would forever be shielded from the fathers in his life. So powerful was this "mama's-boy" fantasy that it often made him oblivious to the dangers he faced in the adult world, something he seems to have realized obliquely toward the end of his years. In a passage dropped from the final draft of his memoirs, Caillaux spoke of his early adulthood in a way that doubtless applied to his childhood as well: "The cushioned and sheltered life I led [living at home] from age twenty-five to thirty-five cloaked me in the livery of a spoiled child, a livery I have had a hard time casting off. Have I ever completely cast it off?"[64] Here, in a passage he was unwilling to publish, Caillaux suggested that his overly protective mother may not have prepared him for the realities of adult life, for the need to take the fathers' power seriously. Did his princely childhood, Caillaux wondered, create a false sense of security? Did it beget illusions of omnipotence that lasted into adulthood, moving him to defy the conventions of his society and the rule of its fathers without taking sufficient note of the consequences for doing so?

Such were Caillaux's most candid perceptions of himself, perceptions echoed by his contemporaries and his biographers. But what Caillaux failed to perceive—what his critics and biographers equally failed to perceive—was that he not only ignored paternal power but actively sought to defy it. Because his father spoke so directly to the negative side of his temperament, Joseph needed not simply to ignore the fathers but to defeat them. He had to prove endlessly that his mother's image of him was the correct one, that he was a brilliant and worthy prince, not the failure his father believed him to be. To prove his father wrong, to prove himself to be neither weak nor incompetent, he had constantly to win his mother at his father's expense and challenge his father for his mother's affection. This may have been a symbolically ideal way to test his mettle, but by doing so he intensified an oedipal conflict already heightened by the extent to which his parents reinforced his divided temperament. Childhood conflicts as sharp as these could find no normal resolution, and Caillaux was condemned to recapitulate throughout his adult life the oedipal dilemmas of his family life. It would never be enough, therefore, for Caillaux to rewin the love of his mother in a continual succession of women; he would have to take them away from other husbands and fathers. Both his wives had been married to other men when he began to see them; both divorced those men for him. Beyond this direct form of oedipal competition, Caillaux sought to vanquish other men sexually in countless other ways: by boasting of his *liaisons élégantes*, by displaying his mistresses in public, by revealing a connoisseur's knowledge of women's most intimate apparel.

Still, for all these elaborate means of establishing his mother's image as the true image, his father's vision nevertheless remained unshakably real, confirmed in the depths of Caillaux's own temperament. The vision could not be undone. But it could perhaps be banished from the perceptions of others and then, with no one to reflect it, from Caillaux's consciousness itself. Such perhaps was Joseph's fantasy, for he made his career not in the anonymous world of public administration for which he was trained but in the highly public realm of politics where he could use his position and his power to shape the perceptions of others. He created, in his political life, an actor's self, an artificial external self of grandeur and power designed to convince his audience—and ultimately himself—that his mother's image was the only image. If acting is a way of exerting power over the perceptions of others, then Caillaux sought to use that power to create the self he wanted to be. To do so, he used parts of himself to fashion a persona that was more than himself, drawing on the trappings of his aristocratic background and milieu to assume the role of a modern-day member of the French noblesse. As Fabre-Luce wrote, Caillaux "created this [aristocratic] character with the embellishments that the size of his following demanded. . . . He made himself coquettish, uppity, chivalrous; he would have *histoires de femmes*."[65]

This aristocratic persona of power and grace may have helped Joseph Caillaux to impose a measure of control over his volatile personality and to cope with the emotional contradictions of his upbringing. It seems as well to have helped him win elections in the Sarthe where the seigneurial image lent him legitimacy and respect. But in the long run it left him ill-equipped for adult life, especially the Hobbesian life of Parisian politics he chose as his own. His fantasy of omnipotence and invulnerability, combined with his relentless need to humble figures of authority, led him to underestimate his political opponents, even to tempt them, however unconsciously, by needlessly exposing himself to political attack.

It is difficult to explain otherwise why he not only created but took pains to preserve documents as potentially damaging to his career as the letters he wrote to Berthe and Henriette while each was still his mistress. These letters documented his adulterous affairs with them and left written evidence of his political opportunism. The "Ton Jo" letter to Berthe, composed in 1901, boasted of a politically damaging duplicity concerning the income tax, while the *lettres intimes* penned to Henriette eight years later compromised him even more. Not only did they declare his adulterous love but they insulted his constituents by mocking their rustic accents and outlined the cynical political calculations that would govern his separation from Berthe. "When I met you, my love," Joseph wrote Henriette, "I felt attracted to you with the force of my entire being. I would have resisted my feelings, however, . . . had I been happy at home. But I wasn't happy, I was humiliated and torn apart by the act [i.e., marriage] I had endured. . . . I therefore threw myself toward you with a passionate fervor or rather with a fervent passion." He was careful to add, however, that although he hoped "to regain my liberty [through divorce], in no case will I move before the elections."[66]

Shortly after sending these letters in September 1909 he asked Henriette to return them, out of fear, as he put it at the trial, that she "could misplace them or that someone would steal them from her." But having retrieved them, poste restante, Caillaux then "committed the error of not burning them immediately." Instead he put them in an accessible drawer where Berthe discovered them the next day: undue prudence had given way to carelessness in the extreme. It was as if he had wanted to test the limits of his fantasized invulnerability, something he seemed to do throughout his career. And because he did so he needed constant protection, first from an amended father-figure and later from surrogate mothers and a familial following of loyalists who enveloped him as his real mother once had done with perhaps too much success.

As soon as Caillaux left the secure and familiar world of the Sarthe to assume national prominence as minister of finance he found protection in a political mentor who resembled his father just enough to replace Eugène but whose personal qualities could compensate for what his father had lacked. Joseph found the good caring father he wished his own had been in René Waldeck-Rousseau, his prime minister in the government he joined in 1899. "What warmth of feeling," Caillaux wrote of the man credited with restoring republican France in the aftermath of the Dreyfus affair. "How he lavished delicate attention almost without seeming to! How he supported, how he encouraged! When he had to make a [critical] observation to a collaborator whom he was fond of and whom he knew loved him, he did it with an infinite tact. Having made his constructive remark he immediately added words of comfort, discreet words of praise that consoled and strengthened."[67] Waldeck appears here the polar opposite of Eugène Caillaux, the ideal mate for his mother, the kind of man Joseph, no doubt, wished he himself had been.

It is significant that Joseph turned to Waldeck-Rousseau just months after having been rendered parentless with the death of his mother in 1898 (Eugène had died two years earlier). Alone in the world, Joseph fastened himself emotionally to the elder republican statesman who would become his political mentor and idealized father, the happy rewrite of the man he wanted to forget.[68] Both his father and his prime minister were solid members of the haute bourgeoisie, professional men who had turned reluctantly to politics. But where Eugène had joined a government hostile to the Republic, Waldeck-Rousseau dedicated himself to preserving its existence. And Joseph, a timid, even reluctant, republican before his association with Waldeck-Rousseau, became one of the Republic's most ardent defenders, moving increasingly to the left with each passing year. By 1914 he was the leader most closely associated with the Radical Republic, a position that made him the prime target for all those who opposed it.

Perhaps because his movement to the left made him such a political target, Caillaux surrounded himself after the death of Waldeck-Rousseau in 1904 with surrogates of the mother who had done so much to nourish his princely self. From the *liaisons élégantes* of his early adulthood to the furtive affairs of his later years, he sought constantly to please women, to win their love and emotional support, only to drop them when they no longer served his purposes— perhaps to prove to himself that he was not as emotionally tied to his mother as he feared.

But his ties to Anna Caillaux were strong indeed, so strong that parts of Joseph's personality were regularly described in words commonly applied to women of his era. If Caillaux was bi-polar in the eyes of his contemporaries, then one pole was male and the other female. Like so many women of the Belle Epoque, Caillaux was seen as emotional and nervous, as vain and fastidious in his dress, as a charmer who captivated the crowd. Fabre-Luce, it has been noted, referred to Caillaux as "coquettish," linking his many *histoires de femmes* to a certain feminine power of seduction.

These powers helped him attract a steady succession of women, prompting Fabre-Luce to suggest that at each stage of Caillaux's political ascent he acquired a new woman as a trophy of his success.[69] He may also have wanted a new and, as it turned out, more socially prominent woman at each level to mirror back to him the heightened self he believed each new echelon justified. His affair with Berthe Gueydan, renowned for her beauty, accompanied his promotion in 1899 to minister of finance. His marriage to the wealthy Henriette Claretie came shortly after he was named prime minister in 1911.[70] And, when it seemed Caillaux would become prime minister again three years later, rumor had it that his second marriage was in trouble and that there was another woman in his life.[71]

To complement the series of women, Caillaux surrounded himself with a group of loyalists whom he expected to treat him like a prince. His prewar assistant François Piétri likened him to an enlightened member of the old regime's *noblesse de robe*, and Louise Weiss, long a Caillaux intimate, referred to him in her memoirs as a "seigneur."[72] Clearly Caillaux thrived on such deference and suffered without it. He boasted to the journalist Joseph Dubois that, before 1914, when he arrived at the train station in Le Mans "the stationmaster himself always hurried to meet me. He did not want to give the honor of carrying my bags to anyone else." But after the war, with his political fortunes in decline, a stationmaster's unwillingness to hurry to his side made him feel like a "sunken man."[73]

As with his women, Caillaux abandoned his old associates and appointed new ones with each political promotion.[74] And when he came under violent attack, as in the Agadir crisis of 1911 (discussed below), he often chose not to defend himself but to rely all the more on his artificial family of loyalists, adding new members willing to preserve his illusion of invulnerability. In 1913 he went so far as to admit the unsavory Bolo-Pacha, a swindler and future German agent, into his sanctum of advisors and confidants because Bolo flattered him with consummate skill.[75] Commenting on this entourage, Henry de Jouvenel wrote that Caillaux judged those around him, "not according to their qualities but according to their attitude toward him."[76]

Just as his mother had, those around him may have made him feel powerful and invulnerable, but they also left him open to attack. Rather than make him aware of the difficulties he confronted, his wives and associates allowed him to see only the magisterial self he wanted to project. In his testimony before the *Cour d'assises*, Caillaux revealed that at the height of Calmette's attacks he had gone so far as to instruct "every member of my staff that no one except my chief aide was authorized to speak to me of these press campaigns, and that he could do so only in the gravest of circumstances. . . . This interdiction I extended to include my wife."[77]

By 1914 Joseph Caillaux had become one of France's most controversial—and therefore most vulnerable—figures, as much for his personal as his political life. And because he remained so insulated from negative elements in his own personality and in much of the world around him, he left himself especially exposed to the unprecedented dangers of the trial. Caillaux's nature would not, of course, have mattered as much had he not moved so far to the left relative to his social origins. Had he remained with Poincaré and Louis Barthou comfortably ensconced in the republican *juste milieu*, wrote Fabre-Luce, he might have been one of those "brilliant opportunists" who succeeded in appeasing the democrats with their rhetoric and the conservatives with their economic and financial orthodoxy.[78] But then he would not have been Joseph Caillaux. The very personality traits that made him feel so charmed, even invincible, were precisely those that had moved him to defy political convention and bourgeois complacency to turn against the privileges of his class. In his moments of self-exaltation Caillaux believed himself capable of reforming a country desperately in need of change, capable of overcoming political and economic obstacles that seemed insurmountable to most of his political peers. And he was not alone in this assessment of himself, for political commentators of all stripes tended to view him as the sole man of the left whose leadership might move France toward reform. Caillaux alone, wrote Fabre-Luce, possessed the energy, the expertise, and the personality to place himself "at the center of the epoch and draw all its passions to him."[79]

   This Caillaux certainly did, especially after 1906 when as minister of finance under Georges Clemenceau he resolved to take up one of the thorniest problems of his day: the reform of France's antiquated tax system. From this point on he came to embody an activist republicanism of social reform, a republicanism in which the state would be taken seriously as an agent of (gradual) social change. Such activist republicanism did not sit well with most of those in positions of economic power—bankers, railroad owners, captains of industry—nor did it consistently win the support of more than half the members of France's lower house, the Chamber of Deputies, or more than one-third of France's senators. Even the adherents of Caillaux's Radical party, an organization officially dedicated to the egalitarian republic (at least with respect to the rights of men), proved reluctant to tamper with the existing order of things. Radicals were zealous only in their devotion to anticlericalism, to the political decline of organized Catholicism. When challenged with proposals to help the poor, to improve working conditions, to ease the pain of old age, sickness, and unemployment, they found it difficult to pass constructive legislation. Every year at their annual party conferences the Radicals expressed a ritualized commitment to address all these problems, but when it came to action they were unable to agree on specifics.

This disarray especially marked proposals to overhaul France's archaic and grossly unfair tax system, based in large part on the needs and resources of the early nineteenth century. Landed property was assessed according to a cadastre completed in 1830, and dwellings were taxed by the number of doors and windows they possessed. Manufacturers and members of the liberal professions paid taxes not on the basis of revenue or profit but according to the business they owned or profession they exercised. Adjustments were made for enterprises at the extremes of poverty or prosperity, but the documentation required for demonstrating the one or the other was rudimentary at best. Taxation, moreover, was not uniform across the country, allowing some departments and communes to enjoy lower effective tax rates. And perhaps worst of all, about half of all the government's revenues came from regressive indirect taxes on articles of common consumption.[80] Not only was the system unjust, it failed to meet the requirements of a modern industrial society. France desperately needed a new system of taxation. Many on the political left believed it should be an income tax; between 1871 and 1898 more than one hundred proposals for a tax on personal income were submitted to the French parliament. None had a chance of passing until 1906 when Joseph Caillaux decided to give his all to the effort.[81]

Even though such an impost already existed in England and Germany, Caillaux's legislation was enormously controversial in France, where opposition to a uniform system of direct taxation possessed a long and venerable history.[82] Such opposition had weakened the absolutist state in the eighteenth century and had helped cause the French Revolution itself. Political leaders in the nineteenth century took note of these developments and did their best to avoid proposing the kind of tax renovation that had stirred up so much trouble in the past; tax reform became politically taboo. Especially forbidden was the income tax, a reform that would require individuals not just to report their earnings but to open their books to the state. The income tax, opponents argued, represented an unacceptable level of state intervention into private affairs, amounting to nothing less than a "fiscal inquisition." Senator Jules Roche, a political moderate, called it "a national peril," and Raymond Poincaré, until then Caillaux's friend and political ally, denounced the income tax as "the handmaiden of socialism."[83] The worst reform of all was progressive taxation, supported by the far left and considered by Senator Roche to be "the seed of an entire social revolution."

Views such as these guaranteed that the opposition to Caillaux's income tax would be fierce indeed, so fierce that its foes succeeded in blocking passage in the Chamber of Deputies for nearly three years and for an additional five in the Senate. But Caillaux held firm; his parliamentary efforts were tireless. He managed, ultimately, to rally virtually all the Socialists and enough of the Radicals to push the bill through the Chamber in 1909. Five years later, in July 1914, it cleared the Senate, albeit in truncated form.[84] Caillaux had overcome powerful opposition from entrenched interests; without his work it is unlikely that prewar France would have seen such a measure.

These uncompromising efforts to create a more equitable system of taxation marked him as a man of the left and earned him the enmity of the Parisian elite, despite—or perhaps because of—his social status and personal wealth.[85] Before 1909 centrists and several on the right had tolerated Caillaux, even respected him for his budgetary prudence and financial expertise. After 1909 there would be no more such indulgence; Caillaux became pure enemy.[86] When his bill passed the lower house, the noted economist Paul Leroy-

Beaulieu went so far as to claim that Caillaux's income tax would be "as catastrophic as the revocation of the Edict of Nantes," Louis XIV's seventeenth-century law outlawing Protestantism in France. Caillaux might have survived the enmity of the elite had he been a more cautious person, but he failed to take sufficient note of the influential enemies he had made, especially among those who had once been his friends. Caillaux had now to face the mounting opposition of Poincaré and that of two other political giants of the era, Aristide Briand and Louis Barthou. He also faced the hostility of the enormously powerful mass-circulation press, whose wealthy owners had fought the new tax with all their ample means. But Caillaux was enormously proud of his political achievement, proud now to be considered a leader of the highest stature, and he saw in this situation "only the summits," as the journalist Claude Pierrey put it, "not the precipices."[87]

Caillaux's preference for the summits made him particularly vulnerable to the penny press. Not only did its directors part company with him over the income tax, but they found him insufficiently nationalist as well. Historians have long characterized the years from 1905 to 1914 as an era of "nationalist revival," as a time when French men and women exalted in a new patriotism tinged with feelings of aggressiveness and hostility toward Germany.[88] And even though recent work has questioned the magnitude of the phenomenon, raising doubts that a new nationalism extended very widely or deeply into French society, it remains clear that the Parisian press, and especially the mass-circulation press, was often stridently nationalistic during this period.[89] The directors and leading journalists of the *grande presse* had by 1910 grown highly suspicious of Germany and of any French politician who sought a rapprochement with the conquerors of Alsace and Lorraine. When Caillaux, who became prime minister in June 1911, successfully negotiated a treaty with Germany during the Agadir crisis of that year, the nationalists turned against him their considerable journalistic force. They helped to ensure the collapse of Caillaux's government in January 1912, and from then on the former premier remained a favorite target, especially after he was elected president of the Radical party in October 1913.

In the meantime, a nationwide controversy over a piece of defense legislation intensified the anti-Caillaux feelings of nationalists, moderate to extreme. Responding to a German military buildup, a parliamentary majority voted in July 1913 to increase the term of France's compulsory military service from two years to three. But it did so only after months of intense debate. Virtually all the Socialists and many left-leaning Radicals had vehemently opposed the three-year law, and the newsprint nationalists along with the center-right forces of Barthou, Briand, and Poincaré feared that if Caillaux returned to power he would be skillful enough to achieve its repeal.

Poincaré and his allies worried in general that a left-leaning government headed by Caillaux would undermine the tough new military and diplomatic posture, embodied in the three-year draft, that the president had adopted in the wake of Agadir.[90] As prime minister in 1912 and as president of the Republic from 1913 on, Poincaré sought not just to bolster the country's defenses against a possible German assault but to prepare France for its own offensive war. Not that Poincaré intended to strike Germany first. Rather, he endorsed a new French military theory built upon an offensive strategy, upon the idea that the best defense was a good offense. Any German attack—so the theory went—the French would meet in kind, launching an offensive of their own. These plans were complicated, however, by a German military buildup announced in early 1913; France's offensive strategy now required a much larger conscript army than the country had possessed in 1912. France needed not just a sizable invasion force to strike enemy territory but an inflated contingent of "covering" troops to hold back an expanded German army while it did so. A purely defensive strategy would have required fewer French forces because their sole task would have been to interdict a German invasion. Poincaré needed therefore to raise a larger army, and he could do so only by preserving the fragile three-year draft, about which many voters and their deputies remained skeptical.[91]

When Caillaux overthrew the center-right government of Louis Barthou in December 1913, returning himself and his party to the political limelight, conservatives and moderates began to worry that he would realize their worst fears. Poincaré confided to his diary that Caillaux's action in defeating a cabinet so closely tied to the new nationalist foreign policy had "broken the charm and shattered the national movement."[92] According to republican precedent, Poincaré should at this point have appointed Caillaux prime minister, but the president refused to take this step, elevating the ineffectual Gaston Doumergue instead. Still Poincaré could not prevent Doumergue from naming Caillaux minister of finance nor from allowing the minister to dominate the new cabinet and the parliament it controlled.

There is no evidence that Caillaux actually meant to repeal the three-year law. But because Poincaré, Barthou, and their allies believed the Radicals might achieve the power and the discipline to do so under Caillaux's leadership, he was targeted for political extinction. He became, as Maurice Barrès put it, "the most hated man in France."[93] After all, Caillaux had managed to negotiate a peaceful solution to the conflict over Agadir at a time when nationalists in both Germany and France were prepared for war, even yearned for war. Then, having been elected president of the Radical party, France's largest political organization, Caillaux managed to impose an uncharacteristic level of discipline on them while making political accommodations with the Socialists to their left. Separately neither the Radicals nor the Socialists could achieve much concrete social or political change. The Radicals were too diverse and divided ever to agree on a firm plan of action, paralyzed by the conflicting legacies of individual liberty and republican citizenship they had inherited from the French Revolution.[94] And the Socialists, themselves divided into two often hostile factions, had with their rhetoric of class conflict and social transformation placed their party too far outside the mainstream for effective parliamentary action. Caillaux alone, it was widely believed, was capable of disciplining the individualistic Radicals while bringing the Socialists under their umbrella of republican respectability.[95] Such a grand coalition of the left could undermine Poincaré's tough military and diplomatic posture and dash the revanchist hopes of all those still smarting from the German victory in the Franco-Prussian War of 1871. As Barrès saw it, Caillaux possessed the ability "to bring Jaurès's pacifist dream down from the clouds, to make the theories of working-class internationalism and the fraternity of all people both practical and realizable."[96]

Caillaux was careful, however, not to reject the three-year law altogether, maintaining only that the increased military expenditures it required should be financed by a more equitable fiscal policy, namely the income tax. In this, he enjoyed considerable support both within the left and among centrists.[97] Despite parliament's passage of the new military law, the country had not turned sharply to the right. If France was to expand its military, voters widely believed, then those with the means should pay. Nor did the three-year law prove that a majority of French men and women—or their parliamentary representatives—had embraced a resurgent militarism and endorsed the rabid nationalism of the far right. Poincaré and Barthou had kept the army's new offensive strategy secret, so sharply did it depart from accepted republican military doctrine. They justified the three-year law purely in terms of France's traditional and largely uncontroversial principles of republican defense. Just as the nascent First Republic of 1792 had had to adopt firm military measures in the face of monarchical forces invading from the east, so now, they suggested, did the Third Republic need extended military service to protect itself from the kaiser's authoritarian designs.[98] The Socialist leadership saw in this argument a cover for a new policy of domestic reaction designed to contain labor militance with an expanded army. But the Socialist rank and file was susceptible to such a venerable appeal to republican sentiment. And even more so was the rank and file of radicalism, enabling the likes of Poincaré, Barthou, and Briand to use the emotional resonance of republican defense to great effect. Still, they did so without converting the bulk of the population to a more aggressive stance vis-à-vis the Germans or even to particularly strong support for the three-year law.[99]

In the legislative elections of April and May 1914, opponents of the law actually won a majority of the seats though not quite a majority of the popular vote. Thus, on the eve of the First World War, most French voters* appeared to eschew military confrontation without rejecting patriotism itself.[100] The country was not polarized into two hostile camps of the right and left, as historians have often argued.[101] The bulk of public opinion floated in a fluid center that could drift in either direction, toward the moderate nationalism of Poincaré or the patriotic pacifism of Caillaux. Depending on the circumstances, the great French majority could

---

* In 1914 women did not yet possess the right to vote, so the voting population included only adult men.

endorse the policies of one or the other not because the country was divided down the middle but because it remained so unified. All this actual and potential support for Caillaux's pacific politics of reform is what made him seem so dangerous to the center and the right. So, as we have seen, did his ability at times to turn his ideas into reality even while under strenuous attack.* In these circumstances Caillaux's willful indifference to the forces arrayed against him helps explain his success, for his fantasy of omnipotence enabled him to persevere when others would have admitted defeat. The leaders of the national movement wanted him off the political stage, and Calmette's crusade against him, with its unprecedented violence and disregard for the truth, was intended to achieve precisely that.

From 10 December 1913 when Caillaux became minister of finance to 16 March 1914 when his wife shot Calmette, *Le Figaro* ran no fewer than 110 articles, anecdotes, and cartoons hostile to the Radical leader. Some did no more than stir up the journalistic grime for which Parisian newspapers were notorious. But most of Calmette's articles went much further. They were designed not just to attack Caillaux's views or question his political competence but to impugn his character and morality. *Le Figaro* seemed bent on presenting Caillaux as morally unfit to govern, then or in the future. Nevertheless, as violent and persistent as Calmette's unprecedented campaign was, he proved unable to sway French opinion against Caillaux as long as he drew his evidence, however sensationalized, from the realm of public political life. Caillaux's views enjoyed too much support for him to be vulnerable to attacks that could be construed as purely political.[102]

As late as mid-March 1914, after three months of a relentless journalistic campaign against Caillaux, no one in the Chamber's Radical and Socialist majority called for his resignation from the cabinet; nor did his position as president of the Radical party seem any less secure. Even worse for Caillaux's enemies, the left was widely expected to win a substantial victory in the approach-

* In the middle of *Le Figaro*'s campaign against him, Caillaux seemed unperturbed as he brought his tax legislation before the Senate and succeeded in making it more progressive in the Chamber (see Allain, *Caillaux*, 1:260–69; Krumeich, *Armaments and Politics*, p. 174).

ing two-round legislative election to be held on 26 April and 10 May 1914.[103] Briand had organized a center-right electoral coalition called, hyperbolically, the *fédération des gauches;* despite Briand's personal popularity, the federation was no match for Caillaux's well-entrenched Radicals or for a thriving Socialist party. Not until Calmette revealed aspects of Caillaux's personal life by publishing the "Ton Jo" letter did Caillaux's opponents begin to loosen his hold on power. To undermine Caillaux's position, Calmette ultimately had to leave the terrain of traditional politics to attack him where he was much more vulnerable: his private life, his personality, and his social standing. By making Caillaux's private life public, Calmette could hope to succeed where the traditional approach had failed.

Nonetheless, Calmette undertook his descent into Caillaux's private life only belatedly, even reluctantly, for the editor was well aware of the Third Republic's unwritten strictures against the publication of private correspondence.[104] The "Ton Jo" letter represented an attack of last resort; for the first twelve weeks of his press campaign Calmette held it in reserve, in the belief, no doubt, that Caillaux would fall under the weight of *Le Figaro*'s relentless barrage of financial and political accusations. Appearing almost daily, the paper's allegations fell into three categories. The first portrayed the finance minister as a "demagogic plutocrat"—an epithet borrowed from Briand—who took advantage of connections in international finance to line his own pockets and those of his friends, mostly "foreign" (meaning Jewish) financiers.[105] A series of articles accused Caillaux of using his position as chairman of two overseas financial institutions, the *Crédit foncier égyptien* and the *Crédit foncier argentin,* to collect illicit kickbacks on three continents. *Le Figaro* neglected to mention, however, that Caillaux had resigned those positions before rejoining the government in December 1913. Beyond these accusations, Caillaux was said to have used his power as finance minister to extort 400,000 francs from French banks and to remove high civil servants who displeased his wealthy banker friend Spitzer, "recently naturalized and of Jewish origin," as Calmette put it.[106] There were other allegations as well, allegations that Caillaux had illegally listed foreign stocks on the Paris Exchange and then made a fortune from them, that he had channeled government money into his own political coffers, and so forth. No hard evidence existed then or emerged since to sustain these claims.

Still, Caillaux was a wealthy man who lived well from his investments, and Calmette's charges struck newspaper readers as entirely plausible.

They became more so in early March when Caillaux startled the Senate with a document suggesting that interest from government bonds might not be taxable under the proposed new impost on personal income. Senators were startled because just three months earlier Caillaux had overthrown Barthou's cabinet for its plans to allow precisely the same exemption. When news of Caillaux's document reached the Paris stock exchange, the value of government bonds rose sharply. To his enemies it seemed as though Caillaux had used his position as finance minister to manipulate the market for his own benefit. What is more likely is that he had introduced an ambiguity into his language to win additional votes. But when he produced no satisfactory explanation for his "coup de bourse," Barthou suggested in the Chamber that "not everyone suffered a loss from it."[107]

Calmette's second line of attack was more serious, for it raised questions about Caillaux's patriotism. In four articles entitled "Caillaux in the Eyes of History" *Le Figaro* insinuated that as prime minister in 1911 he had made a treasonous secret deal with Germany to end the Agadir crisis, France's diplomatic dispute with Germany that had almost triggered a war over Morocco. France had been trying to seize exclusive control of the territory's economy, and Germany considered its interests there in jeopardy. On 1 July 1911 the kaiser retaliated by sending the gunboat *Panther* to Morocco's port of Agadir. French opinion was scandalized, but the truth was that their country's moves in Morocco had violated at least two different international accords.[108]

Caillaux lacked experience in foreign affairs, but as soon as he grasped the military and political situation he determined to resolve the crisis peacefully. Legend had it that Napoleon always refused to go to war unless he felt there was a 70 percent chance of winning, and when France's chief of staff General Joffre could not guarantee such a percentage in 1911 Caillaux opened negotiations.[109] Without consulting his own foreign minister, who seemed ready, even eager, to risk war over Morocco, he took the unusual but not unprecedented step of entering into secret personal discussions with German representatives. Though word of the talks leaked out, forcing

Caillaux to endure an ugly confrontation with officials from the Quai d'Orsay, he was able to reach an agreement: France would relinquish its portion of the Congo in exchange for Germany's promise not to interfere in Morocco. Given France's weak military position—it lagged behind Germany in both armaments and manpower—Caillaux had made a shrewd arrangement.[110] He had avoided a war France was militarily unprepared to fight while giving up territory in the Congo that promised scant economic return. In exchange Caillaux had achieved exclusive French control over a colony, Morocco, that possessed real value, economic as well as strategic. Still, the nationalists who dominated the ministry of foreign affairs and much of the press never forgave him for ceding territory that had belonged to France and perhaps for averting a war they were impatient to fight. Shortly after Caillaux signed the Morocco agreement on 4 November 1911, the press service at the Quai d'Orsay told a group of journalists, "It was war that we needed."[111]

The nationalists were convinced that Caillaux had committed treason by signing the accord of November 1911. Calmette revived their allegations three years later by insinuating in his press campaign that Caillaux had been illicitly involved with Germans during the whole of the Agadir crisis. Calmette's intimations were based on three German telegrams—intercepted and decoded by French intelligence agents—from the foreign ministry in Berlin to the kaiser's ambassador in Paris. The French transcripts of the intercepted German telegrams were typed on light green paper and became known as les verts. These were classified documents, but Calmette had obtained copies from government officials hostile to Caillaux. The first two verts, sent in late July 1911, outlined the unpublicized conversations taking place between Caillaux's representative and his German counterpart.[112] On reading the transcripts, France's foreign minister, Justin de Selves, immediately protested to Caillaux for having excluded him from the negotiations. Selves became even more outraged a few days later when he learned that Berlin had suddenly changed its diplomatic code. He knew that diplomats establish a new code only when they discover that the existing one has been broken. And because Caillaux was engaged in secret negotiations with the Germans, Selves decided it must have been the prime minister himself who revealed that his own intelligence service had deciphered their code. At this point, the foreign minister's accusations against Caillaux changed from violation of institutional turf to violation of national secrets. Selves became all the more convinced of Caillaux's treachery when a third telegram, written in the old code and deciphered in November 1911, praised Caillaux for his efforts to solve the Morocco crisis and for easing tensions between the two countries. This document alone was enough to convince nationalists in the French foreign ministry that Caillaux was guilty of treasonous contacts with the enemy. More objective officials wondered, however, why Berlin had written this third cable in a code they knew had been broken. Jean-Claude Allain, the best recent historian of the Agadir crisis, explains this apparent lapse by suggesting that Berlin, knowing the cable would be intercepted, wrote it to cause trouble within the French government.[113]

No evidence proving treasonous contact between Caillaux and the Germans has ever surfaced, nor is it plausible that the prime minister would have wanted to aid the kaiser in this way. But Caillaux showed extraordinarily bad judgment by entrusting his delicate secret negotiations to one Hyacinthe Fondère, a businessman with little diplomatic experience. According to the latter's German counterpart, the diplomat Oskar van der Lancken, Fondère thoughtlessly revealed to him that the French foreign minister had learned of their discussions from a *decoded German dispatch*. No experienced diplomat would have made such a revelation, for it alerted the Germans to the need to change their code, something they did immediately but with a shrewd twist. German intelligence devised a new code for correspondence their diplomats wanted to keep secret but reverted to the old one when it suited their needs, as in the case of the third *vert* designed to create conflict within the French government. Lancken's own dispatches from the period make clear that Caillaux himself played no part in alerting the Germans that French intelligence had broken their code.[114]

Nonetheless, Caillaux's role was ambiguous enough to give his enemies considerable ammunition, and in January 1914 Calmette determined to use it. The editor was about to publish the *verts* when Poincaré, at Caillaux's insistence, intervened to prevent him. To publish them, Poincaré realized, would have been to admit openly that French intelligence had deciphered Germany's diplomatic correspondence. Both sides, of course, knew that each did its best to learn the other's secrets. But to make public France's success in doing so would have embarrassed the Germans, creating an incident so serious, the German ambassador later told Gaston Doumergue, that a "bomb would explode."[115] In this instance Caillaux was saved by the hypocrisy of international relations; Calmette managed nonetheless to allude to evidence of Caillaux's supposed treason, and these insinuations took their toll. They resurfaced, once again, at Henriette's trial.[116]

Just before Caillaux's testimony on the second day of the trial, *Le Figaro's* Louis Latzarus reported from the witness stand that in January 1914 Calmette had shown him a pair of documents "of extraordinary importance." Both, Latzarus claimed, were so compromising to Caillaux that "any good Frenchman who read them would be convinced of the infamy and the treason" of the former prime minister. The reporter was referring, of course, to the *verts* that Caillaux had succeeded in preventing Calmette from publishing the previous winter. In his own testimony, Caillaux appeared to take Latzarus's remarks as a new threat to reveal the *verts*, and the Radical leader countered with a threat of his own. "Let everyone realize that, resolved to defend myself, to prevent outrages against my honor, or indirectly, that of my wife, I will bring to bear everything that will be necessary."[117] This was no idle menace on Caillaux's part, for he possessed some compromising—and theoretically classified—documents of his own. Caillaux had removed from the Ministry of the Interior decoded Italian and Spanish government cables that showed Poincaré in a politically embarrassing relationship with the Vatican and Calmette in the pay of Spain. And if these were not enough, the *New York Times* reported that Caillaux had sent emissaries to the United States in search of compromising information on the American who had been Madame Poincaré's first husband.[118] For months Caillaux had been threatening to release all these documents, to bring about a personal and diplomatic embarrassment neither Poincaré nor Viviani, who had succeeded Doumergue as prime minister in June, wanted to risk. The result was a dramatic and bizarre statement from the government, composed during an all-night cabinet meeting between the second and the third days of the trial and read in the courtroom on the third day: "The pieces [*les verts*] . . . are nothing more than faked copies of documents that do not exist and that have never existed. In no way can they be used to question the honor and the patriotism of Monsieur Caillaux."[119]

The statement was dramatic because it gave Caillaux the patriotic absolution he had long been seeking, bizarre because so many government officials and journalists, not to mention German diplomats, knew the *verts* existed. Beyond this, Caillaux himself acknowledged their reality toward the end of his testimony, just hours before the government was to send them down an Orwellian memory hole. "Monsieur Piétri . . . my former chief of staff, told me that he knew M. Calmette was going to publish in *Le Figaro* some important diplomatic documents. . . . A few days later, he arrived at the office with the documents themselves. . . . M. Barthou told me later that his telephone call at eleven P.M. gave him just enough time to stop a publication fatal not just for a particular individual but for the *patrie* itself."[120] With this testimony on the record, Caillaux's victory concerning the *verts* was Pyrrhic at best.

Calmette may have been unable to publish the *verts*. Yet these did not exhaust his supply of government documents potentially harmful to Caillaux. In particular, Calmette possessed the *document Fabre*, a piece of evidence revealing genuine wrongdoing on Caillaux's part. In the spring of 1911, Attorney General Victor Fabre* had drafted a statement accusing Caillaux of illicit political motives in forcing Fabre to postpone the appellate case of Henri Rochette, a shady financier seeking to overturn an earlier conviction for fraud.[121] Fabre confided the document to Briand, then minister of justice, who passed it on to his successor, Louis Barthou. Several copies were known to have circulated to the press, but before Calmette no one had ever threatened to make it public.

Caillaux does not seem to have been directly associated with Rochette, though they shared a number of political friends including the attorney Maurice Bernard. The latter was Rochette's lawyer in the fraud case and had been Caillaux's attorney in the divorce from Berthe, concluded shortly before Bernard paid Caillaux a visit concerning Rochette. Joseph had been pleased with Bernard's work, for it permitted him to marry Henriette Rainouard. And Bernard took advantage of Caillaux's good spirits to ask for a favor: would he arrange for Rochette's case to be postponed? Attorney General Fabre had rejected Bernard's request for more time, and the defense lawyer wanted him overruled. This Caillaux's inter-

---

* France's attorney general is a high civil servant who ranks below the cabinet level.

vention readily accomplished, moving Fabre to compose the memorandum in which he condemned Caillaux for compromising judicial independence and for "humiliating him as never before" in his life. Fabre could hardly have felt much better nine months later when the trial of Rochette finally convened, for Bernard immediately moved for acquittal citing the statute of limitations. The ploy was too obvious, however, and the court refused to take it seriously; Rochette's original sentence was increased from two years to three.

In this instance, unlike most of the others, Calmette could base his accusations on solid evidence, though he embellished it for his own purposes. The editor was correct to claim that Caillaux had pressured the attorney general and that he had abused his ministerial authority at the behest of a privileged friend. But Calmette neglected to mention one key detail: the court had sentenced Rochette to prison, rejecting as spurious Bernard's attempt to hide behind the statute of limitations. In Calmette's version, financial corruption found its quid pro quo in judicial absolution. What is more likely is that Caillaux intervened not so much to rescue Rochette as to accommodate an influential member of the legal profession who might be useful to Caillaux in the future.[122]

Still, Caillaux's behavior had indeed been corrupt. His enemies intended to make the most of the document that proved it. At Madame Caillaux's trial, the Fabre report took on even more importance than the *verts*, for Chenu focused much of his case on the contention that Madame Caillaux had assassinated Calmette to prevent the *document Fabre* from seeing print. Shortly before Joseph Caillaux's testimony on the trial's second day, Chenu asserted: "The fear that the Fabre document would be published [was] one of the essential motives of Madame Caillaux's crime." And in his summation on the eighth day he went even further, declaring, "It is because M. Gaston Calmette had the Fabre document, it is because this document was about to be published, that the crime was committed."[123] Louis Latzarus, Calmette's friend and confidant at *Le Figaro*, testified that his editor had carried the Fabre document in his billfold at all times and had indeed wanted to publish it, perhaps as early as January 1914. He did not do so, Latzarus told the court, because Calmette had, in his words, "given my word of honor not to." The witness did not reveal to whom Calmette had made this promise, but we know from President Poincaré's unpublished di ary, only recently made available to historians, that Louis Barthou had given Calmette a copy of the *document Fabre* on the condition that he agree only to refer to it, not to print it.[124] Barthou possessed the document illegally, as it rightfully belonged in the government's archives, and he did not want the public to know that he had pilfered official documents for his own political use.[125]

Calmette kept to the letter of his agreement but not the spirit. On 10 March 1914 he published a long article in *Le Figaro* accusing Caillaux of corruption in the Rochette affair. Two days later he referred explicitly to a document written by Victor Fabre, presenting it as proof that Caillaux had used his political power in an effort to spare the swindler Rochette the rigors of France's judicial system.[126] By 12 March, therefore, the whole sordid Rochette affair, duly embellished by Calmette, was before the public. Caillaux did not, nonetheless, want the actual document to be revealed; on 14 March he asked Poincaré to intervene on his behalf.[127] Since the president had prevented Calmette from publishing the *verts*, Caillaux could hope that he would do the same for the *document Fabre*. Even so, Caillaux could not be confident that no one else would print it. As Henriette and then Joseph explained at the trial, they both knew that other journalists beside Calmette possessed copies of the document. Edmond du Mesnil of *Le Rappel* had told them on 14 March—two days before the assassination—that the Fabre report was to be published not by *Le Figaro*, which came out in the morning, but "by an evening paper," either *La Liberté* or *L'Intransigeant*, both right-wing journals. How, the Caillaux asked on the witness stand, could the desire to prevent the Fabre document's publication have motivated Henriette's act when she knew Calmette was not alone in possessing it?[128]

Of course the Caillaux might have discovered the existence of multiple copies of the memorandum only after the assassination of Calmette. Independent confirmation shows that such was not the case. Gustave Téry, one of Caillaux's most ferocious journalistic enemies, admitted that Caillaux had learned on the weekend before the crime that he and Léon Bailby of *L'Intransigeant* possessed copies of the Fabre report.[129] Beyond this, in Joseph's conversation with Poincaré on 14 March the finance minister made it clear that he knew Barthou possessed the original. And another of the discussions Poincaré recorded in his diary on 14 March (but expunged from his published memoir) suggests Caillaux may have suspected that Maurice Bunau-Varilla, principal owner of *Le Matin*, had also procured the document.[130] In that conversation, Bunau told the president he had warned Caillaux "that [Caillaux] was done for and . . . this document [Fabre] will be published; it must be."[131] From all this, Joseph concluded in his testimony, it would be absurd to imagine "that my wife would have gone to find M. Calmette to suppress this Fabre report, when he had only a copy of it."[132]

Given the persuasiveness of this evidence, why did Chenu persist in maintaining that Madame Caillaux killed Calmette to prevent publication of the document? The answer has, once again, to do with prevailing cultural attitudes toward women. Parisian juries tended to sympathize powerfully with women whose honor and *pudeur* were threatened. A woman, overwhelmed by emotion, who killed to preserve her reputation could hope to be excused; one who killed for political motives could hope for nothing. For this reason, Chenu had at all costs to undermine the defense's contention that Madame Caillaux had killed Calmette out of fear the *lettres intimes* would be published. He had, instead, to give her political reasons, motives for which no one, not even a "real woman," could be absolved.

But despite Chenu's impressive efforts to deflect attention away from the *lettres intimes*, the Calmettes' attorney nonetheless returned again and again to the all-important "Ton Jo" (figure 7). Perhaps Chenu was more concerned with bringing down Joseph Caillaux than with convicting Madame Caillaux, for he risked damage to his own case against her by reading aloud in court the letter that Henriette claimed had driven her over the emotional edge. To a hushed courtroom Chenu read the lines that Calmette had published with great fanfare four months earlier. "I pulled off a handsome success," Joseph Caillaux had written in 1901 to Berthe Gueydan. "*Today I crushed the income tax bill while seeming to defend it.*"[133] Chenu continued, still reading from Caillaux's letter:

> I received acclamations from the right and the center without doing too much to upset the left. I succeeded in blocking the progress of the right, which was indispensable.
> Today, I had yet another session this morning in the Chamber that didn't end until a quarter to one.
> Now here I am in the Senate. . . . The session tonight will no

La véritable déclaration de M. Caillaux
relative à l'impôt sur le revenu

7. The "Ton Jo" letter, a personal note with political implications. Calmette published a facsimile in *Le Figaro* on 13 March 1914.

doubt be closed to the public. I will be harassed, brutalized, almost sick, but I will have done a great service for my country.

Ton Jo

Le Figaro's publication of the letter on 13 March 1914 had coincided with Caillaux's efforts in the French Senate to secure final passage of the income tax bill, and his earlier claim of having "crushed the income tax bill" seemed to mark him as the ultimate hypocrite. But Calmette neglected to mention that Caillaux had written this line in 1901, five years before he committed himself to the task of pushing an income tax bill through parliament. When Caillaux wrote the "Ton Jo" letter, he did not yet believe the Chamber—or the country—was ready for such a tax bill, so he maneuvered skillfully to table it while signaling to the left that he supported it in principle. Hence Caillaux's famous line that Chenu read in court. Caillaux's tactics displayed the shrewd pragmatism that was to be a hallmark of his political career. But the "Ton Jo" letter revealed another, more problematic, side of him, the boastful self-importance that alienated friends and foes alike and plunged him into difficulties that he could easily have avoided. Almost every sentence of the letter featured the pronoun "I," and as a whole the note read as though the junior cabinet member were head of government. What is more, it appeared to confirm the damning label Briand had pinned on him: "demagogic plutocrat." Here was the young aristocrat, secure in his inherited fortune, crushing the income tax while appearing to defend it, preserving his wealth while seeming to sacrifice it to democracy.

The recital of the letter and the way Calmette characterized it must have wounded Caillaux, for he devoted considerable attention in his testimony to undoing its effects (figure 8). How, Caillaux asked, could any personal letter of this sort have purely political implications? No! "It was an incursion into my intimacy, into my private life that had been committed. My wife, quite naturally, was very troubled by it." He went on, ignoring the income tax question altogether, in order to evoke sympathy over the kind of campaign Calmette had waged. It was a cowardly campaign and a dirty campaign, he suggested, a campaign that sought not to criticize his politics directly but to "get at me politically through my honor, my honorableness, and at the same time to get at my wife through her honor, because it was our household itself that he was after." Caillaux must have considered this point crucially important for he returned to it twice within the next few minutes: "I repeat, it is my honor that is in question, it is the honor of my wife, it is our honor, together, as a couple. . . . These violent attacks called into question not my projects or my doctrine, but my honor, my honorableness."[134]

Throughout his testimony Caillaux tried to counter Calmette's challenge to his honor and to the questions raised about his marital fidelity by presenting himself, in highly emotional terms, as Henriette's loyal and loving husband. "Never," he declared, "could I feel a happiness more complete and more absolute than the one I have found in this union [with Henriette]. She has been and is for me not only the most tender and most affectionate wife there could be, but she has been the most diligent, the best informed, the wisest partner one could have. We have lived and will continue to live in a close intimacy of heart and spirit."[135] This declaration won Caillaux enormous sympathy, for such apparent emotional candor was virtually unprecedented for a political leader of the Third Republic.

8. Joseph Caillaux testifies on the second day of the trial (*L'Illustration*, 25 July 1914).

The journalist Geneviève Tabouis, one of the few women admitted to the early sessions of the trial,* recalled years later that when Caillaux began to talk of love "a thrill ran through the courtroom."[136] Even *Le Figaro*'s Georges Claretie, committed to the defense of Gaston Calmette and all he stood for, had to acknowledge that Joseph succeeded in making himself appear "sweet and mild, timid and humble."[137] He managed, according to *Le Petit parisien*, "to profoundly move his auditors, to reveal a bit of his broken heart."[138]

It may be that by telling "the story of my intimate life from my first marriage until the painful events that have resulted in my presence before you," Caillaux had decided to hinge his and his wife's defense on the way in which the jury judged their personal life.[139] If such was his decision, the advantages were great but so too were the risks. If Caillaux could evoke the jury's sympathy by appearing to defend his wife's honor and by maintaining that Calmette had violated the inner sanctum of their personal life, Henriette might be saved. Yet by reminding the court and the public at large of his history of adultery and divorce, he made himself vulnerable to a mounting cultural conservatism that identified allegiance to the traditional family with allegiance to the fatherland. And in doing so, he appeared to confirm the view that he was too emotional to be entrusted with political power.

Vibrant emotion may have helped him triumph in the courtroom, but it was the last thing the majority of French citizens sought in their leaders, especially in a time of domestic and international crisis. However brilliant his courtroom performance, Joseph Caillaux was too emotional to inspire the public confidence commanded by Raymond Poincaré, known, as Joseph himself put it, for his "solidity" and his "puritanism."[140] Caillaux undoubtedly believed that a successful defense of Henriette would restore him to political prominence. But in the atmosphere of crisis that surrounded the case, the very aspects of his character and personality that helped him in the courtroom only served to ensure his political demise.

---

* At the opening of the trial Judge Albanel barred women from the audience but could not exclude women attorneys and professional journalists. The presence of professional women apparently set a precedent, for by the middle of the trial the courtroom was so populated with women that male journalists commented on their numbers.

Joseph would emerge from the trial with his political career in shambles.

Nevertheless, Joseph Caillaux possessed so many political skills that he might have tasted a measure of partisan revenge had war not loomed large at trial's end. The party he presided over remained dominant in the summer of 1914; in normal times he might have regained the cabinet post he had been forced, after 16 March, to resign. But the international situation made such an outcome impossible. Caillaux was a man of peace and compromise, a man too complex and troubled for a country prepared, by the beginning of August 1914, for war. Caillaux concluded the second volume of his memoirs by saying that humanity would be preserved from the mass destructiveness of modern war only if governed by leaders "animated by an unyielding will to peace equal to their patriotism." Such men, he wrote, referring to the words of Maksim Gorky, would have to be "foreigners in their own fatherland while being the best of its sons."[141] Caillaux may not have been the best of France's sons, but he did possess the strength and the vision to see beyond the narrow nationalism that afflicted so many of his fellow politicians. In the grim summer of 1914, Caillaux was surely right that France, like its European neighbors, needed patriots who could see their own country from the foreigner's point of view. But rather than empower men like Caillaux whose very eccentricities might have enabled them to behold what others could not, France turned to a leader, Raymond Poincaré, whose horizons extended no further than the borders of France.

Such were the needs and desires of 1914 when France confidently, even jubilantly, entered a conflict it expected to win quickly and easily under the steady, if uninspired, leadership of Raymond Poincaré. But three years later, with the country mired in a murderous and stalemated war, an extraordinary situation called for an extraordinary leader. In its extremity France needed a man who did not fit the standard Third Republic mold, and this even President Poincaré seemed to understand. He himself was too ordinary to break the impasse his policies had helped to create; he realized he had no choice but to turn to one of the Republic's two outcast giants. "I have to choose," Poincaré confided to his diary in November 1917, "between Clemenceau and Caillaux [for the position of prime minister]. My choice is made."[142] The one represented war without compromise, the other the compromise of peace. Both had violated the cultural conventions of Belle Epoque France* but only one could never be accused of seeing his own country from the foreigner's point of view.[143] Clemenceau, elevated to the prime ministership, presided over two more years of war and over a peace settlement destined to disaster; Caillaux, falsely accused of treason, spent the next three years in jail.

---

* Clemenceau had been a prominent political figure for more than thirty-five years before he was elevated to the cabinet in 1906. He owed this delay in large part to the financial scandals of the 1890s and to his tumultuous—and highly public— love affair with an American woman.

Henriette Caillaux
Femininity, Feminism, and the Real Woman

"On 16 March about three in the afternoon a lady walked into Gastinne-Renette . . . 'I am Madame Caillaux and I want to see a revolver.'"[1]

So testified Georges Fromentin, whose statement highlighted the trial's third day in session. Fromentin worked as a salesclerk for Gastinne-Renette, the elite gun shop on the Right Bank where Joseph Caillaux possessed an account. Henriette Caillaux had approached his counter on the afternoon of 16 March explaining that she needed a small weapon for an upcoming automobile trip through the rural region her husband represented in the Chamber. Fromentin gave her a thirty-two caliber Smith and Wesson revolver, which Henriette found difficult to operate. After several failed attempts to make it work, she descended to the shop's basement firing range where the clerk had arranged for someone more expert to help her. There Henriette tried again, only to bruise her delicate trigger finger. Another employee brought her a different pistol, a Browning automatic, known for its simple operation and flexible trigger. This one gave Henriette no trouble and she acquitted herself reasonably well on the firing range: three of her six shots hit the human silhouette that Gastinne-Renette used as a target. "An average score," judged Fromentin's colleague Antoine Derviller who testified next.

Her practice finished, Madame Caillaux returned to the ground floor where she asked Fromentin to load the gun for her. This was against store rules, so with a bit of coaching Henriette loaded it herself. The procedure involved removing a chamber from the bottom of the gun, filling it with six cartridges, and then snapping it back into place. Loaded, the gun was not ready to fire until Madame Caillaux released the first cartridge into the Browning's barrel. This she did as soon as she stepped into the backseat of her chauffeured car. She was careful to move the safety into place, but otherwise the gun was fully armed.

With this testimony the Calmette family lawyer, Charles Chenu (figure 9), began his prosecution in earnest, focusing the court's attention on Madame Caillaux's gun purchase and target practice just hours before she had herself driven to *Le Figaro*. But he did so in a curious way. Though the episode smacked of premeditation, Chenu emphasized two other elements: the technical difficulty of using the Browning automatic and, more important, Henriette's emotional state. Chenu asked Fromentin to demonstrate how to ready a Browning automatic for action. "You hold the pistol in the right hand," explained the salesclerk, "with your arm taut. You turn it slightly to the left and with your left hand you grab the weapon by the grooved part at the end of the slide chamber and then you pull it hard and fast. Let go, and the cartridge should be in place." Chenu then asked each juror to try it himself, adding, "I do not promise that you will succeed."

The lawyer's intention was subtle, but Madame Caillaux understood it at once. With this elaborate demonstration Chenu hoped to suggest that the Browning was so complicated a weapon that even the members of the court's all-male jury would have trouble figuring it out. Was this not therefore something that ought to be beyond the competence of a normal woman? Henriette agreed, explaining that she could do it only because of unusual circumstances. "I would like to tell the jurors that it is perhaps somewhat less extraordinary for me than for most other women to be able to operate weapons from Gastinne-Renette." She had never actually fired a revolver before—"Never, never," she exclaimed—but since her childhood she had known how to use rifles and carbines. "My father was a great hunter and he taught me how to make his hunting cartridges. I myself hunt." Henriette meant these comments as an explanation of her apparent departure from female propriety, suggesting that she could handle guns only because of an idiosyncrasy of her father, not because she was unfeminine. It goes without saying that Chenu and the rest of her opponents were not convinced.

With this line of questioning Chenu returned to an idea that he had raised from the start, that Henriette Caillaux was not a "real

9. Sketch of Maître Charles Chenu, attorney for the Calmette family
(*L'Illustration*, 25 July 1914).

woman." A real woman does not, he suggested, know how to use guns; a real woman does not practice marksmanship; and a real woman does not carry a loaded weapon in her handbag. *La femme, la vraie femme*, was for most French men of the era a creature governed by her emotions. Her intellect was limited, her practical and technical abilities restrained. The real woman acted not in the exterior world of politics and business, or even of literature and the arts, but in the inner sanctum of the home. She did not make a spectacle of herself—actresses, known for their sexual license, were not real women—nor did she seek to upstage her husband. This womanly woman had no ambition beyond that of caring for her husband, her home, and most important of all her children. She was frail and frivolous, given to transports of childlike sentiment. But her disposition, frustrating as it might occasionally have been for a husband, was as it should be. For the real woman needed not to shape the world but to secure the family.

The lawyer's purpose in attempting to deny Henriette status as a real woman was to undo her defense by crime of passion. That defense rested not just on the Belle Epoque's popular psychology and its romantic imagery but on its male view of women. Only a real woman, one ruled by emotions and nerves, could commit a crime of passion. Thus, Chenu's task—and that of his supporters in the press—was to portray Henriette as more man than woman, as lacking the emotionality and the vulnerability that supposedly made Belle Epoque women what they were.

This "real woman" against whom Henriette was to be compared existed, of course, only in the imaginations of the (mostly male) writers, lawyers, and commentators who had created her. The lives of France's flesh-and-blood women were far more complex. As Bonnie Smith shows, even the most traditionalist of women, those most committed to home, family, and Church, hardly spent the whole of their lives indoors and out of sight. Well-to-do ladies of the leisure class devoted considerable effort to charitable works—feeding and clothing the poor, organizing schools and clubs for young working-class girls, and providing kindergartens and crèches for children. All these efforts took money, and prominent women raised impressive sums through tireless fund-raising activities in their communities. In northern France these charitable endeavors became so successful by the late nineteenth century that municipal officials of the Third Republic, hostile to the charities' Catholic tone and spirit, did their best to dissolve them in favor of secular and bureaucratic alternatives.[2]

But all this evidence of women's strength, initiative, and responsibility was irrelevant to Chenu's argument, for his case against Henriette Caillaux rested on pure stereotype. After Chenu finished the practical demonstrations with his Browning automatic, he made a point of asking both of Gastinne-Renette's salesclerks about Madame Caillaux's emotional state. She had bought the gun less than three hours before firing it into Calmette's abdomen, and the attorney wanted to know whether she seemed distraught or exhibited behavior bizarre in any way, whether she appeared to be driven by passion. "During the course of all these operations [testing the gun, loading it, readying it for use], did Madame Caillaux remain calm, normal, attracting no attention?" "Absolutely," responded Fromentin. With this question Chenu left nothing to chance. He sought not an independent description of Henriette's emotional state but Fromentin's agreement with his own. When he repeated the question to Fromentin's colleague a few minutes later he did not need to cue him so directly. "What was Madame Caillaux's demeanor?" The answer: "Very calm."

Though Chenu paid the most sustained attention to Henriette's emotional state on this, the trial's third day, it was not the first time he had broached the issue. The day before, he had made a point of asking each witness to describe Madame Caillaux's manner immediately after her arrest. "As far as her attitude was concerned, was it impassive?" he asked M. Giraudeau, an editor present when Henriette's six shots rang through *Le Figaro*'s offices. "Absolute calm, indifference; she gave the impression of being absolutely detached from what had just happened." Giraudeau, a friend and colleague of Calmette's, had already said as much in his opening statement: "Madame Caillaux remained immobile in the corridor, impassive, still, showing no emotion whatever." Other *Figaro* employees seemed to fix on one of the words used by Chenu and Giraudeau, volunteering that she seemed "impassive."

Had they been coached? We cannot know with certainty, but it seems likely that Chenu had stressed beforehand to these close collaborators of Calmette's the importance of Henriette's unemotional state. Another *Figaro* editor referred to her absolute "self-control" after the crime, "an attitude that horrified me." And yet another, a veteran of the *fait divers*, testified that in all his years of crime reporting he had "never seen anyone as calm as Madame Caillaux." Most assassins, he said, rant and rave after their act; Henriette exhibited an "absolute tranquility."

Such testimony seemed to say that Henriette was not the kind of woman who merited the indulgence of men. Where, Chenu queried, was the spontaneous emotionality in an individual who chose her weapon with such calculated care? And where was the feminine vulnerability in a woman whose familiarity with guns seemed to surpass that of the average man? French men of the Belle Epoque claimed to owe nothing to females who acted more like men than women, who were more attached to the external masculine world than the familial womb of hearth and home. Chenu's strategy could not have been more apt, given France's notorious indulgence for the crime of passion. And Maître Labori (figure 10) took great pains to counter it, to convince the jury of Henriette's all too feminine emotionality. The stakes, after all, were very high. As a "real woman" Henriette might go free; as a man-woman she was sure to be condemned.

Immediately after Chenu finished with his witnesses, Labori introduced a parade of people who swore that Henriette had been anything but calm.[3] Joseph's chief of staff, Emile Labeyrie, testified to being shocked by Henriette's demeanor when he saw her at noon, some six hours before the assassination. She looked, he said, like "a hunted animal." Henriette seemed so visibly upset that Labeyrie became worried, upset himself. As he greeted her, "she looked at me vacantly, hardly even saying hello." The witness then proceeded to counter Chenu's picture of Henriette as calm in the immediate aftermath of the crime. "My impression was just the opposite." Other witnesses could find her calm only because they did not know her. "I knew Madame Caillaux, and I was able to discern in the words she uttered, in her look, in the way she carried herself, the color of her skin, many things that others could not see." Anyone who knew her, he said by way of conclusion, could see that "this was a being no longer in possession of herself."

Next Labori called Yvon Delbos, editor in chief of the left-leaning *Le Radical*. As Labeyrie had, Delbos disputed the characterization of Madame Caillaux as coldly unemotional. What seemed like calm, he said, was really a severe depression brought on by Calmette's

10.   Sketch of Maître Fernand Labori, Henriette Caillaux's attorney (*L'Il-lustration*, 25 July 1914).

revelations. Just hours before her fatal act, he "found her slouched across her armchair, her look stiff and despondent." Still, Delbos continued, nothing in what she said or did made him suspect for an instant what she was about to do. "She was extremely depressed, but this was precisely the opposite of that exultation, that sort of lucid insanity that took hold of her [the very next day]."

After Delbos, other witnesses testified to Henriette's extreme emotionality during the days before she assassinated Calmette (figure 11). Madame Chartran, one of Henriette's close friends, found her "extremely nervous, wounded by the article [in *Le Figaro*] that had appeared the day before." On 15 March, that is twenty-four hours before Henriette Caillaux shot Calmette, Madame Chartran believed her friend had descended into "a terrible state of depression." Henriette, Madame Chartran explained, had just been to a reception where someone had insulted her, citing information from *Le Figaro*. "She looked anguished, the pain evident on her face. She must have been trembling because I said to her, 'Calm yourself, my good friend; this will all settle down in time.' "

The litany of depositions continued with Isidore de Lara, a composer of music who was friendly with both Madame Caillaux and Gaston Calmette. Lara had lunched with Henriette on 13 March, the day *Le Figaro* published the "Ton Jo" letter. "I noticed in Madame Caillaux a huge change. She seemed indignant and in the grip of an extreme nervousness." Two days later Henriette expressed fears for her husband's life. "They will end up by killing my husband," she told Lara. Still, he concluded, despite all her fears and anxieties, "I have the profound conviction that on Sunday [the day before the assassination] Madame Caillaux had not the least thought of committing an act of violence."

Henriette herself endeavored to confirm the impression Labori was trying to evoke. On the trial's second day she made several interjections—without being called to testify—disputing the opposition's efforts to portray her as unruffled and emotionless. "The gentlemen from *Le Figaro* [who swore to her impassivity] did not know me, so it was perhaps more difficult for them than for others to see the emotion that gripped me. Not everyone expresses emotions out loud."[4]

After these attempts to establish that Madame Caillaux was anything but calm before and after visiting Calmette at *Le Figaro*, Labori next seemed to elicit a testimonial to her femininity. The attorney asked Eugène Moran, another long-standing friend of Henriette's, to describe her character. Moran had been among Madame Caillaux's luncheon companions on 13 March. "Never before had I seen in her such sweetness, such an absence of violence." His next statement seemed at first to damage Labori's case: "No matter what the subject of conversation, Madame Caillaux responded calmly,

11. Henriette Caillaux listens to a witness (*L'Illustration*, 25 July 1914).

with extreme sweetness, without ever getting agitated or nervous." But despite her characterization as calm, it was a sweet feminine calm fully consistent with the Belle Epoque's male image of true womanhood, not the masculine absence of emotion that Chenu hoped to portray.

As *La Revue*'s Jean Finot had made clear in a 1911 article, "The Psychology of Women," men of his era viewed women both as highly emotional and as soothing, sweet, and passive.[5] The contradiction was only apparent, for emotionality and sweetness formed the two sides of the same feminine coin. As long as women remained insulated from worldly stimulation they were subdued, sweet, and loving. But because their nervous systems were so fragile, so vulnerable to the least upset, their serenity readily gave way to waves of passion that took charge of them, body and soul. A woman could be sweet and composed one moment; depressed, anxious, even violent another. That Madame Caillaux was said to display such shifts in mood—sweet on 13 March, overexcited two days later—provided just the evidence of feminine character Labori sought. (It need hardly be said that Labori's witnesses did not portray Monsieur Caillaux's equally dramatic shifts in mood in similar terms.) Especially useful was Moran's conclusion, an ode to Madame Caillaux's femininity almost worshipful in tone. "Madame Caillaux reminded me of one of those eighteenth-century portraits of women shown with an infinite sweetness, particularly those pastels that have a great sweetness of expression." With this statement, Labori's witness endowed Henriette with the artist's ideal of womanhood, with a kind of feminine perfection as far removed as possible from the picture Chenu had drawn.

A few months earlier, the *Petit parisien* had evoked precisely the same image of Madame Caillaux by publishing a lengthy interview with one of her oldest friends. The latter, who had known Henriette for some twenty years, described her as "simple, sweet, loving, incapable of rebellion—even, I would say, without will. . . . She lived the tranquil existence of a proper and gracious *parisienne* of the bourgeoisie." Still, Henriette had her moments of extreme emotionality. "I witnessed scenes where she showed a deep nervousness, a moodiness that could shade off into anger." The friend hastened to add, however, that "these were explosions that subsided quickly, the kind of explosions that we women find ourselves subject to all too often."[6]

After Moran came Labori's best witness, Pierre Mortier, the youthful director of *Gil Blas*. Mortier testified that he had been saddened, after "Ton Jo" appeared, to see Henriette's sweetness vanish in favor of a "certain state of exaltation," "a gripping anxiety," "a state of great agitation." The director had been one of the first of Caillaux's friends to arrive at the police station; there, in her state of nervous exhaustion, Henriette told him that she had "only wanted to teach Calmette a lesson." But waiting in a dimly lit room at *Le Figaro*, listening to conversations among editors about their hunting dogs and about "an expensive campaign" made her "lose her head as she entered [Calmette's office]."[7] Mortier had already made clear in an editorial that women "with all their weakness, their apprehension, their suffering" should be judged differently from men.[8] In court, he endeavored to show that Henriette epitomized just such a woman.

It may be that these friends and cronies of Joseph Caillaux had taken their cues from the former finance minister himself. Their testimony sounded many of the same chords as had his highly personal monologue of the previous day. On the stand, Joseph portrayed his wife as too sheltered and too feminine to withstand the day-to-day combat that marked his own political life. Repeatedly the embattled politician referred to her as "ma pauvre enfant" and "ma pauvre créature."[9] In late 1913, just before *Le Figaro's* attacks began, Henriette had begged him not to accept a new cabinet post, citing the inevitable strain on her and on their marriage. But he had dismissed her worries and moved back into the Ministry of Finance. Joseph testified that he had failed to notice his wife's fragile emotional state, and when the press campaign began in earnest he ignored her growing despair. To make matters worse, Joseph later realized, the gag rule he had imposed on his entire retinue had devastated his wife who, unable to voice her fears, "withdrew into herself." In Caillaux's words, "as any woman who loved her man would do, she complied with the order," the order, that is, to remain silent.[10]

Meanwhile the journalistic pressure on Caillaux continued to mount. As an experienced political animal, Joseph could bury himself in work and channel his anger and anxiety into the ongoing parliamentary battle. But Henriette could only sit at home and fret, especially since she had been "ordered" not to confide in her husband. On the few occasions when she did, Joseph only deepened her anguish by promising to "casser la gueule à Calmette." With this promise Henriette acquired yet another worry—that her husband would kill Calmette and ruin their lives.

At the trial Joseph expressed his wife's dilemma in terms of the difference between men and women, between the male's active engagement in the world and the female's impotent distance from it. "You're a man; you live in the midst of political battle; you deliver blows and receive some in return; you are absorbed by your work . . . by the problems of the struggle." Men "armor themselves with the pretense of invulnerability." But what men fail to see, Joseph continued, is that women, weaker to begin with, have no such outlets for their fears and anxiety. "I failed to see the ravages caused by this press campaign [against me] . . . but right next to me there was a poor creature who was suffering, who hid her sorrow." When asked what was wrong, "she responded that she didn't feel well. She transformed her emotional suffering into physical pain. I didn't understand. The fire smoldered unseen beneath the ashes, and then one day the flame shot out."[11]

Caillaux may have composed this statement for the jury's benefit; it nonetheless depicted, eloquently, not just the patriarch's insensitivity but the emotional consequences of cloistering women at home. Its immediate purpose, though, was to portray Henriette as having embraced the Belle Epoque stereotype of femininity so important to the French man's view of himself.

According to the era's vast number of books and articles on the psychology and biology of women, on feminism and femininity, to be a woman—precisely as all the trial's principals suggested—was above all else to be a creature of emotions.[12] Whether for biological or psychological reasons, women were regularly described as hypersensitive, nervous, volatile, irrational, and lacking in self-control.

Among the writers most involved in communicating such views was Charles Turgeon, the influential law professor and critic of feminism. "Because of a nervous system more excitable, more sensitive, more vibrant than that of men," Turgeon wrote, "women are more open to worries, to tenderness, to passion." These qualities, he added, gave women their appeal as well as their defects, for tenderness and passion made them "alluring but dangerous, pacific but explosive, maternal but selfish."[13]

Men often benefit, Turgeon contended, from women's flights of passionate intensity, for this is what makes them so devoted, so caring, so loyal. But at the same time their propensity to flash out of control was what made them so weak, so incapable of willful self-control, so undeserving of masculine trust. It could even cause them to display a "feline malignity" that stood as "a sign and an effect of their weakness and their nervousness." The main casualty of all this was women's strength of will, which Turgeon defined as the ability to "subordinate natural impressions and instinctive impulsions to a mechanism of control that one imposes upon oneself." Men possessed such strength, women did not. And that was why the "weaker sex" vacillated between being the "plaything of diverse impulses that agitate her tumultuously and being the victim of a single but vehement impulse that dominates her imperiously."[14]

Nature had made women this way, Turgeon claimed, and feminists needed to accept that reality, a reality men had long understood. He did go on to admit, however, that a small number of highly educated women seemed to depart from this description. These women displayed a certain rationality, a certain worldly competence. But they confronted a grave danger, the danger that "intellectuality [will] develop at the expense of tenderness, . . . [that] intelligence will vanquish emotion." Turgeon worried that if this were to happen on a large scale, women would cease being women. "Love would become the enemy," marriage would decline and so would the birth rate. "A lettered woman, one . . . interested in nothing beyond the perfection of knowledge and the refinement of intellectual sensibility would not only risk breaking with the habits of her sex, but she would risk separating herself from humanity itself." By mastering her natural emotionality, Turgeon seemed to say, the educated woman neuters herself, renders herself sterile—literally as well as figuratively—and leaves ordinary humanity behind. Such an eventuality would destroy love and weaken the nation. What France needed, Turgeon concluded, was "women, simple and *real* women"—not educated and unemotional asexuals, but real women with all their passions, their volatility, their flightiness, their need for direction and control.[15] A woman was ruled by her emotions or she was not a woman at all.

These themes were repeated again and again between 1900 and 1914. Jean-Paul Nayrac, a disciple of the eminent psychologist Pierre Janet, wrote that woman's "hypersentimentality [was the] cause of all her weaknesses." She was "habitually passive and emotive," a condition that "rendered her a slave and an inferior in the face of modern civilization." And because her "brain was less well organized [than man's], her nervous system reacted nonstop, allowing her to be carried away by the least emotional shock."[16] All this emotional vulnerability made her a likely candidate for crimes of passion; once gripped by anger or jealousy or hatred, a woman easily lost control. Men possessed the ability to resist emotional stimuli, to tame them through the sheer force of rational will. Women, by contrast, enjoyed no such power, for their "affectivity destroyed all their meager resources of will and character . . . often leading them to commit excesses and even crimes."[17]

Lest anyone think these writers produced their works in hopes of changing women, of making them rational rather than emotional creatures, most hastened to affirm the desirability, even the charm, of feminine emotionality. The journalist Henri Marion stated outright that what men liked most about women was precisely the weakness their passions caused. "This basic weakness is what makes them women, very much women, in our eyes." Men enjoyed women's need for control and direction, and "no one likes to see in them an independence of spirit and action."[18] As the writer Octave Mirbeau put it, "women are characterized not by their brains but by their sex, and that is what makes them so desirable."[19] Weakness, vulnerability, irrationality, dependence, such were the qualities that made a woman really a woman.

These conceptions found confirmation in novels from the period, even in those written by women. Colette Yver, one of the period's most prominent women writers, took great pains to warn her readers against the dangers of too much masculine education. *Princesses de science* (1907) told the story of a woman doctor, Thérèse Guéméné, whose successes as a practitioner and a scientist estrange her from her husband, a doctor himself. The more their marriage deteriorates the more he diverts his attention and his affection to a widow of softness and simplicity, a "real woman," in the words of Geneviève Gennari, who devotes some interesting pages to Yver's work.[20] But luckily for Yver's heroine, just as Monsieur le docteur is about to leave her she realizes the error of her ways. At long last she understands that to save her marriage—and her life—she has to abandon her profession. This wise, if belated, action allows the book to end happily: the doctoresse regains her womanhood, the husband his wife.[21] For readers who somehow missed the point, Yver has one of her minor characters recite the moral of the story. "A woman-doctor has no heart, a woman-doctor has no sensitivity, a woman-doctor is not a woman."[22]

Why the need to portray women as so weak and so lacking in emotional control? Why the need to define which women were "real" and which were not, to attempt to ensconce them in their domestic role while punishing those who tried to escape it? This male discourse of the late nineteenth century was far from new, but it seems to have become especially virulent and widespread during this period. For it was in France of the Belle Epoque that the nineteenth century's hierarchic system of gender relations began seriously to break down. Men struggled with increasing difficulty to reserve citizenship, economic prowess, and familial authority exclusively for themselves; male commentators of all kinds reacted sharply—and defensively—to change. That the decline of the old gender order accelerated in the aftermath of the revolutionary Paris Commune and France's humiliating defeat in the Franco-Prussian War (1870–71) is far from coincidental.

The gender order that had done so much to shape French society in the nineteenth century was established during the French Revolution and its Napoleonic aftermath. Though it is a cliché of modern history to associate the French Revolution with the rights of man, what is noted less often is the extent to which that revolution virtually nullified the rights of woman. As Joan B. Landes shows, aristocratic women of the ancien régime possessed a certain power and standing that the male leaders of the French Revolution took away and then refused to extend to any other women.[23] Before 1789, women who inherited noble estates not only could administer them in their own names but in some regions enjoyed the right to vote in local and regional assemblies that such property conferred.

As late as 1661, aristocratic women could still receive titles of no-bility in their own right, and they exercised the prerogatives of their rank by sitting as members of the *parlements* that dispensed justice under the old regime. Dozens of noble women retained seats in various provincial *parlements* until the eve of the French Revolution itself.[24]

Such privileges accrued, it need be said, only to a tiny minority, but a considerably larger group of prominent women enjoyed ex-tensive informal power and influence in what Landes calls the "absolutist public sphere" of the late seventeenth and eighteenth centuries.[25] This sphere consisted largely of urban salons organized and animated by aristocratic women. In these salons intellectual figures, writers, nobles, high government officials, and other mem-bers of the urban elite came together for conversation and conviv-iality in a setting distinct from the much more restricted and hier-archic life of the royal court. All conversation revolved around the female *salonnière* or hostess, who in animating her salon established standards of dress and comportment that her mostly male guests were expected to observe. Thus, in founding these intimate theaters of social and intellectual life, women of the ancien régime not only created an arena of public experience that had never existed before, they made themselves the cultural arbiters of an emerging polite society of cultivation and taste.

Such female prominence, Landes maintains, began to annoy many of the male writers and Enlightenment thinkers who congre-gated in the woman-centered salons. These men of letters came to associate the *salonnières* with the royal mistresses and confidantes, the ladies in waiting and female conspirators, whom "enlightened" men widely believed to exercise undue power at court. In the hands of Jean-Jacques Rousseau, the prophet of virtue, purity, and mod-esty for women, this protest against the aristocratic woman's cul-tural and political power became a critique of the old regime itself. French society and politics were corrupt, Rousseau maintained, because they had become effeminate. Not only had the king's abso-lute power "domesticated" all other men, feminizing them through their inferior status with respect to the patriarch of France; men had also become the vassals of aristocratic ladies. "Every woman in Paris," wrote Rousseau, "gathers in her apartment a harem of men more womanish than she." The grave and virile discourses so characteristic of ancient Greece and Rome had ceased to be heard, Rousseau maintained, in monarchical France, where men had become acculturated to the mannered and superficial chatter of women. Such was not the case, Rousseau added, in the all-male clubs of his own republican Geneva, where "the turn of conversation becomes less polished, [but] reasons take on more weight."[26]

By condemning the absolutist monarchy for empowering women and emasculating men while praising the republic for its grave masculine reason, Rousseau did much, as Landes makes clear, to shape the later discourse and action of the French Revolution.[27] After 1789, and especially after 1792 when the First Republic was declared, revolutionaries set out to eliminate all remnants of an aristocratic culture they believed to be decadent and corrupt. They resolved to replace an effeminate monarchy of artifice and ornament with a virile republic of virtue and reason. To do so, the revolutionaries undertook to banish women from all public life.

In 1793, the Revolution's Jacobin leaders dissolved political organizations composed mainly of women and then banned women from attending any political meetings at all. That same year Olympe de Gouges, author of the "Declaration of the Rights of Woman" was sent to the guillotine for supposed acts of treason while another early feminist, Théroigne de Méricourt, was publicly whipped.[28] Of Gouges's execution a semiofficial newspaper exclaimed, "It seems the law has punished this conspirator for having forgotten the virtues that suit her sex."[29] In 1795 women were forbidden even to sit in the visitors' gallery of the National Convention, and after a violent demonstration in which women were prominently involved, the Convention singled them out for a special kind of punishment, namely confinement to the home: "Be it decreed that all women should retire . . . into their respective homes; those who . . . are found in the streets, gathered in groups of more than five, will be dispersed by armed forces or arrested until public calm is restored."[30]

This was the harshest, most repressive side of the Revolution's treatment of women, the most negative consequence of its desire to keep women from the public sphere. But there was another side to this "privatization" of women, one that was much more positive. For even as revolutionary leaders consigned women to the home, they joined with feminists in declaring that women had something of unique importance to do there. The role of women in the new revolutionary order was to produce the virtuous and patriotic citizens who would people it. Women, especially women of the middling classes, were exalted for their status as "republican mothers," for the crucial part they would play in nurturing and educating the Republic's newborn citizens.[31]

Here, the influence of Rousseau was profound once again, for in his overwhelmingly popular novels *La Nouvelle Héloïse* (1761) and *Emile* (1762) Rousseau extolled the importance of female virtue and of the mother's unique responsibilities for the care and education of her children.[32] But in praising women's contribution, Rousseau insisted that they should limit themselves to their motherly and domestic duties, to the purely private world of family life. In this the French revolutionaries would later agree. "Each sex is called to the occupation that is fitting for it," proclaimed the Jacobin leader André Amar, and women's role was "to begin educating men, to prepare children's minds and hearts for public virtues."[33] Mary Wollstonecraft, the advocate of women's rights who observed the French Revolution, strongly agreed, only she sought to make the belief in republican motherhood into a genuine source of advancement for women. "If children are to be educated to understand the true principle of patriotism," she wrote in *A Vindication of the Rights of Women* (1792), "their mother must be a patriot. . . . But the education and situation of woman, at present, shuts her out" from the knowledge and training that make republican patriotism possible.[34] Women, Wollstonecraft concluded, need to have the same education as men and to enjoy the rights and responsibilities that would make their motherhood meaningful.

Although the French Revolution did not fulfill Wollstonecraft's wish, feminists throughout the nineteenth century would hold fast to the idea that the responsibilities of republican motherhood entitled women to equal rights within the family and to a serious education outside it. The struggle for these rights would be long and hard, for with the exception of new inheritance laws that treated daughters and sons equally, the French Revolution left women worse off than they had been before. No earlier regime had gone so far as to make it a crime for women to appear in public. That ban was lifted, of course, but its spirit remained. Less than a decade later Napoleon was to create a system of laws, the Napoleonic

Code, designed to erase women from public life—if not from the streets—altogether.

Like the revolutionaries who made his ascension possible, Napoleon looked back to the ancient republics and particularly to Rome for inspiration as he set out to found a postrevolutionary legal order. What impressed Napoleon and his advisers about ancient Rome was its patriarchal and paternal authority, the nearly absolute power it gave husbands over families and their wealth. In structuring society this way, the Roman Republic seemed to avoid the excesses of female power that philosophes and revolutionaries alike identified with weakness and corruption. Napoleonic law, like Roman law, would keep women in their place, while raising men high above them.[35]

The Napoleonic Code (1804) was a system of written laws in which judicial decisions were to be made according to statutes, not precedents as in the English and American cases. The code was concerned primarily with the disposition of private property, but its first two sections took up the problems of citizenship and family life in elaborate detail. Perhaps the most characteristic provision of these two sections is the infamous article 213: "The husband owes protection to his wife, the wife obedience to her husband."[36] Throughout the nineteenth century, French courts consistently interpreted this provision to mean, among other things, that the husband possessed the right to determine where the couple would live and to compel his wife to move to his chosen residence. Husbands, moreover, were granted widespread conjugal privileges including the right to force their wives to have sexual intercourse whenever they desired it. The code did not recognize marital rape.[37]

Other specific provisions of Napoleon's civil code added to the husband's sexual rights. A wife's adultery could be punished by imprisonment, a husband's only by a fine—and then only if the wife could prove that her husband's adulterous partner lived in their marital home. A husband who killed his wife after having caught her in *flagrant délit* was not a murderer according to the law, but a wife who surprised her husband in similar circumstances could be charged with a capital offense. The code allowed men to impregnate unmarried women with impunity, for it included no provisions for compelling fathers of illegitimate children to support their offspring. Napoleonic law was so unbalanced with respect to male and female sexuality that it could easily have been based on Napoleon's own notorious sexual conduct. But more generally, the double standard it enshrined was designed to give women the entire responsibility for maintaining the republican ideal of female virtue and purity. The law took any transgressions against that ideal to be women's fault.

If the code gave women sexual responsibility, it endowed men with responsibility for virtually everything else. Under Napoleonic law men possessed complete control over the family's financial affairs, including the right to manage any money, securities, or property that their wives brought to the marriage in the form of a dowry or other personal wealth. In marriages governed by community property, as most marriages were, the husband enjoyed the right to sell any of his wife's personal belongings save her real estate, from which he could nonetheless enjoy the rent. Even in marriages governed by the separation of property, the wife could not alienate her own real estate without her husband's consent. Under both marital regimes, any wages a woman earned belonged by law to her husband, and a woman could not engage in a business or even open a bank account without her husband's permission. Once a woman had gained her husband's permission to start a business, the risks of her enterprise accrued to her while the benefits went to her husband: she could be sued in the case of business disputes, but any profits that she earned passed directly to her husband. At her death, the assets of her business became part of her husband's estate; he alone had the right to determine who would inherit them. Married women, therefore, possessed no more economic independence than did their minor children, for even when they earned their own livelihoods, the law rendered them completely subject to their husbands' control.

As for the realm of law and politics, there women were equally disenfranchised. Not only did they lack the right to vote, they were forbidden from initiating lawsuits, from serving as witnesses in court, and from witnessing such public acts as births, deaths, and marriages. Women, moreover, possessed little legal control over their own offspring. Their husbands alone controlled any property belonging to minor children; fathers alone possessed the right to decide whether children could marry. In addition, fathers could order the arrest and imprisonment of their own minor children for up to six months (one month in the case of those under age sixteen) if they decided such discipline was needed. Fathers retained all these rights even if they no longer resided in the same household with their children. Finally, if a husband died before his wife, the widow automatically retained custody of her offspring only if she did not remarry. If she married again, it was up to the deceased husband's family to decide whether she could keep her children.[38]

With all these rights for men and restrictions for women, the Napoleonic Code, like the French Revolution itself, took the Rights of Man quite literally. And even if the French Revolution did not, as historians once believed, bequeath a new society ruled by the bourgeoisie, it did create a new order governed by men. The Napoleonic Code did much to divide French society by gender, giving it two separate but unequal spheres: a privileged public realm of law, economics, and politics reserved exclusively for men; and a private sphere of sexual virtue, reproduction, and the home where women would reside.

Those who framed the Napoleonic Code clearly intended it not merely to confine women to the private realm but to confirm what most men believed to be women's natural inferiority. Women were excluded from public life because God had not endowed them with the rationality and strength needed to fulfill the responsibilities the larger realm required. The code did not, of course, create its neatly ordered gender hierarchy overnight. As Bonnie Smith demonstrates, in the commercially important north of France women retained a significant role in the management of the region's largely family-owned firms until the midnineteenth century. Before then businesses tended not to be geographically separated from the homes of their owners; women as a result were able to maintain a presence in both realms. Wives often saw to the day-to-day operations of a business while their husbands took to the road in search of new clients and new markets. In one typical case, Monsieur Motte-Brédart spent his days negotiating with customers while Madame directed the operations of their cotton mill.[39] By 1850, however, the mores of the code and the eclipse of family firms, together with a growing male desire to remove women from a marketplace increasingly seen as amoral, conspired to deprive women of their once prominent business roles.

According to the feminist critic Mary Poovey, the nineteenth-century separation of male and female spheres, of a public world of work from a private nest of domesticity, enabled men both to compensate for the amorality of their marketplace and to overcome the alienation it necessarily produced. By barring women from the economic sphere, imprisoning them in a pantheon of domesticity, men sought to make women into goddesses of moral perfection, into the ethical opposites of those whose economic role required them to abandon all values to the pursuit of material gain. Because capitalist competition turned men into objects, separating them from their essential selves, Victorian men, Poovey suggests, sought above all else to recapture an undivided precapitalist humanity. They imagined they could do so by establishing domestic refuges of wholeness and purity designed in the image of Woman, in the image, that is, of the unproductive—and therefore unalienated—being whose nature destined her for the home.[40]

Woman could remain unalienated, it went without saying, only by remaining untainted by the marketplace; those females who refused to be consigned to a home-sweet-home of feminine purity threatened this entire masculine construct and inevitably became the objects of considerable anger and scorn. Victorian men had convinced themselves that their own moral well-being depended on the purity of women, a purity whose inevitable fragility left men feeling anxious and vulnerable.[41] Moreover, as the nineteenth century wore on, women increasingly turned the image of purity itself against the men it was supposed to serve. By framing a discourse of love and compassion and extending their nurturing role outward from the family into a variety of charitable works, middle-class women challenged the capitalist ethic in the name of the very morality intended to legitimize it.[42]

Thus, despite their banishment of middle-class women from the public sphere, men could not relegate them to the wholly inferior status that the Napoleonic Code formally maintained. The French revolutionaries—and their Napoleonic successors—had conceded a certain superiority to women in the crucial areas of motherhood and the management of the home. And by the late nineteenth century women had succeeded in transforming these two acknowledged strengths into sources of genuine power and influence.

As work increasingly took middle-class men away from the

home, women gained more and more effective control over their children and responsibility for their well-being, despite the formal authority the code gave to fathers. Moreover, because men largely abandoned the private sphere of the home to their wives, women, often termed "ministers of the interior," assumed responsibility for the family's everyday life. Bourgeois wives managed the household finances, supervised servants, furnished and maintained the interior—often with distinctive style and taste—entertained family, friends, and business associates, and saw to a good part of their children's education. Women fulfilled all these responsibilities in addition to giving birth to several children and caring for them in the increasingly child-centered family of the industrial era. By the late nineteenth century, middle-class women no longer sent their babies out to wet nurses to be fed and raised through infancy.[43] Bourgeois women were firmly in charge at home, and their role there testifies to women's rationality, responsibility, and resourcefulness, male discourse notwithstanding.

By the later decades of the nineteenth century women appeared to have acquired so much power in the domestic sphere that some male commentators began to complain that their own lives paled by comparison. Day in and day out, men had to leave their homes for jobs they found increasingly boring, even demeaning, as industrialization and bureaucratic expansion stripped even educated middle-class employees of initiative and responsibility. "Our material life," wrote the journalist Théodore Joran, "is becoming more and more cramped, formal, and devoid of all initiative."[44] Women, by contrast, in charge of children and the home, seemed to live fuller lives and wield more power than men. As the novelist Marcel Prévost put it, "Women are, at home, the mistresses of their time. They have as many responsibilities as men, but these responsibilities they fashion for themselves. Women have more independence and leisure [than men]."[45]

How far things had come from the days of the Napoleonic Code! The women it had deprived of political and economic rights now seemed to enjoy in the home itself the very freedom and independence the code had endeavored to take away. As if women had not already turned the tables, they began in the last third of the nineteenth century to infiltrate the public realm as well. First they extended their maternal and domestic responsibilities to charitable work beyond the home; soon they moved into the paid professions themselves, especially the field of education.

As the secularization of the schools after 1879 gradually removed nuns from the classroom, thousands of teaching positions became available throughout the country. Women, already responsible for nurturing and educating young children, were the logical individuals to assume the new posts. Teaching, therefore, became the first profession open to significant numbers of women. Between 1876 and 1886 the number of female elementary school teachers more than doubled, and their numbers continued to rise until 1914.[46] To prepare these *institutrices*, normal schools were established in each French department, and to train the teachers' teachers an elite Ecole normale supérieure was created as well. A law of 1880 added a system of women's secondary schools designed to provide an education that went beyond the three Rs. None of these institutions, save the Ecole normale supérieure, was designed to prepare women for the world of work, much less for a serious life of the mind, but many did so unintentionally. Even though the girls' secondary schools were less rigorous than the boys' lycées, concentrating as they did on the "domestic arts," these institutions inevitably expanded the horizons of their pupils.[47] In growing numbers, girls with a secondary school diploma went into teaching and some began to use what they had learned to make their way into journalism and the arts. A few even went on to the university and to the exalted professions of medicine and law.

It was not until 1880 that women were allowed to attend lectures at the Sorbonne and 1884 that the first women entered the Paris faculty of law. Still, by 1913 there were some 4,250 women enrolled in French universities, nearly 10 percent of the total number of students.[48] Women gained the right to practice medicine in public hospitals in 1885 and the first woman lawyer, Jeanne Chauvin, was admitted to the bar in 1900. Although women progressed very slowly in the legal profession, representing by 1913 a mere 0.25 percent of all lawyers, they moved faster in the field of medicine, a profession that extended women's traditional nurturing and healing role into the wider society. By 1906, France possessed 573 women doctors, 3 percent of the total.[49]

Though the numbers of professional women remained relatively low in the years before World War I, the very existence of women teachers, lawyers, and doctors represented a startling change from what had been the case before. To many men, these female professionals, few as they were, stood as symbols of a new and threatening world of opportunity for women, a world in which women seemed to assert their equality with men. That much of the impetus for these changes came from a newly active feminist movement only made the male reaction against them all the more virulent.[50] It is likely that the explosion during the Belle Epoque of a male literature that insisted upon the emotional and physical weakness of women, upon their rational and intellectual incapacity, came as a reaction against the female advancements of this era.

It should be added that some of these advancements were embodied, albeit timidly, in changes to the Napoleonic Code. The most important of these revisions was the legalization of divorce in 1884 (see chapter 4), a reform made possible in part by a feminist movement that sought to release unhappily married women from the strictures of Napoleonic law. Beyond legalized divorce, women gained the right to open postal savings accounts in their own names and to withdraw money without their husbands' consent (1895). In 1897 single women were granted the right to witness public acts. A decade later married women acquired full ownership over the wages they earned and new legislation obliged their husbands to consult them before alienating family property.[51]

Within the family itself, changes to the code gave women considerably more status. In 1857 a ruling by the *Cour de cassation* ended the father's monopoly of authority over his minor children by granting grandparents and other family members rights under certain circumstances. A law of 1907 reduced fathers' authority further still by granting mothers equal rights over minor children and full "paternal" authority in the case of illegitimate children. Finally, a code revision of 1912 granted advocates of women's rights one of the reforms they had desired the most: the right to initiate paternity suits. With the passage of this bill feminists achieved a crucial victory, for the new law finally required men to assume financial responsibility for their illegitimate children.[52]

All these improvements in the status and condition of women, achieved in large part through the efforts of a growing feminist movement, created intense feelings of fear, hostility, and vulnerability among France's male commentators of the era. Exacerbating these feelings was a lingering sense of impotence stemming from France's disastrous defeat at the hands of Prussia in September 1870 and from the bourgeoisie's momentary collapse some six months later at the hands of Paris's revolutionary Communards; both events moved middle-class French males all the more to assert their superiority over French women. French males—defeated in war, vulnerable to a potent working class—feared deep down that foreigners saw them as lacking in the honor and warriorlike virility still widely believed to embody masculinity itself.[53]

Such collective masculine insecurity could perhaps be cured in the long run through a new war with Germany or in new confrontations with militant workers. In the short run it could be assuaged only by women. French men of the Belle Epoque, like most people in most times, tended to define themselves in relation to those around them, especially to those they saw as other than them, opposite to them. Thus, the more they could persuade French women to conform to a masculine idealization of the *vraie femme*, submissive, obedient, emotional, unthreatening—sexually or otherwise—the more French men could feel the virility to which they aspired. To consider themselves men of the world, French males had first to enforce sex roles at home.[54]

French male insecurities stemming from defeat in war, both international and interclass, found their way explicitly into the journalistic commentary of the Belle Epoque. The influential daily *Le Gaulois* devoted its front-page editorial on New Year's Day 1900 to the New Woman and to what she portended for the French future. Her effect, the editors wrote, would be monumental. "Of all the changes that have undone and reconstructed the appearance of every element of our country, the most important is the one that has modified the nature of woman and deflected her from her past." In the space of a century, they maintained, the French woman had transformed herself from the archetypal female of Napoleon's time to the masculinized intellectual of the new twentieth century. Under Bonaparte's Empire, members of the fair sex were "women down to the marrow of their bones." Which meant that they "submitted themselves willingly to their men, men who asserted a maleness more magnificent than in any other era." Napoleonic women, moreover, were "calm and patient, sweet and dulled by the constant companionship [of women and children], and by the inertia of their lives." And perhaps most important, the Empire's women were overwhelmed "by the intense and magnificent whirl of activity accomplished by men who returned home between two battles to get them with child, only to hasten back to the front having left behind the overpowering image of conquerors." None of these women, the article added, were particularly intelligent, but their beauty more than compensated. Besides, "history did not need women of genius; the heroism of men was enough."[55]

This statement cut to the heart of men's fears in the Belle Epoque, for the editors made clear that for them masculinity and femininity were inextricably linked, that the nature of one defined the nature of the other. Napoleonic women, they suggested, were "real" in an archetypal way precisely because their men were so "magnificently male." The real woman was explicitly paired with the virile (and perhaps brutal) conquering man, a male who treated his women with the same spirit of conquest he displayed on the battlefield. But if each sex was defined by its opposite, if men were magnificently male only when women expressed their femininity in willing submissiveness, then what would happen to men as women began to assert themselves? Did not, in other words, the emancipation of women imply the subjugation of men, the strengthening of women the weakening of men? And most ominous of all, it seemed to follow that the decline in French power abroad after 1815 directly paralleled the decline in men's relative position at home. Having lost the ability to rule their women, French males were no longer man enough to rule the world. The editors of *Le Gaulois* believed it was no coincidence that French men had never exerted so much authority over their women as when they held all Europe in their hands as soldiers of Napoleon. The gender order established by the Napoleonic Code seemed to parallel the Napoleonic order created by the emperor's victorious armies. The masculinization of women since that time seemed to signal not just the feminization of men but the emasculation of France.

All of this was confirmed, the editors continued, in the aftermath of France's humiliating 1870 defeat at the hands of Prussia. The new women of the late nineteenth century, they wrote, "grew up in the depressed atmosphere of defeat that the conquering Prussians had left in their wake." And in this atmosphere French women saw their men with new eyes, eyes that had been opened by a democratic system of education new to the era. "Women experienced the fearful contact of ideas . . . and having grown accustomed to seeing the world's truths, even to making bold use of them, they became masculinized. And the first thing they did with the new intellectual abilities we gave them was to judge their men, *diminished as men were by all that women had conquered.*"[56] Not surprisingly, the editors added, these budding new women looked to France's humbled male and asked themselves, "*That* is the master we're supposed to respect?" What could there be to respect in a "man, demoralized by the acceptance of defeat," and by the wan permissiveness of the Republic it had made possible?

It is important to note that the word "conquest" appeared over and over again not just to describe the Prussian victory in 1870 but to characterize the emancipatory gains of women. These writers felt that women's conquest of men went hand in hand with Prussia's conquest of France. The connection was reciprocal, the weakening of men vis-à-vis their women both explaining and being explained by the military disaster at Sedan. Men had lost the war abroad because they were losing the battle of the sexes at home, and they were losing the battle of the sexes at home because they had lost the war abroad. No longer was France the land of "magnificent males" to whom women and nations submitted. Now it was French men who found themselves on the bottom, in effect the overpowered women of Europe.

These were not isolated sentiments. Similar views appeared regularly in surveys of public opinion published in the daily press. One of the most extensive of these was an *enquête* devoted to the question, "Is there a crisis of love?" sponsored by *Le Matin* and later republished in a volume entitled *Un homme qui comprend les femmes* edited by the journalistic notable Hugues Le Roux. In his commentary Le Roux focused on what he called the new hermaphrodites, the large number of men and women who in the turmoil of contemporary France seemed to have lost all gender identity. Women, he claimed, had become masculinized—mostly through education— and men feminized to the point that both appeared to meet in a uniquely French space of gender neutrality.[57] Le Roux's purpose in making this point was to alert his compatriots to the sexual superiority of Germany, still the home of real women and virile men. That country possessed only a tiny elite of women intellectuals, and unlike their French counterparts, these sexless beings were outcasts in their own country, outcasts because German men had become so masculine, so brutally male in their triumphant return from the Franco-Prussian War. "The German hero, having returned from the war bloody, jack-booted, half drunk from his victory and from French champagne, had repelled these learned women with their military ways. They were afraid he would annex them as if they were simple provinces."[58] As a result, these women never married and now, Le Roux claimed, they wished they had never been educated at all.

This remarkable statement reveals the extent to which French male fears about Germany were related to gender and sexuality. For Le Roux explicitly drew a connection between the fate of France and the fate of women at the hands of supermasculine men. The Prussian conqueror had dealt with both in precisely the same way, annexation. France's prize provinces of Alsace and Lorraine had been annexed—that is, conquered—in the same way as the German maiden's virtue. German soldiers had been able to compel France's feminized men to submit to superior force, to the force of real men capable of imposing their will and planting their seed. French men, Le Roux suggested, were the women of Europe, and that is why France as a nation was so vulnerable.

The question, then, for Le Roux and for many others in France was how to prevent such a violation of the nation's manhood from happening again. French men needed to restore their collective masculinity, and they sought to do so by stemming the tide of women's emancipation. If the French woman could become a real woman once again—much as Bonapartist myth had characterized her—then the French man would necessarily regain the virility believed to characterize the Napoleonic age.

These attitudes concerning women and the connection between masculinity and femininity shaped the cultural environment in which the *affaire Caillaux* unfolded. Almost everyone connected with the trial, from the extreme right-wing *Action française* to the revolutionary *Guerre sociale* (feminists were the notable exception), agreed on what constituted a real woman and on the naturalness of this image of femininity. Virtually all concerned believed that real women should not be judged according to the standards of men. The problem for Madame Caillaux was that not everyone agreed she conformed to the proper female image. Even before the trial began, views of Henriette Caillaux's status as a real woman broke down along right-left lines. For conservative papers like the *Action française* and *Le Figaro* Madame Caillaux was more man than woman and as such deserved no special consideration. But for Caillaux's allies on the Radical and Socialist left, Henriette epitomized the sheltered and childlike woman to whom the masculine rules of justice did not fully apply.

In a pretrial editorial *L'Action française* referred to Madame Caillaux as "a capable and determined woman," as a woman, that is, with masculine qualities. And reporting on the case's first day the paper made its position even clearer. Decent men, the editors wrote, naturally feel sympathy for a (real) woman accused of major crimes. "We know full well what [the real woman] has done, but still we expect to feel a conflict between our knowledge of the facts, our reason, our sense of justice on the one hand, and our human sentiments on the other." In Madame Caillaux's case, however, they felt no such conflict. Her self-assured, haughty, almost masculine manner absolved them of chivalry's demands. "She enters [the courtroom] with assurance . . . [speaking] with perfect ease," poised like a parliamentary "orator." "This criminal," they concluded, "is no 'femme fatale.' "[59]

The editors of *Le Figaro*, individuals with personal as well as ideological hostility to Madame Caillaux, appeared more determined even than the *Action française* to deny Henriette status as a real woman, to portray her as calm, rational, and coldly unemotional. In one page of newsprint, *Le Figaro*'s *chroniqueur* used the word "calm" no fewer than eight times. And he returned again and again to words like "unemotional," "cool," "controlled," "lucid," and to typical passages such as these: "Her face showed no apparent emotion. . . . Without emotion, Madame Caillaux contemplates the twelve men who will judge her." "During three solid hours of testimony, this woman demonstrated more calm, more control, and more mastery of her nerves than anyone in the history of the *Cour d'assises*. Never did tears light her eyes . . . never did her heart pound or her voice—always sure of itself—strangle in her throat." "Try as she might to cry, she knew not how."[60]

What *Le Figaro* wanted to emphasize above all with these statements was Henriette's fundamentally unfeminine nature. "She tried to summon the sentimentality habitual in the *Cour d'assises,* emphasizing her words for effect: I was a *mother,* I was a *woman.* But instead all that emerged from this testimony was a speech utterly lacking in sensibility and steeped in a disconcerting calm." In the editors' view, Madame Caillaux had left femininity behind for the masculine world of ambition, power and politics. "What we hear in [her speech] is the tones of parliament; never do we discern the voice of a woman."[61]

The contrast between *Le Figaro* and the press sympathetic to the Caillaux is so startling as almost to suggest an entirely different case. For *Gil Blas,* a paper of the moderate left, Henriette was the quintessential woman: weak, vulnerable, prey to her emotions. In court, *Gil Blas* reported, she appeared too helpless and too fragile to answer the charges against her. The paper's *chroniqueur,* a lawyer named Campinchi, called Henriette a "simple woman overwhelmed with suffering . . . an anguished woman [condemned each night] to the gloomy darkness of the Conciergerie." Throughout the trial "she cried silently."[62]

The *Petit parisien,* having described Madame Caillaux as "the victim of an inconceivable overexcitement," credited her testimony with a "tone of sincerity." Whereas *Le Figaro* claimed she had shed not a single tear, the *Petit parisien* emphasized that "sobs punctuated her tale."[63] Finally, the left-wing *Hommes du jour* invoked—with appropriately delicate language—the ultimate excuse for feminine weakness and emotionality. "On the morning of her crime this overexcited woman was prey to what is familiarly called her period. This is yet another reason to see that she was bewildered to the point of irresponsibility."[64]

That the two portraits of Madame Caillaux were so utterly opposed testifies to the high stakes involved in viewing her one way or the other. And if this press commentary were not proof enough, the *Journal des débats* confirmed the extent of concern, in and around the courtroom, with her emotional legitimacy as a woman. "People [observing the trial] reproach Madame Caillaux for the levelheadedness with which she presented certain details. As for her effort to give a certain effect, for her overall bearing, these are hotly debated in the corridors."[65]

Neither the image of fragile female nor of hardened New Woman, of course, could capture the reality of an existence far more complex than either side in the case wanted to admit. The absence of sources makes it impossible to know the details of Henriette Caillaux's life, to perceive the fullness of her thought and emotions, but what little can be discerned makes it clear that she conformed to neither of the masculine myths that had been used to portray her. Her father's interest in having her learn to hunt and shoot suggests an upbringing removed from that of the idealized real woman depicted by the defense, as perhaps does her attraction to such a flamboyant figure as Joseph Caillaux. Moreover, her willingness to become sexually involved with the Radical leader while still married to her first husband—and then to chance the social stigma of divorce—is characteristic not of timidity and a retiring nature but of a certain independence of spirit and willingness to take risks. Nevertheless, none of these characteristics made her the cold and calculating *hommesse*, the stereotypical New Woman of her opponents' imaginations. Henriette Caillaux had married while still in her teenage years and, saving a short period after her divorce, remained married until her second husband's death. Madame Caillaux spent virtually the whole of her adult life as a mother and a homemaker; she appears not to have received a secondary education or to have prepared in any way for the world of work or the professions. Nor is there evidence of any association on her part with feminists or with any branch of the feminist movement. Like other women of the wealthy upper middle class, Henriette Caillaux enjoyed certain freedoms and opportunities denied women of more modest income but in no way used her wealth to become what contemporary feminists would have considered an emancipated woman.

This absence of feminist ties did not prevent Madame Caillaux's opponents from claiming that she sympathized with the women's movement or from blaming the emancipation of women for her act of violence against Calmette. Thus, closely related to the battle over Madame Caillaux's status as a real woman was her putative connection to feminism. Those who saw her as more man than woman called her a feminist, whereas her defenders sought to distance her as much as possible from any taint of new womanhood. If she was a real woman, she could hardly be a feminist.

Writing in *Le Journal*, the conservative columnist Lucien Descaves was one of those who attributed Henriette's act to the Belle Epoque's newfound emancipation of women. His article, "Other Mores," recalled the good old days when men fought their battles for themselves and women remained above the fray. During the Paris Commune, wrote Descaves, feuding activists left their wives at home and settled things for themselves. Their wives thought enough of the men to believe them "capable of meeting their adversaries and triumphing." In those days men were men and women stayed home where they could comfort their husbands and, if need be, attend to their wounds. Wives never said [as Madame Caillaux did], "There is no justice in France." Nor did they go out and buy a revolver and practice firing it. In times past, the wife launched her husband into battle; now he launched her. Not, Descaves neglected to add, that the men had performed so well back in 1870 and 1871. But that, of course, was precisely what made writers like himself so sensitive to the idea of women's fighting men's battles in their place. For this conservative writer, to open politics to women did not merely upset the sexual balance; it robbed men of their very masculinity.[66]

With statements such as these, right-wing commentators trapped themselves in something of a contradiction. On the one hand they blamed feminism, which for them meant the masculinization of women, for Madame Caillaux's crime. But on the other they attributed that crime to the female's supposed childishness and irrationality. Pierre Mille, the prominent journalist, maintained that in an age of female emancipation to give women access to guns was to guarantee that guns would be used. When women were confined to the home there was little danger. But now that they participated in politics and public life, Madame Caillaux's example would become the norm. The problem, Mille claimed, was that "women are impulsive beings who have no idea what they are doing. They are just as likely to kill you with a gunshot as to hurl a saucer at your head."[67]

What gave such arguments a ring of plausibility for right-wingers was a notorious statement about women and guns by the radical feminist Madeleine Pelletier. In *L'émancipation sexuelle de la femme* (1911), Pelletier wrote that "women should adopt the habit of carrying revolvers for evening outings and walks in the country." Beyond providing protection in case of danger, "the revolver creates a psychic aura of power; the simple fact of feeling it on you makes you stronger."[68] Pelletier clearly recognized the symbolic power firearms had long held for men, which helps to explain why they condemned her almost to a man. Most mainstream feminists, it should be added, condemned her as well, for they feared that her extreme views—especially her belief in sexual liberation—would discredit their movement.[69] Their concerns were justified; Pelletier provided a convenient target for antifeminists who used her rupturous commentary to dismiss feminism as a whole. Unwittingly, she contributed considerable ammunition to the opponents of Madame Caillaux.

Two months before the trial *Le Figaro's* new editor, Alfred Capus, claimed it was feminism that drove Henriette Caillaux to kill Gaston Calmette.[70] Women had been urged to carry guns, Capus wrote, and because Henriette did so Calmette lay dead. That Capus could provide no concrete evidence of any feminist influence on Madame Caillaux underscored the contradiction that had snared other conservatives as well. Capus attributed Henriette's act of violence both to a manly engagement with the world and to a childlike departure from its rules, to the feminist quest for worldly power and to the traditional woman's supposed lack of self-control.

Such a distorted notion proved too much for France's feminist leaders, who departed from their characteristic caution to denounce its inconsistencies. Jane Misme, editor of France's leading feminist newspaper, joined with Henriette's supporters in maintaining that feminism had nothing to do with her crime. Without condoning the assassination, Misme argued that crimes like Madame Caillaux's occurred because France's ideal of the "real woman" kept them in a state of political immaturity, not because of any new feminine independence. Even the most elementary sense of politics, Misme continued, would have prevented Henriette from taking the action she did. But because she had been excluded from public life, she "understood nothing of the battle" her husband confronted. As a result, she reacted to adversity first by becoming "enervated, then frantic, and suddenly she committed murder."[71]

Antifeminists claimed, Misme wrote, that impulsive behavior like Henriette's "represents what is essentially feminine and that this is what we should expect on a larger scale if women succeed in penetrating the political realm." But the reality was just the opposite. "Madame Caillaux," the editor declared "is emphatically not a feminist. She epitomizes the traditional woman, so completely 'feminine' as to remain exempt from all interest in intellectual or social life." Her act expressed a frustration born of ignorance and powerlessness; in no way did it represent the emancipation of women. Crimes like Madame Caillaux's subjected men not to the "new woman" but to the explosive rage of the femme fatale. Only education and equality, concluded Misme, "could make women into the conscious allies of men and no longer their unconscious enemies."[72]

Misme might have added that given the moral pedestal upon which women had been placed, Henriette Caillaux may have shot Calmette in part because she believed she possessed the right to exact justice herself. If women were purer and more moral than men, as nineteenth-century commentators often maintained, then why should Henriette not imagine she could punish Calmette for his transgressions? Indeed, immediately after shooting Calmette, Henriette Caillaux described what she had done as an act of personal justice, as a protest against a society in which official justice had ceased to exist: "Because there is no longer any justice in France," she had executed Calmette. Her actions testified to the confusion that could arise in women from being encouraged to feel morally superior while being unable to experience the full possibilities and limits of the public realm.

In most of her comments, therefore, Misme appeared to bolster Henriette's claim to be a real woman, but in other respects she took her distance from both sides in the *affaire Caillaux*. To voices on the right she maintained that feminism, far from provoking acts of violence, would add to civic responsibility by initiating women to public life. And to commentators on the left she suggested that Henriette's predicament, and thus Joseph's as well, was the logical consequence of their own feminine ideal. Finally, to the men on both sides her words contained an implicit warning: beware of the traditional woman. If you fail to grant her standing and responsibility she may target you next.

Femininity and feminism. Because no controversy existed over whether or not Henriette Caillaux had killed Gaston Calmette, she would be judged in large part through the meanings and associations suggested by those two words. The jury would decide her guilt or innocence by considering evidence that related as much to her character as to her actions on 16 March 1914. Did she qualify as a real woman? And if so, to what extent did her femininity itself or, to be more precise, the way her culture judged that femininity constitute the extenuating circumstances that might diminish her guilt? The peculiar nature of this case explains why both lawyers devoted as much time as they did to Henriette's emotional state and to her connection with feminism. But these two issues did not exhaust the question of whether or not Henriette qualified as a real woman. Other aspects of her character were important too, particularly her marital bond, her domesticity, and, above all, her sexuality. France's middle-class morality remained quite stern in the early years of the twentieth century, and though bourgeois men and women violated it often enough, a real woman took great care to disguise her sins. If Henriette could be portrayed, therefore, as a proper bourgeoise, as a woman devoted to home and husband, protective of her children, careful about her reputation, she would be viewed all the more as *vraiment femme*.

Just as Henriette was about to finish her testimony two days earlier, on the trial's first afternoon, she had added a coda intended to convince the jury of her standing as a good and proper bourgeois lady. This statement served as her summation, as the part of her discourse she hoped the jury would remember best. In it what she stressed above all was her claim to real bourgeois womanhood. Madame Caillaux wanted to leave the lasting impression that her "honor as a woman," her propriety, and her reputation defined the whole of her character.

"Oh I know," Henriette told the jury, "that people have often criticized me for being a bourgeoise, that people tease me all the time. But everything they say is true, and I'm not embarrassed by it. I am a bourgeoise." It was for this reason that she worried so about the possibility Joseph's love letters would be published, for they represented her "dearest and deepest secrets." To make them public would have been to "strip [her] naked" before all the world.[73]

So concerned, Henriette testified, was she to preserve her reputation that when Berthe Gueydan had first seized the intimate letters in September 1909, she and Joseph had decided to break off all relations rather than have the documents divulged to the press.

"Both of us preferred to renounce our great affection rather than see our intimacy displayed." Later on when Calmette printed the "Ton Jo" letter and with it threatened to reveal the others, Henriette feared for her entire (bourgeois) way of life. "We had extended dinner invitations to a group of important civil servants and to some foreign ambassadors. Three weeks later I was to be presented to the king and queen of England. What a humiliation [the letters] would have been for me, because all these people read *Le Figaro*."[74]

Even worse, Henriette concluded, the letters would have wounded her daughter where it would surely have hurt the most, her carefully nurtured purity. This nineteen-year-old, unmarried and untouched, "would herself have been affected by the publication," by its evidence of her mother's errant past. "What a disillusionment for someone so pure of heart," Madame Caillaux declared, to learn from "journalists moved by hatred and desire for revenge" that her mother had not lived up to the moral principles by which she had raised her daughter. There would have been no way to keep the newspapers from her, and Henriette "imagined the silent reproaches that would have shown on her face." Henriette would have been forced to admit wrongdoing, even hypocrisy, in front of her daughter. This she could not abide. "No, there are things that must never be asked of a mother."[75]

As it turned out, of course, Henriette was forced to admit all this and more. By killing Calmette she guaranteed the revelation of precisely those documents she had wanted so desperately to keep secret. Henriette's opponents might have used this contradiction against her, except that she had already effectively disarmed them by making it part of her defense. To have assassinated a leading journalist in an effort to shield her private life from the news was nothing if not irrational. What better proof, she suggested, that her crime had been motivated by passion alone—that she was a real woman ruled by real emotion.

With her statement concerning what the letters might reveal, all that remained of Henriette's testimony was to apologize for the "great unhappiness" she had caused and to declare that she "would have preferred to have almost anything published rather than be the cause of what has happened." It is significant that save for this penultimate expression of regret, de rigueur before any *cour d'assises*, Henriette ended with an appeal to the exigencies of bourgeois morality. What was so frightening, she maintained, about the publication of her guilty correspondence was its ability to show her lacking in the morality she wanted so much to represent.

How plausible and how potentially successful, given what can be discerned of the Belle Epoque's middle-class standards, was such a defense? The authority on this question is Anne Martin-Fugier whose illuminating work on the era's bourgeois womanhood helps put Madame Caillaux's professed outlook and ideals into proper historical perspective. Martin-Fugier makes it clear that to be correctly a bourgeoise required at least the outward adherence to a strict set of standards. Above all, marriage and motherhood were essential, for both were seen as every young woman's ultimate goals. To reach the midtwenties without having accomplished either was to render oneself déclassé. Once married, the new bourgeois wife was charged with providing her husband a comfortable "nest," with fashioning a refuge beyond his world of travail. For this reason, the middle-class woman did not work outside the home. To do so was enough in itself to disqualify her from real bourgeois womanhood.[76]

The period proliferated with books of advice on how to be such a woman. By far the most popular belonged to a series written by Baronne Staffe, who sought to train women of middling means in the ways of the true bourgeoisie. Her volumes ranged from *Customs of High Society: Rules of Modern Savoir-vivre* to *The Mistress of the Home, My Secrets to Help You Please Others and Be Loved,* and finally to *The Woman in the Family.*[77] An advertising brochure promised that the last would "show the woman the role she must fill in the paternal home." Its message, the baronne wrote, marked the culmination of all her other works, for it taught women how "to introduce joy, comfort, and well-being into the home, how to make it into a nest so warm and so sweet as to be almost painful to leave." The home was the "royaume de la femme" in which no sacrifice was too great for the benefit of its inhabitants.[78]

Beyond sacrifice, the bourgeois woman needed to please. In a chapter entitled "How to Please Him," the baronne explained the winning ways of the real woman. "To be loved by a man, a woman must not have the slightest masculine trait, either mentally or physically. . . . To be really a woman, she must have plenty of grace and virtues, the most important being self-abnegation and devotion."

What do men want? Staffe asked, displaying an impressive grasp of the era's male insecurities: "They want a companion who is amiable, gay, serene, and accommodating." They want a woman who is more heart than head. "To please him, hide half of your brain but show him the whole expanse of your heart." Above all, "never seek to outshine your husband; to relegate him to second place is not to be a real woman."[79]

By these standards Henriette appeared to do quite well. The comfort of the Caillaux' "nest" was legendary, as was the efficient way she managed their home. Of his marriage, Joseph wrote, "Henriette brought me a large dowry, and even more important, she introduced into my household a strong measure of order and economy."[80] It goes without saying that Madame Caillaux did not work and, unlike Joseph's first wife, did not try to outshine her husband or even to stand out in any way.[81] As Madame Caillaux's long-standing friend had explained to an interviewer from the *Petit parisien*, "As a married woman, [Henriette] was always faithful to her duties. She was a perfect woman of the interior, an excellent mother . . . she was even deeply *popote* (a homebody)."[82]

The real woman, as the advice books made clear, devoted herself to her husband's well-being. And Henriette represented herself as having taken this advice, explaining her action against Calmette as motivated by love and self-sacrifice. Joseph had told her he would kill his rival if *Le Figaro* published more personal letters, and Henriette claimed she became so worried he would make good his threat that she had decided to act in his place. "The fear of seeing my husband kill a man, of seeing him arrested . . . [ellipsis in original] of all the consequences that would follow, all this gave me the idea to undertake a supreme effort myself." Hers, Henriette suggested, was an act of devotion, a sacrifice of the self in favor of her husband, his political career, and ultimately the nation: "France and the Republic need you," Henriette had written Joseph just prior to leaving for *Le Figaro*, "so it is I who will commit the act." Henriette had resolved to "do justice" in hopes of sparing Joseph the need to defend her honor. She would sacrifice herself for the greater good of her husband and of the Republic he embodied.[83]

Here was an explanation the male jury could find compelling: a husband was prepared to risk everything to defend his wife's honor, and to protect him a wife took action herself. As always in the Caillaux case, it is impossible to know whether this part of Henriette's defense had been planned beforehand. If so, the strategy was brilliant, for it enabled Madame Caillaux to make what seemed to be premeditation pure and simple into an act of devotion worthy of Baronne Staffe herself.

On the whole, Henriette's testimony and that of her friends made a strong case for her real womanhood, for bourgeois virtues seemingly above reproach. But there remained one crucial part of her life story that raised considerable doubt: her sexuality. Madame Caillaux, after all, was an adulteress. She had cuckolded her first husband, ultimately divorcing him to involve herself with a married man who would divorce to wed her. Such were not the ways of the true bourgeoise. According to Martin-Fugier a real woman, one who upheld the era's cultural ideals, was expected to maintain a facade of sexual indifference, even after marriage. Respectable bourgeois wives were not supposed to enjoy sex—certainly they would never divorce over it—and sexuality could never be a topic of conversation, not even between mothers and daughters. The pleasures of the flesh were to remain the pure province of mistresses and prostitutes, for the Belle Epoque had raised the old distinction between mother and whore to a matter of principle. As Jules Renard's Monsieur Vernet says in *L'Ecornifleur* (The sponge), "Une femme n'est pas une femme."[84]

One's wife was not to be an object of sexual desire, since to desire her was to degrade her. Worse, male moralists of all persuasions warned that those who stimulated their wives sexually risked losing them to adultery. "With the habit of pleasure in a marriage," wrote J. P. Dartigues, "[women] slide imperceptibly into adultery." If one's wife was treated as a mistress, men were told, she was bound to become mistress to another. Such masculine fears betrayed more than a desire for order within the family; they revealed a sexual uneasiness of serious proportions.[85]

Again and again commentators cautioned husbands to have only the most uninspired sex with their spouses. And women's nighttime fashions seemed to oblige, allowing married couples to procreate with their clothes on. Popular among bourgeois wives were long nightgowns that left only the hands and feet exposed. A slit was strategically located in the midsection so there would be no fleshy display to create undue excitement. In 1901, a newspaper advertised these nighties with the sobriety they deserved: "[Our night-gowns] have at the bottom of the hips a slit in the antero-median six to seven centimeters in length, coquettishly fringed with a delicate lace."[86] There is little coquettishness in such attire—lace or no—and its prevalence helps, perhaps, to explain why France's birth rate declined during this period.[87]

It is notable as well that most French feminists accepted the reigning culture of sexual repression. They differed from male commentators on this subject only in the belief that men should respect this sexual culture as much as women did. Like other bourgeois women of the late nineteenth century, feminists had been trained to repress their sexual feelings, but they were also acutely aware of the risks that sexual intercourse involved: pregnancy, the pain and physical danger of childbirth, and the venereal diseases that men often communicated to their wives. Many feminists, moreover, resented male sexual practices that paid too little attention to what women might find pleasurable.[88]

The era's distinction between mothers and whores, between chaste wives and sullied mistresses, loomed large, therefore, for bourgeois women of Henriette Caillaux's standing. Only a respectable woman could be received in society, and the standards of respectability were high indeed: once a whore, always a whore. Martin-Fugier recalls Proust's Odette de Crécy who had been a demimondaine before marrying the estimable Swann. After their marriage the great salons remained open to him but only if he came alone. For Parisian high society nothing, not even the most exalted of marriages, could make an "honnête femme" of Odette de Crécy.[89]

It goes without saying that not all women of the bourgeoisie lived up to these standards; adultery was one of the Belle Epoque's favorite diversions. Only a small percentage of French women actually indulged, but talk of it was everywhere. The theater was obsessed with adultery, and novelists seemed unable to construct plots without it.[90] Even those readers who shunned the more risqué authors such as Octave Mirbeau or Paul and Victor Margueritte, found steamy scenes of adultery in Paul Bourget, perhaps the most devoutly Catholic of France's well-known novelists. Like government censors who compile elaborate compendiums of pornography to "study" the problem, Bourget justified his pulsating pages by claiming the need to expose his era's immorality. And in order to uphold that morality, Bourget always had his adulterous characters come to a bad end. This was an agreeable arrangement for Bourget's mostly female readers, who could enjoy a certain titillation without turning to writers of ill repute.[91]

Such fascination with illicit unions suggests that sexual repression and adultery went hand in hand during the Belle Epoque. The one sustained the other, with the result that the era could maintain its austere standards only with the help of hypocrisy. Publicly, almost everyone endorsed the official morality; privately, some observed precepts of their own. Strict sexual mores continued to reign within the bourgeoisie only because most French men and women tacitly agreed to keep their transgressions out of sight. The latter could come to the surface only in theater, literature, and the courts. In real life, the key—especially for women—was not to be caught.

Because this outward austerity was possible only to the extent that the more libertine reality remained hidden, Madame Caillaux's worries about her checkered past were far from exaggerated. What threatened her good bourgeois standing was not the existence of her prior adultery, nor the fact that her intimates knew about it, but that it might be revealed to the public at large. According to the norms of the Belle Epoque's bourgeois culture, to reveal in public acts officially considered immoral was to transform those acts from mere aberrations of behavior into something that threatened to redefine one's basic character. Like venial sins in the confessional, private transgressions could be readily forgiven, the individual's moral character left unchanged. But once made public, the sin became far more serious because it was now more difficult to dismiss as mere aberration. Private sexual behavior, therefore, possessed a wholly different status and meaning from public sexual behavior, and exposure was what Henriette dreaded most of all. Because this was so, Henriette Caillaux had good reason to fear not solely for her own position in polite society but for her relationship with her daughter as well.

Young women of the good bourgeoisie were to know nothing of sex, in mind or in body, and Henriette Caillaux's nineteen-year-old daughter was no exception. Louise Weiss, also nineteen at the time of the Caillaux Affair, wrote in her memoirs that her parents considered her much too young to know anything about it. After Calmette's assassination, Weiss overheard her relatives "whispering about the case." But as soon as they noticed her eavesdropping, silence descended.[92]

Alain Decaux has written that during the Belle Epoque middle-class parents "watched over their [daughters'] virginity in much the same way the count of Monte Cristo guarded his treasure."[93] Virginity was a capital without which no daughter could negotiate the bourgeois marriage market. And to maintain this all-important chastity, parents took no chances. Girls were sent to convent schools where nuns took the preservation of innocence to extremes that they alone could devise. Outside the convent, young women were accompanied at all times by an adult; never were they to be left alone with a male, not even their fiancés. Baronne Staffe explicitly warned parents of the betrothed always "to keep them in plain sight."[94]

The consequences of such strict rules and unrelenting parental surveillance were grave for both sexes. Young women entered marriage wholly ignorant of sex, while their mates had experienced little more than the brothel's furtive pleasures. This situation made for wedding nights of disgust and terror for the era's virginal brides. Colette's description of hers is justly famous: "The husband, tight and graceless, undertook his assault on the nuptial bed, his face illuminated by excessive appetites. He stank of stale cigar and chartreuse liqueur, and as he claimed his due he showed all the gallantry of a sailor on shore leave." Another account, sensational enough to be a *fait divers,* told of an innocent young bride's wedding night with a husband she barely knew. He entered their railroad compartment completely nude; having never seen so much as an undraped painting she tried to flee. The husband, "claiming his due," pulled her down on the bed and raped her. The next day she tried to commit suicide.[95] Such narratives abounded, as all too many innocent wives found themselves imbued the morning after with an "insurmountable disgust" for their mates.[96]

Such then was the cultural perspective from which Henriette Caillaux contemplated the revelation of her letters, letters that would have made public her adulterous affair with Joseph Caillaux. In elaborating all her worries, Madame Caillaux doubtless hoped to evoke sympathy from the members of her jury. These men of the middling middle class would have understood her desire to keep buried a past of which they did not wholly disapprove but whose consequences, once made public, they could have fully imagined. If the jurors could be made to see her as a real woman governed by emotion and committed to bourgeois appearances, they might find it in their hearts to excuse her crime.

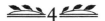

Berthe Gueydan

The Politics of Divorce

The fourth session was the one for which everybody had been waiting. Madame Berthe Gueydan would at long last lay her side of the story before a public increasingly avid for the details of Caillaux's private life. Would the now famous *lettres intimes* be revealed? Would Joseph's two wives relive their rivalry in open court? And who would be the more sympathetic, the more genuinely feminine of the two? Journalists of all stripes intended to comment on these questions, but those on the right would do much more. They would use Gueydan's tale of abandonment and divorce to castigate Joseph and Henriette Caillaux for crimes against the family and against the nation created, they believed, in its primordial image.

Joseph Caillaux was known for his *liaisons élégantes*, a celebrated divorce, and for twice marrying mistresses who had left their husbands to be with him. Henriette Claretie, likewise, had violated her own marriage and that of another woman by her relationship with Joseph Caillaux. As two of France's most public figures in the years before 1914, both found themselves potentially vulnerable to charges of hastening the decay of France's moral life, of transgressing against the duties of marriage and family. Their vulnerability on personal and ethical grounds stemmed from a conservative revival that marked pre-1914 France, a revival that found expression not only in a new nationalism but in a backlash against the secular republic's moral relativism and against its apparent challenge to the traditional family.

By 1914 the Catholic church and other conservative groups had gained considerable strength from a politically and religiously charged debate over marriage, divorce, and the family that began with the 1884 law permitting divorce and took on new intensity at the turn of the century.[1] Conservatives may have been defeated in the Dreyfus affair, but they staged a rapid comeback after 1900 when rekindled concerns about French degeneration and German prowess allowed them to focus new attention on the family. France's moral decay, commentators claimed, had spread to the family itself, an institution progressively weakened by feminism, individualism, and divorce. Depopulation was the inevitable result, so much so they said, that France could soon be overwhelmed by a fecund German empire.[2] In this context, efforts first to establish legal divorce and then to allow it on demand provoked a traditionalist backlash that idealized the family of yore and gave conservatives a cultural issue potent enough to fuel a robust political resurgence. By raising the family question, anticlerical republicans enabled conservatives to shift their challenge to the radical republic from political to cultural grounds—that is, from a terrain on which rightists enjoyed little support after 1900 to one from which they could build widespread public assent. In this setting Calmette's ability to open the Caillaux' private life to public inspection menaced them perhaps even more than the editor himself may have realized.

But on the fourth day of the trial, before these deeper issues could be aired, there was first the battle of the wives, a part of the courtroom drama that even the most dour of dailies could not but sensationalize. It goes without saying that *Le Figaro* took up the cause of Berthe Gueydan, whom the editors portrayed as a pure and humble woman overpowered by the Machiavellian politician who had once been her husband. Madame Gueydan, *Le Figaro* wrote, entered the courtroom fortified by her "lofty and valiant soul." But she was "alone against everyone . . . having suffered the abandonment of the husband she had loved and the torture to which triumphant slander subjects the righteous." She had fallen into all the traps so carefully laid by Joseph Caillaux because her modesty and simplicity had left her unschooled in the ways of the world. "Simple and beautiful," she told a story of innocence betrayed and of the "lost illusions of her love." Suffering had hardened her features, but she remained "very pale, burdened by emotion, and very simple." The editors fixed on her supposed simplicity, a quality that emphasized the vulnerability of a woman who had "no one to protect her, and no one to sustain her. She is a woman and she is alone." Everything about her, *Le Figaro*'s account suggested, betokened a state of extreme fragility, almost helplessness.

In the witness box her voice trembled, and her whole body trembled with it. As she recounted the tragedy of her life she "appeared as if naked." Her tale was so compelling, her suffering so palpable, wrote *Le Figaro*, that witnesses in the courtroom audience, initially hostile, "listened on the edge of their seats to the story of this broken life." In the end Berthe Gueydan won their sympathy.[3]

As *Le Figaro* portrayed her, Madame Gueydan was the opposite of Madame Caillaux. The editors had pictured Henriette as cool, calm, and collected, sure of herself and utterly in control of her emotions. Berthe appeared in these accounts almost as Henriette's opposite, as frail, feeble, and fatally feminine. Henriette found herself condemned for being an *hommesse*, Berthe indulged as the quintessential woman.

Not surprisingly, *Le Figaro*'s sympathizers and associates endeavored to do the same thing. The well-known playwright Henry Bernstein, a close friend of Calmette's, echoed *Le Figaro*'s description of Madame Gueydan in his own testimony on the fifth day. Berthe had come to him for help shortly after her divorce, Bernstein told the court; he claimed to have been intensely moved by her plight. "In a veritable state of pathos, she traced for me her entire story. She laid bare her weakness in the face of the omnipotence of her husband; she told me of the abandonment in which she found herself, the feelings of solitude and terror she felt so profoundly." Bernstein, it seems, found in Berthe's tale of woe not just an individual's tragedy but material for dramatic art. "From a purely artistic point of view," testified the playwright, "I found this somber tableau very beautiful. I found very beautiful all of her appeals, the smallness, the weakness of this being who stood before me against this great wall of hostility and silence."[4]

Such was the portrait drawn by *Le Figaro* and its most ardent supporters. What makes it particularly notable is that virtually no one else saw Madame Gueydan this way. No one saw her as weak, helpless, and inescapably feminine. Commentators outside *Le Figaro*'s orbit—even those quite hostile to Henriette Caillaux—presented Berthe Gueydan as tough, aggressive, and capable of caring for herself. If anything, Berthe was perceived as the more masculine of the two women. The *Journal des débats*, nearly as unsympathetic to the Caillaux as *Le Figaro*, revealed none of the latter's insistence on stereotyping Henriette and Berthe as polar opposites on a scale of true femininity. "Madame Gueydan, with her pale coloring, her regular features, the long face whose straight nose highlighted her kind of looks, her taste for sober but elegant clothes [contrasted with] Madame Raynouard [*sic*], blonde and rosy, indolent, ostensibly passive, without anything that revealed much of a personality at all."[5] With this description of the two rivals, the *Journal des débats* appeared to give Berthe Gueydan an aura of seriousness and credibility that Henriette Caillaux supposedly lacked.

L'Illustration, the conservative paragon of photo journalism, could not paint Madame Gueydan in the colors of suffering femininity, much as it would have liked to see Henriette condemned. Instead, *L'Illustration* called Gueydan an "exceptional woman," one whose "silhouette is tall and beautiful, with a face whose regular features suggested willfulness and drama, a powerful and confident regard that impresses." True, the magazine presented her at the same time as "one of those heroines of passion whose tragic simplicity modern drama has been unable to depict." But they described her this way not because of any feminine frailty but because of an emotional power to be found only in the theater of the ancients.[6]

Henriette's supporters went even further in this direction. For *Les annales politiques et littéraires*, Berthe was cleverly political and brilliantly manipulative, fully capable of inventing a tale of martyrdom and humiliation to sway the jury, the press, and public opinion. The journal spoke of the "shadowy maneuvers of which she was known to be capable" and dismissed her tale of woe as little more than a theatrical ploy. Everything about her rendered her unappealing, even dangerous. "Her stature, her somber and fatal beauty, the fire of a regard charged with rancor, the hardness of her fixed and bitter profile, enveloped her as if with mystery and terror."[7] How far we have come from the picture of feminine helplessness sketched by the editors of *Le Figaro*! Here instead was something of a feminist femme fatale, a civilized Amazon whose dark beauty and fiery anger linked her all too closely with the females of antifeminist paranoia described above.[8]

The *Annales* was far from alone in presenting Berthe Gueydan this way. In the words of *La Lanterne*, even more sympathetic to the Caillaux, "there was something about [Gueydan's] beauty, hardly faded at all, that was troubling and diabolical." Such was the magic, the "superior art," of this fearsome New Woman that the "eloquence and the subtlety of the two eminent barristers was reduced to nothing."[9]

Just as *Le Figaro* had tried to condemn Henriette by picturing her as unfeminine, so the pro-Caillaux papers sought to sway opinion against Berthe by associating her with the furies of feminism. This was, of course, a grotesque distortion but one that was based on a grain of truth. Though no direct evidence exists to link Berthe Gueydan with feminism, it is clear, nonetheless, that she was energetic, intelligent, and independent in ways utterly unknown to the second Madame Caillaux. Joseph would admit as much in his own testimony as did a number of more independent commentators.

Berthe Gueydan's background was as modest as Henriette Caillaux's was well-to-do. The youngest of six girls in a family of eight children, Berthe grew up in a world that knew no luxury.[10] Her father had moved the family to New Orleans in the 1850s, but he did not succeed in making the fortune he had sought in the new world. Shortly after the Franco-Prussian War, the Gueydans returned to France where Berthe's father took a modest position in a Grenoble bank.

We know nothing else of Berthe's parents or her early life except that she, like all her sisters, was sent to the convent of the Sacré-Cœur, where she received, as Isabelle Couturier de Chefdubois put it, "an education that was too elementary." She learned the basics of grammar and history, but her course of study "devoted most of its attention to the domestic skills and embroidery. There was little else."[11] This was perhaps an overly negative view of convent education, for Bonnie Smith has found that in the north at least the sisters of the Sacré-Cœur were far more demanding. Their curriculum included not only the *arts d'agrément* and lessons in the social graces but formal course work in literature, history, foreign languages, arithmetic, and religion. The goal of even this latter part of the curriculum, however, was not to open students to intellect or science but to give them just enough knowledge to make them pleasing and competent bourgeois wives.[12]

The convent's daily routine was austere, with mass at dawn, meals eaten in silence, and a long succession of twenty-five-minute classes each begun and ended with prayers.[13] For a young woman as spirited as Berthe Gueydan, there could be little happiness within the confines of such a strict regime. Most likely she left the convent at age thirteen, marrying just three years later. At her parents' urging, Berthe accepted a proposal from Jules Dupré, the son of a well-known artist who held a modest position at the Ministry of Fine Arts. "Everyone [else] considered this [marriage] an act of folly," wrote Couturier de Chefdubois. Berthe's "character and education were certainly not ripe for marriage," and especially not for the child she bore less than a year later. Berthe "was incapable [at age seventeen] of properly caring for her son."[14] Couturier de Chefdubois claimed that Berthe agreed to marry Dupré only because she was enamored of his father, but the explanation may be more benign than this. Without a dowry to second her good looks, the sixteen-year-old Berthe was in no position to reject her parents' or her suitor's wishes. Like so many marriages of the era, Berthe's conformed to her parents' sense of practicality, not to romantic impulse. The latter she would find some thirteen years after her marriage in a liaison with Joseph Caillaux.[15]

Berthe Dupré and Joseph Caillaux met in 1900 when Joseph was already in his second year as minister of finance in Waldeck-Rousseau's government of republican defense. It is not clear exactly how they came together, but Joseph would certainly have known Berthe's husband, who in 1900 served as deputy chief of staff for another cabinet minister, Alexandre Millerand. Berthe's marriage was by this time a mere formality, and Joseph apparently jumped at the chance for an involvement with a woman his colleague Paul-Boncour described as "a magnificent creature."[16] Not only was the now twenty-nine-year-old Gueydan renowned in Paris for her great beauty, but her involvement in the artistic and intellectual world of Jules Dupré père had helped her, as Couturier de Chefdubois grudgingly wrote, "compensate for the gaps in her background and education."[17] Berthe had become quite worldly, quite the *parisienne*, by the time she met Joseph Caillaux, who was drawn to her all the more because she already had a husband.[18] She would be ideal for a busy man weary of his encounters with women in "specialized establishments" but not yet ready for the commitment of marriage.[19]

It was in the flush of this affair that Joseph Caillaux wrote the self-important letter, signed "Ton Jo," that would crown *Le Figaro*'s case against him thirteen years later. Joseph should have found other ways to dazzle his mistress, but in 1901, when he penned the letter, Berthe had no reason to show it to anyone. If anything, the political power it revealed contributed to her desire to make him hers. In 1904 against Joseph's wishes she decided to divorce Jules Dupré, and gradually her lover found himself drawn toward what he later called a "marriage of resignation." Caillaux began to ask himself "whether a man could really live his life alone" and whether he could deny marriage to a woman who had divorced for him. The wedding finally took place in August 1906 after his resistance had evaporated altogether in the wake of his "nervous troubles" and his near defeat in the parliamentary election of that year. Later on, Caillaux would write that he realized "in moments of clarity that [the marriage] would not last."[20]

Whatever the truth of Caillaux's ex post facto claims, it did not take friends of the couple long to notice that all was not well. Magdelaine Decori, the longtime mistress of Raymond Poincaré, noted in her journal that Joseph always arrived very late to the "brilliant and very Parisian" receptions given by his wife. Gueydan held these soirées at the residence of the minister of finance, which she had lavishly redecorated; there she held court, her niece wrote, "dressed with perfect taste and showered with homage and adulation."[21] One evening, Decori chided Caillaux for his tardiness, and his response revealed a hostility toward Gueydan couched in the discourse of republican virtue and simplicity. "My wife does me wrong with these receptions, given my [democratic] political views." That evening, Decori wrote, she told her husband that "the Caillaux' marriage is falling apart" and that Joseph was "jealous of Berthe's success as the hostess of a great Parisian salon. Instead of taking advantage of it, he will divorce her."[22]

Decori may have invented the story after the fact; if not, she was more accurate than she knew. Not long before this particular reception, Joseph Caillaux had begun an affair with Henriette Claretie, an attractive blonde who possessed none of the flashy worldliness that made Gueydan such a Parisian success. Echoing the French revolutionaries' critique of the aristocratic *salonnières*, Joseph voiced resentment of his wife's ability to stand out, her conversational éclat, her links to the world of high art and high culture.[23] And though he did his best to boycott Berthe's parties, she seemed little inclined to give them up. He found himself drawn, he would later explain, to

Henriette as an antidote to Berthe Gueydan. Henriette promised to be an altogether different kind of wife, quiet, deferential, far more provincial than the eminently Parisian Madame Gueydan. Joseph Caillaux had become a republican politician in the French revolutionary tradition, and he wanted a wife of whom Rousseau would have approved.

Meeting in court four years after the collapse of their marriage, Joseph and his first wife bristled in each other's company. So hostile was their exchange that an uninformed spectator might have believed it was their defunct marriage at issue, not the murder of one of Paris's leading newspapermen. This was especially true in that Caillaux's controversial testimony two days earlier had already seemed to direct the proceedings more toward him and his personal history than Henriette and her crime. When Madame Gueydan began her testimony (figure 12), it was almost as if the actual defendant had ceased to exist.

As a witness Berthe did not impress. She appeared cold, haughty, brittle; her refusal to cooperate with the judge alienated spectators and journalists alike. Madame Gueydan, reported *Le Petit parisien*, "assumed an aggressive stance from the start and she maintained it, nuanced here and there, for the duration."[24] She opened her testimony by sparring endlessly with Judge Albanel over her desire to use written notes. The law forbade her to do so, but she insisted anyway. At one point Labori intervened to declare that "Madame has already testified several times [i.e., during the *instruction*] with considerable force and authority" and did not, therefore, need to use notes as a crutch.[25] In making this statement, Labori's intention was twofold: to move the proceedings forward and to reinforce the idea that Berthe Gueydan was a tough individual who could take care of herself.

Gueydan's stalling tactics did little to evoke sympathy from the courtroom audience, yet when she finally consented to testify "spontaneously and without notes," as the law required, observers could not but feel some compassion over the way Joseph Caillaux had treated her. Berthe testified that early in their marriage she believed it to be "the happiest and most committed that anyone could see." Only later did she realize that Joseph had been playing a double game almost from the start. He may have kept up marital

12. Berthe Gueydan spars with Judge Albanel (*L'Illustration*, 25 July 1914).

appearances, but before their first anniversary he was already involved with Henriette Claretie (married to a literary critic of modest
reputation, Léo Claretie). It took Berthe about a year to discover the
affair, and even then she gave her husband the benefit of the doubt.
This other woman meant nothing, he told her, he had succumbed in
a moment of weakness. He would see her no more; he and Berthe

would take a "grand voyage" together to leave the whole mistaken affair behind.

But the trip never took place. Instead Gueydan spent the summer of 1909 alone in Switzerland. Upon her return to Paris in September she received an anonymous letter saying that a blonde divorcée was trying to take her place. Confronted with this new bit of evidence, Joseph claimed that the blonde was merely a friend. "I was astonished," testified Madame Gueydan, "for we had too close a union for him to have a friendship without telling me about it and I told him so." At this point, Joseph became "very irritable, and though I didn't realize it at the time he was planning to smother me, just like, if I dare say so, just like Desdemona."[26] She went on to say that Joseph threatened to kill her a few days later, and whether or not this was true, her reference to Desdemona was telling. Berthe cast herself in the role of tragic heroine, as the loyal and long-suffering wife of a powerful man whose character flaws had condemned her to oblivion. Virtually all the commentators referred to the trial as a great piece of theater, and Berthe, like Henriette, played her character to the hilt.

Despite her accusations, Gueydan continued, Joseph remained unwilling to own up to his affair with Henriette. To convince Berthe that Henriette was merely a friend, Caillaux fabricated several letters designed to make their affair appear innocent. Joseph left the phony letters in the top drawer of his desk, which he left partly open. "I saw a drawer halfway open," Berthe told the court. "I was amazed because Monsieur Caillaux was very orderly. And then I thought that if this drawer is halfway open that's because it is some kind of trap." She did not fall into it but, inexplicably, Joseph himself would. A few days later Berthe looked into her husband's study and found the same drawer locked. She opened it with the key to another piece of furniture and this time she found real letters, ones so explicit that there could be no question about Joseph's affair with Henriette nor about his intention to divorce her when the political moment was right. "There is only one consolation, one lone succor [in life]," Joseph had written Henriette in one of the letters Berthe discovered. "It is to think of my little one, to see her in my arms as at Ouchy (God, what delicious moments!)." Joseph's closing words to his mistress must have shocked Berthe Gueydan the most: "A thousand million kisses all over your adored little body."[27]

After recovering from the initial impact of revelations like these, Berthe realized she possessed some weapons of her own: the letters themselves, which she confiscated; and the threat of an immediate divorce that might sabotage Joseph's electoral chances. "I said, let's get divorced right away. Immediately he threw himself at my feet and crawled on his knees begging me not to divorce him." He claimed that the affair was all a mistake, that she was the one he really loved, and because this was so, she should return the letters to him. But Berthe had already taken the precaution of mailing the letters to her sister, who proceeded to have them photographed.*

Joseph had, at all costs, to convince Berthe not to divorce him. A divorce scandal could easily turn his peasant constituents against him, and to avoid the risk of electoral defeat he had no choice but to affect a reconciliation, replete with promises of fidelity, a second honeymoon, a new life together, and so forth. In exchange, Caillaux asked Gueydan to burn the guilty letters she had seized. This she dutifully did—in an auto-da-fé attended by witnesses for both sides—but without including the photographic copies, knowledge of which, she later claimed, had been kept from her. Meanwhile Joseph took the precaution of having a private detective tail his wife in hopes of obtaining some ammunition of his own. Mistrust to this extent seldom heals an ailing marriage, and once safely returned to office in the spring of 1910 Caillaux moved to dissolve it.[28]

Joseph abandoned Berthe for good on 29 June 1910. It was not until the following day, Berthe testified, that her sister gave her the photographic copies of the letters burned the previous year. Until that point, Gueydan said, she had not known the copies existed. Berthe testified that if she had known about them she would certainly have given them to Joseph Caillaux. Why? Because she was a loyal wife who loved her husband in spite of everything. "My sister . . . told me nothing because she knew my character. She knew that I would have told my husband about [the photographic copies] during the eight months I lived with him between the day the originals were destroyed and the day he left me." Throughout her testimony Berthe portrayed herself as a woman so loving, so loyal, so trusting that she believed everything her husband told her.

* These letters were later introduced as evidence in the case against Henriette Caillaux and became part of the transcript of her trial.

When a letter from Henriette was delivered to their house, she readily agreed to dismiss it as a fraud. When the anonymous letter arrived telling her that a rival wanted to take her place, she believed Joseph's claim that the affair meant nothing to him. And even after finding the letters that told of a conspiracy to divorce her, she wanted to return them to Caillaux. "Everyone told me never to return those letters. But I wanted to give them back because I loved my husband."

Time and time again, Gueydan presented herself as the trusting wife victimized by a powerful and unscrupulous husband-politician intent on divorcing her against her will. Despite all his machinations, she testified, "when he saw me, all he saw was a soft and sweet woman who loved him." She had been willing to do anything to avoid the pain of divorce, to maintain the sanctity of her home even though her husband had committed adultery. "I had already divorced my first husband out of love for M. Caillaux, who had begged me to divorce for his sake. I thought about the fact that I was a mother, about how hard it was to be a woman alone, and I resolved not to divorce, not to break up our home." But none of her concessions, none of her efforts to preserve their marriage, meant anything to Caillaux, who abandoned her the minute his parliamentary seat was safe. "I was thrown out of my house, and another woman took my place." Ultimately, she had no choice but to agree to a divorce. "I was a woman alone, defenseless, caught in a net like a bird . . . I lacked the strength to go on."

Berthe had indeed been the victim of a powerful and mendacious man. And at the trial she did her best to relive that victimization for all its dramatic effect. Asked at one point to speak more loudly, she answered as if to confirm the commentary of her sympathizers who portrayed her as a weak and overwhelmed woman. "You must understand that this whole story is so painful for me that I am giving it every ounce of my strength." Still, there is considerable evidence that she was not so simple and loyally feminine as she made it seem. If she had been as naively loving as she maintained in court, why did she decide to force open the locked drawer of Joseph Caillaux's desk in which she found a pair of incriminating *lettres intimes*? And why, on finding them, did she immediately send them off to her sister for safekeeping instead of returning them to her husband? Finally, is it plausible that she knew nothing of the existence of photographic copies until after Joseph had ended the marriage and, further, that once she took possession of the copies she showed them to no one? The answer to the last question will never be known, for Berthe's sister Madame Robert was conveniently abroad in the United States at the time of the trial. Several witnesses did testify, however, to having seen parts of these letters and to being familiar with their contents, confirming the subsequent claim of Madame Gueydan's niece Isabelle that Berthe had shown the "Ton Jo" letter to "many political personalities" as well as to Bunau-Varilla of *Le Matin*.[29] What is more, a journalist named Vervoort testified that at the urging of Madame Robert he went to see Berthe Gueydan after her divorce and that she showed him copies of all the letters in question.[30] Finally, there remains the problem of how Calmette had been able to obtain a facsimile copy of the "Ton Jo" letter if Berthe had not given it to him. When Judge Albanel asked her this question, her evasive answer demonstrated anything but naïveté. "If you can tell me how [Calmette] got hold of the *document Fabre* and the German diplomatic dispatches, then I will answer you."

With the question of the *lettres intimes* before the court, Albanel and Chenu made an effort to convince Berthe to submit them as evidence in the case. She had been unwilling to do so during the pretrial *instruction*, a position she seemed at first to maintain before Albanel. But the potential importance of these letters made Albanel and Chenu unwilling to drop the issue. Albanel wanted to see whether there was any truth to the Caillaux' claim that the letters were so compromising that the very fear they would see print had moved Henriette to deranged violence; Chenu hoped to use them to remind the jury of his opponents' moral transgressions against marriage and the family. Asked again whether anyone beside herself and her sister had ever seen the letters, Berthe responded that since the divorce they had been in a deposit box at a branch of the Société Générale bank on the Champs-Elysées.

"Until when did they remain there?" asked the judge.

"Until now," Berthe responded.

"They're still there?"

"I didn't say that. I said up until this moment."

With this answer, Berthe added even more to the suspense surrounding these letters, suggesting, cleverly, that she might be persuaded to reveal them. There ensued considerable wrangling over whether or not she would agree to submit the letters as evidence, when Chenu heightened the suspense even more.

"Where are the letters at this moment?" he asked.

"They are right here," she responded, pointing to her handbag.

"Have you changed your mind about whether to give M. le Président [Albanel] the photographs you earlier refused to submit to the *juge d'instruction?*"

"I prefer not to," Berthe answered, citing her unwillingness to compromise Madame Caillaux.

At this point Chenu tried to convince her to reveal the letters and Labori, apparently relieved that she persisted in her refusal, intervened to thank her for her delicacy with respect to his client. But Gueydan, unwilling to let him off so easily, then turned to the jury and asked if they wanted to have the letters read aloud. Silence. In that case, said the judge, Madame Gueydan can step down. This decision did not at all please Chenu, who asked Berthe, again, to reconsider. She turned to Albanel. "Now, Monsieur le Président, I would like to propose another solution. I could perhaps put the letters in the hands of Maître Labori, who can do with them what he wants."[31]

This was a poisoned gift if ever there was one, for Gueydan had checkmated Labori with a maneuver of considerable brilliance. If he suppressed the letters he would arouse too much suspicion. But if he read them, he would be in the position of mortifying his own client. Perhaps Chenu had devised the idea of giving Labori himself the unpleasant responsibility of revealing the letters; Berthe's actions in the courtroom suggest that she may have planned it herself. If so, this was not the work of a fragile female. Labori, of course, had no choice but to submit these letters to the court and ultimately to read them aloud before all assembled.

Joseph Caillaux's reputation had hardly been enhanced during Berthe Gueydan's hours on the witness stand. After she had been dismissed he asked to be heard. There was little Caillaux could say in his defense so, skilled politician that he was, he took the offensive (figure 13). This former prime minister was nothing if not audacious, for he dared not only to launch a public attack against the woman he had wronged but to seek justification for his past be-

13. Joseph Caillaux defiantly faces a courtroom audience filled with murmurs of protest (*L'Illustration*, 25 July 1914).

havior in the Belle Epoque's masculine views of women. In a courtroom packed with journalists and politicians, a courtroom from which women spectators had originally been barred, Caillaux told Gueydan—for the public record—why she had been unfit to be his wife. "Between a man to whom everyone grants authority, vigor, and power," said Caillaux turning to confront Madame Gueydan directly, "and you in whom these qualities are overdeveloped as well, it was impossible that things would last." Joseph told Berthe and the world that she was too forceful, too strong-willed, and too intelligent for his needs. How, he asked, could he have remained with her given their "conflict of natures at once opposed to each other and too similar?"[32]

With Henriette, Joseph continued, everything was different, balanced, natural; for unlike Berthe she was a "bourgeoise . . . from my sphere in society . . . with a character and a nature I could attach myself to."[33] In the cultural climate of 1914 Caillaux had no trouble admitting that what he needed was the kind of wife most of his male compatriots would have agreed was a real woman—one who was soft, quiet, and retiring, who shared none of the quintessentially masculine qualities "overdeveloped" in himself.[34]

Joseph Caillaux, a man who seldom admitted to mistakes in the political realm, readily confessed the error of wedding a woman too much his intellectual peer. And because he had married so inappropriately, Caillaux told the court, he agreed magnanimously to pay for his fault. As part of the divorce settlement Caillaux gave Gueydan the elevated sum of 18,000 francs a year plus investments worth 210,000 francs. The two figures, claimed the former premier, represented half his fortune. When Berthe objected that no amount of money could repair the emotional damage he had done her, his response was so arrogant as to provoke loud protests in the courtroom: "Permit me to remind you," he announced, addressing his former wife once again, "that you possessed not a *centime* when you came into my house."[35] It is important to note that only his pride in economic superiority aroused indignation from the audience. Not so his candid desire for intellectual and emotional precedence over the woman he married. This aspiration seemed so natural to the male audience that it produced not a ripple of dissent.

But clever as these efforts were, none could explain away his personal history of unfulfilled promises and marital deceit. Especially unmoved were the growing number of conservative commentators who identified Joseph Caillaux's moral failings with his presumed political corruption. For them, divorce dissolved the family in the same way that radical republicanism dissolved the nation. Paul Bourget, the popular novelist, wrote in his regular newspaper column that one of the deepest and most tragic lessons of the *affaire Caillaux* concerned the problem of divorce. To him, the testimony in the case "strikingly proved that divorce solves nothing, appeases no one, that it soothes no suffering, dampens no grief." Things were different, he wrote, "when marriage was indissoluble . . . for couples knew that the chain linking them was unbreakable and even those in difficult marriages did their best to accommodate themselves to life's reality." Such unfortunates stayed together not for themselves but for the good of the community, since all societies need the assurance that fundamental relationships will last, that some things are permanent. The durability of families was crucial, Bourget maintained, for political reasons as well. He had written earlier that "for something to be solid and durable it must be natural, and what is natural in politics is the family. The family must be the basis for all our institutions." This is why threats to the family concerned Bourget so much, and why his brief against the Caillaux turned on the question of divorce. The latter, he concluded, "more than any other of the so-called modern reforms" had uprooted French society from its traditions by absolving people of the belief "that certain things are inevitable and must be accepted."[36]

Like Bourget but in more strident terms, the right-wing journalist Guy de Cassagnac linked the Caillaux' divorces with a wider moral and political breakdown. Writing in *L'Autorité*, Cassagnac declared that "ours is a lamentable epoch, one in which divorce has overturned the laws of society and destroyed all respectability. It has precluded a peaceful home life and created a fearful chaos among women, children, and husbands. . . . [It] ignites scandal and stirs up hatred." More than any other recent event, the Caillaux Affair reminded Cassagnac of the evils of divorce. "When I heard Madame Caillaux say 'the first wife of my husband' or 'the son of my husband's first wife' I took my head in my hands, certain that . . . this case represents nothing less than the trial of our secular society, of the rotten and immoral existence that the republic has inflicted on France."[37]

Though right-wingers indulged in the most colorful rhetoric about divorce, journalists for the centrist mass-circulation press made similar pronouncements. The picture weekly *La France illustrée* blamed Calmette's death on "the immorality of our decaying mores, the insanity of emotions that break all bonds and pile divorce upon divorce."[38] And the independent *Annales politiques et littéraires* explained that episodes like the Caillaux Affair could occur in France because of the "evil ferments introduced into our mores by divorce."[39]

Although the trial of Madame Caillaux took up the issue of divorce mainly in connection with Berthe Gueydan's testimony, this press commentary kept the problem alive during the whole length of the proceedings. And on the trial's last day the politics of divorce returned to the courtroom itself when Charles Chenu made it part of his closing statement against Joseph and Henriette Caillaux. The court, he suggested, owed Henriette not a hint of indulgence, for she was little more than a "mistress [who had] triumphed over the legitimate wife." Even less, he maintained, should it credit the testimony of Joseph Caillaux, who "by divorcing [Berthe Gueydan] in March 1911 transgressed against the solemn oath he had given her."[40]

Thanks to Chenu's efforts and to the renewed vigor of French conservatism, with its emphasis on Catholic morality and the traditional family, the Caillaux' seemingly private history of adultery and divorce had become central to France's public political life. The explanation for its prominence lies at the heart of France's attempt, after 1870, to create a fully secular republic.

Dissolution of marriage became possible in France only in 1884 when the new leaders of the Third Republic added divorce to the foundation of laic laws and civil liberties designed to undergird the fledgling republican society. Like the new public education and the separation of Church and state, the divorce law was to produce bitter and lasting conflict, conflict that revealed the fundamental fissures of French society. So troubling was divorce that when the bill's main proponent, Alfred Naquet, first spoke on its behalf, the Assembly erupted in nervous laughter, refusing even to consider it.[41] Nor did its chances improve substantially after the abortive clerical coup in 1877, the *seize mai*. Republicans wanted no part of a bill that might alienate peasant electors. Still, Naquet persisted and so did the leaders of France's nascent feminist movement who had been crucial to this campaign from its inception.[42]

Inside parliament Naquet and his allies hitched themselves to the bandwagon of anticlericalism, maintaining that the family's laic liberation required divorce. In Naquet's words, the "spirit of clericalism" had stamped out the short-lived divorce law of the French Revolution, and now "the sweet revenge of the democratic spirit over the clerical spirit means the reestablishment of divorce."[43] Freedom from an unwanted marriage was as essential to the individual as all the other liberties promised by the secular state. And each French citizen, Naquet declared, must have the right to love, to feel passion and to live life independent of the Church's outmoded restraints.[44]

Attacked on all fronts, Catholic leaders reponded to this issue as forcefully as to the Republic's efforts to secularize the schools. Clergymen viewed the assault upon Catholic education and the revival of divorce as two sides of the same coin; both threatened the stability of society itself. According to Monsignor Charles-Emile Freppel, a bishop who sat in parliament, the Christian family was essential to France's very existence: "With all its vicissitudes and all its agitations, our country has had the sense to consecrate for itself one incomparable element of solidity, of permanence, and of cohesion: namely, the indissoluble family." Without it France would cease to be a "Christian civilization," falling victim to what Freppel called a "Semitic movement" (Naquet was Jewish) against its hallowed traditions. Mgr. Freppel could not resist a *mot* in concluding that passage of Naquet's bill would "consummate the divorce between the Third Republic and the Catholic church."[45]

Freppel did not ultimately succeed, yet his efforts helped dilute the law that finally emerged from the Senate in 1884. In particular, divorce by mutual consent, central to the revolutionary legislation of 1792, was rejected for a much more restricted bill. What would be called the Naquet Law, though its namesake was displeased on several counts, permitted divorce only on one or more of four specific grounds: adultery, cruelty, slander, and a serious criminal conviction.[46] To discourage divorce even more, the Senate prohibited marriage between the accomplices of adultery and, as a concession to the Church, denied Naquet's proposal to allow a simple separation—Catholicism's lone solution to marital discord— to convert automatically into divorce on the request of husband or wife. The pro-divorce deputy Letellier expressed disappointment with the bill's final form but justified it as "another crucial step toward the laicization of the state."[47] For committed republicans, the legalization of divorce, however truncated the measure, stood as a symbol of secularization on a par with Jules Ferry's reform of the schools.

Though the law of 1884 satisfied no one, its restrictiveness allayed the fears of some opponents and allowed the question of divorce to recede from view. But only temporarily; when organized feminism became more vocal in the 1890s, the issue of marriage and divorce resurfaced as part of a larger controversy over the changing role of women in modern society.[48] Most French feminists did not challenge their culture's reigning belief in separate spheres for men and women. Nonetheless, their efforts to open new possibilities for women—within the home and outside it—provoked sharp responses from commentators of virtually all political hues. Even in its mildest version, feminism aroused the most exaggerated and wildly contradictory species of masculine fears, for men persisted in measuring women against an ideal of femininity based more on the effort to maintain male power and masculine self-images than on any female reality. Thus, because male commentators considered the "real woman" unfit for the world of manly professions, men were especially hostile to efforts, however timid, to enable (middle-class) women to work. Because men exalted women for a natural purity, generosity, and altruism, feminist efforts to defend women's own interests were regularly condemned as unnaturally selfish. And most important to the issue of divorce, because men continued to view women as born for marriage and the family, conservative commentators in particular denounced efforts to facilitate divorce as threatening the foundation of society itself.[49]

This discussion raged throughout the Belle Epoque, but it assumed a sharper tone and new voices after the Dreyfusards' victory of 1899. Their success encouraged certain republicans and feminists to demand reforms in family law consistent with what seemed to be an ascendant individualism.[50] In particular, these groups began to advocate a new conception of marriage. No longer was the institution to represent a sacred engagement for which husband and wife relinquished their separate identities to create a new familial unity. Marriage was now to become, so argued its prospective reformers, a legal bond that joined two equal partners without depriving either of the distinct individuality they had brought to the union.[51] To certain Radical republican men, this new individualistic view of marriage now appeared preferable to the old nineteenth-century arrangement in which the male monopoly of the public realm had found its justification in notions of the female's virtuous inferiority, and its complement in guaranteed familial security for women. These Radicals now seemed willing to relinquish the belief in women's dependence on men in order to free males and females alike to enter and leave marriages as they as individuals saw fit.

Feminist women, for their part, tended to support the new individualistic marriage as a way of making their gender's domestic and maternal roles freer, fairer, and more fulfilling. As Karen Offen makes clear, activist women held no brief against marriage and the family but rested their stance on the assumption that the evolution of both would endow the woman's separate sphere with her own individual voice.[52] Such "familial feminism"—Offen's apt term—was not, however, something the Church and its allies on the right and center could accept. For them the family retained its traditions, or it was not a family at all.[53]

France's debate over marriage and the family began to make headlines in the summer of 1900 when participants in the Second International Congress of Feminine Work and Institutions called for the liberalization of divorce. Their hope was to take divorce out of the hands of magistrates and allow the individuals involved to make their own decisions.[54] It did not take long for this and other such projects to catch journalism's roving eye. With divorce back in the headlines the issue was ripe for politicization, especially after some advanced republican deputies introduced a bill to allow the dissolution of marriage by mutual consent.

By refocusing attention on divorce, these events revealed that virtually no one remained reconciled to the legislation of 1884. Republicans, particularly those most tinged with anticlericalism, found it too tied to Catholicism's conception of marriage, one that deprived individuals of the freedom to end unhappy or oppressive unions.[55] Conservatives, both within the Church and without, voiced an opposite view. For them the divorce bill, ill-conceived to begin with, had failed so miserably that the legislature should revoke it altogether. The law's proponents had promised fewer crimes of passion, less adultery, better marriages, higher birth rates, and fewer illegitimate children. But far from delivering these benefits, the conservatives claimed, divorce had simply made the old problems worse. According to Charles Turgeon, "never before have the knife, acid, and the revolver served so frequently and so furiously the rancor of mismatched spouses."[56]

By the end of 1900 this controversy had erupted into a full-scale national debate, into a war of words conducted in the press through a promising new journalistic technique: the *enquête,* or survey of public opinion. The first such survey was sponsored by the novelists Paul and Victor Margueritte—both ardently pro-divorce—who, in 1900, sounded out elite opinion on marriage and divorce in successive issues of *La Revue.* Their effort was far from scientific, serving more to influence public opinion than to gauge it; most of those polled wrote in favor not only of divorce by mutual consent but of divorce granted upon the request of one spouse alone.[57] Shortly thereafter, *La Revue* gave equal space to opponents of divorce. And, almost overnight, samplings of opinion on marriage and divorce became a growth industry, with a dozen major publications, highbrow and low, devoting space to it between 1901 and 1914.[58]

Paul and Victor Margueritte chose their respondents carefully. Most were Radicals, people whose commitment to personal freedom had drawn them first to Dreyfus and now to marital reform. In one typical contribution, the Radical deputy Charles Beauquier wrote that the state ought to have no interest in how long a marriage lasted; he imagined a future in which unions would be based on contracts of limited duration, "three, six, or nine years, renewable like a lease." Marriage, for this parliamentarian, was a contract like any other, one into which the law could intervene "only to regularize and secure the situation of children." Senator Auguste Delpech, also a Radical, went even further. Not only was marriage nothing more than a contract between free individuals, but the state need not concern itself with the children couples produced. "To justify the restrictions built into our current [divorce] law, its defenders invoke the interest of society and of children; this is nothing but sophistry." Another deputy, Paschal Grousset, expressed more concern for the fate of children. He argued that "the legal aspects of marriage make sense only with respect to the child. Everything else about it that restrains individual liberty is a lie and an abominable tyranny." More such libertarianism came from Lucien Leduc, a lawyer attached to the court of appeal: "Modern marriage . . . is nothing more than an ordinary contract through which each party hopes to develop in association with his complement." Even the youthful Raymond Poincaré was swept up in the movement, advocating divorce by mutual consent but not "upon the request of one, though I have to admit that there are cases that would prove me wrong [in this hesitation]." For Gustave Rivet, future editor of *Le Radical*, divorce was a "natural right" stipulated by Jean-Jacques Rousseau himself, who declared that "man must always be the master of his person."[59] Another respondent warned that if the divorce law did not change, people should not marry, for "as marriage is understood nowadays, it is a debasement." Finally, Emile Zola was in favor of "the couple whose love makes their union indissoluble, but if divorce is necessary there should be no obstacles whatever."[60]

In a preface to their *enquête*, the Marguerittes joined their friend Rivet in explicitly associating the right to divorce with the philosophy and individualistic freedoms of the French Revolution. By secularizing marriage, "the Revolution, whose munificent breath of fresh air sent us toward a sun of justice and humanity . . . understood . . . that society and the law were made for the individual, and not the individual for society and the law. The role of both is none other than to safeguard individual liberty, not to destroy it through indissoluble engagements." For them, "marriage was no more than a contract of fidelity, help, and mutual assistance, a free association between spouses." And divorce they advocated with arguments that have become familiar in our own time: it frees children from a home life filled with antagonism; it allows mismatched couples to be relieved of each other's company; and it forbids one spouse to chain the other to a union he or she finds constraining or harmful. For good measure, the authors concluded with the Radical republicans' tireless justification for everything: anticlericalism. Opposition to divorce reform was part and parcel of a "religious reaction" eternally hostile to "the principles of '92."[61]

At first glance it seems surprising that these Radical republicans cast their arguments in the language of pure individualism. Radicals, after all, tended to question the liberalism associated with such individualist positions, expressing allegiance in the 1890s to a new doctrine called solidarism. The proponents of solidarism intended it to correct the ills of classical liberalism while warding off the menace of collectivism. In particular, solidarists proposed that the nation no longer be conceived as an assortment of atomized individuals related to one another only through competition in the marketplace. It ought to be seen instead as a social body composed of interdependent organs, each performing a function necessary to the whole. Given this interdependence, no one could be an island of self-sufficiency, and all the nation's different members owed one another help and support.

Though such a notion ruled out liberal individualism, it did not disown individualism itself. As Judith F. Stone shrewdly points out, the ultimate purpose of solidarism was not to restrain private initiative but to reconstitute the individual sovereignty usurped by laissez-faire capitalism.[62] Solidarists argued that pure economic freedom had created such inequality in the marketplace that workers were now at the mercy of those who employed them. Private property increasingly escaped their grasp, as did the freedom it was believed to guarantee. By stressing cooperation, solidarists sought a rationale for government action designed to redress the balance of economic opportunity and personal freedom. But the ultimate aim remained the protection and enhancement of the individual. As the solidarist spokesman Léon Bourgeois put it, the goal of Radical reform was a perfect meritocracy "in which every man will have reached, within the limits of justice, individual proprietorship."[63] This would be accomplished through progressive taxation, democratic education, and social insurance—reforms, the Radicals believed, that would free individuals from the tyranny of an unrestrained marketplace. These reforms would create a new kind of individualism, one consistent with the realities of modern industrialism.[64]

For Radicals, then, the end of a rejuvenated individualism justified the means of solidarist reform. But when it came to the family, no such elaborate reasoning was required. There, the problem turned not on the existence of too much old-fashioned liberal individualism, as in the society at large, but on the lack of individualism of any sort. The family, Radicals believed—and here Socialists agreed—was a remnant of the ancien régime, with its hierarchic structure, its paternal authority, its Catholic culture of sacrament and ritual. As the writer Jean Joseph-Renaud put it, marriage and the family—unlike republican France's other institutions—suffered from "an unconscious residue of the Christian spirit, [from] the ingrained respect for its sacrament."[65] Likewise, one contributor to an *enquête* in the literary review *La Plume* maintained that "when it comes to marriage, the Revolution changed very little. To marry today, as in the past, is to sacrifice one's freedom."[66] As for individual family members, they "quest with energy, even violence," wrote the editors of the *Revue socialiste*, "for liberty, individuality, and independence, renouncing the chains, rejecting the unnatural servitudes . . . the tyrannies reinforced by all-powerful traditions."[67] For these Radical and Socialist writers, the family needed not a dose of solidarity, but a renovation à la 1789. Its members had to be freed from a tyranny that survived nowhere else.

This chorus of individualist comment on the French family is notable for its absence of female voices. It may be that in considering marriage, republican men, far more than women, valued personal independence over familial solidarity. After all, pleas for the relaxation of marital obligations, for unrestricted divorce and marriage as pure contract, appeared to offer men considerably more than their mates. The remarriage market favored men, since divorce stigmatized women more. And in economic terms marriage was less crucial for men—particularly middle-class men—who were much more likely than their wives to earn a family wage.[68] Beyond this, it may be that for some reformers the rebellion against traditional marriage disguised a deeper male revolt against the responsibilities of wedlock itself, or even a frustration against men's seeming inability to live without it.[69] Whatever the reasons, the Marguerittes explicitly confirmed the masculine bias of this individualist discourse on marriage and divorce. In response to objections that their proposed reforms would be harmful to women, they unabashedly declared, "Let's not suddenly become more feminist than the women!"[70]

There was little danger they would. Feminist and nonfeminist women alike emphasized that marriage involved responsibilities— and solidarities—that made easy divorce less than ideal. In her reply to the Marguerittes' *enquête*, the pioneering feminist writer Juliette Adam confided that growing marital instability gave her second thoughts about divorce in any form. And the novelist Marcelle Tinayre, herself a sincere feminist, told them she favored reforms only if the "material and moral welfare of children and women were taken into account."[71] Both women sensibly realized that in a society such as theirs, unrestricted divorce could devastate women economically, especially middle-class women educated for marriage, not paid employment.[72]

Like Adam and Tinayre, other elite women tended to shy away from the Marguerittes' more extreme proposals, as did leaders of the feminist mainstream, who went no further than divorce by mutual consent. Such caution toward divorce is significant in that women were more likely to request it than men. Women originated about 60 percent of all divorce proceedings, though they did so partly in response to a legal code that, despite some timid changes, still gave married women too few rights of their own.[73] Nonetheless, feminist notables found no panacea in easy divorce. To them, improving marriage for women seemed more important than facilitating its dissolution. As Jane Misme, editor of *La Française*, remarked, "We will solve the problems of marriage not by making it easier to leave our unions but by increasing the possibility of staying. . . . All the demands of feminism—namely, the same physical, moral, and intellectual education for both sexes; economic independence for women; equal marital rights for husbands and wives— help us toward this goal."[74] Feminists took particular umbrage at the idea of dissolving a marriage at the request of one spouse alone. For Marguerite Durand, director of the feminist daily *La Fronde*, this radical version of divorce amounted to nothing less than the right for men to repudiate their wives.[75] If husbands could dissolve their marriages at will, women would be utterly subject to masculine caprice, to men's primordial desire for youth and variety. In the words of Misme, divorce at the request of one spouse would become "the instrument for fantasies of the instinct."[76]

Sensible as they were, these feminist reservations about divorce failed to receive the attention they deserved; the era's male clamor for a more libertarian solution pushed them aside. But as an avalanche of responses was about to show, such radical notions of reform provoked a reaction of fear and anger that soon sent the familial individualists scurrying for cover. By taking the family question to its extremes, the Marguerittes and their allies opened a Pandora's box of emotional issues that conservatives could exploit for political advantage. For now the right could use the new century's "crisis of marriage," its fears about depopulation, the emancipation of women, and the standing of men to shift the terms of political debate to its benefit. Having been defeated in the political realm conservatives now possessed a cultural issue destined to renew their philosophy and help prepare the way for the "nationalist revival" to come.[77]

For the most part, participants—left as well as right—in the journalistic debate set off by the Marguerittes focused their attention directly on the family, on its problems and its essence. But the way they did so was laden with political overtones. We have seen how progressives associated freedom and individualism in the family with anticlericalism and the ideals of 1789. Conservatives, meanwhile, connected the family's health and viability to that of the nation. If the family was in trouble so was the nation; if it could be made whole again so could France. They endeavored, in other words, to reduce all politics to the eternal metaphor of family. And the more they succeeded in doing so, the better positioned they were to attack the Radical republic not just for policies believed to undermine the family but for failing to structure society in the family's idealized image. In this context divorce became central, for conservatives could accuse it of dissolving the institution on which all others were based.

Again and again during these early years of the new century, publicists of the right identified the fate of the nation with the fate of the family. For the writer Maurice Maindron, "A nation is nothing other than a tightly unified family whose members must continually make sacrifices to the grandeur and the honor of its name." Abbé E. Carry defined the *patrie* as a concept "borrowed from the paternal household to designate an enlarged family." And F. A. Vuillermet, the author of books on youth and virility, extolled the family as the "essential foundation for the life of a nation and the necessary condition of its expansion."[78]

In general, conservatives claimed that whatever menaced the family menaced fatherland and state as well. Writing in *Le Figaro*, Arvède Barine (pseudonym of Mme Cecile Vincens) declared that "divorce is at this very moment working to bring about the fall of the Third Republic." An anonymous contribution to *Fémina*, the popular women's magazine, blamed divorce for "destroying family and with it the fatherland itself." And the antifeminist author

Charles Turgeon summed up all the conservatives' worst fears about the relationship between *famille* and *patrie*. "Revolutionaries and feminists," Turgeon wrote, "now understand that the way to overturn our social order is not to bring down the government. As soon as one falls, another rises in its place." Our revolutionaries realize, he continued, that the real target, "the grand enemy that must at all costs be undermined and then destroyed," is the family, "that ancient domestic power which stands as the last refuge of social authority."[79]

For conservatives, paternal authority constituted one of the pivotal issues. Because divorce freed a woman from her husband's tutelage and awarded custody of children to mothers, it led, argued the legal scholar Jacques Peltier, to the decline of paternal power.[80] This development worried the likes of Charles Turgeon, who was already concerned about the era's other inroads into the husband's exclusive control over his wife and children. "We are losing the sense of authority," he lamented. "So enamored have we become of equality and independence that we can hardly tolerate—let alone honor—*le patronat*, the leadership or even the preeminence of fatherhood." Nothing was more regrettable for Turgeon than "the weakening of authority in the family."[81] By sapping authority at its very source, divorce and the ills that accompanied it drained fathers everywhere of the strength to command.

Beyond these moral and ideological admonitions, conservatives responded to the call for easier divorce with some alarming statistics. The annual number of divorces, modest in the new law's early years, was beginning to rise sharply. The courts had dissolved some five thousand marriages in 1887 and ten thousand in 1903, growing to nearly seventeen thousand in 1912. Even more troubling than actual divorces was the annual number of requests for divorce: 4,600 in 1885, 19,000 in 1912—more than a fourfold increase in less than three decades. The number of marriages per year stayed about the same during this period, producing by 1913 a ratio of about one divorce for every eighteen marriages. This figure, low by our standards, was worrisome for many in a country new to divorce, especially for Parisians whose rate doubled that of the country as a whole: one divorce for every nine marriages.[82]

By themselves, the mounting divorce statistics disturbed conservatives enough; viewed side by side with the plummeting birth rate, they created a furor. Between 1880 and 1901, the number of live births per 10,000 inhabitants declined by nearly 14 percent from 250 to 216 and would drop another 13 percent by 1911. These figures provoked the fear that the population of France would soon be the smallest of any major European power and half that of Germany.[83] Most contemporary studies on depopulation after 1900 blamed it in part on divorce.[84] A short marriage, commentators argued, logically produced fewer children than one lasting a lifetime.[85] And the possibility that a marriage might not endure encouraged young couples to limit the number of children they bore. Divorce, conservatives added, was yet another manifestation of the pernicious individualism that made French men and women unwilling to sacrifice personal pleasure and material comfort to repopulate the nation.

When people on the right began to insert their own *enquêtes* into the French press, they used the occasion not just to oppose divorce reform but to challenge the right of divorce itself. The director of a prominent 1903 survey, one Frédéric de France, objected to liberalized divorce on grounds of the male's instinctual quest for variety. Men, he wrote, have "a vague instinct for conquest, a latent desire for caprice." And for that reason the idea that men could end a marriage whenever they wanted "frightens me like a horse without reins."[86] Other respondents took a similarly dim view of liberalized divorce. For the economist Anatole Leroy-Beaulieu, the Marguerittes' reform would lead to a "serial polygamy" that would "sacrifice the essential interests of society and the family not, as some say, to the individual's interest but to his whims and his passions." The writer Jules Bois was convinced that women would suffer much more than men from divorce on demand; Madame Alphonse Daudet, echoing many of Frédéric de France's respondents, believed divorce in any form "martyrs and demoralizes our children." Finally, several writers argued that the campaign for divorce was, in reality, a campaign for the *union libre*, the free union whose transitory coupling amounted to little more than free love. As the sociologist Gabriel Tarde put it, "as soon as we begin down the road to divorce, logic commands us imperiously to go all the way, all the way to mutual repudiation for no particular reason. If we seek to judge and reform marriage from the individualistic stance of providing the greatest happiness for the spouses, then our ideal, whether we realize it or not, is the free union."[87]

Emile Durkheim, writing in the *Revue bleue,* echoed his fellow sociologist's reservations about the campaign for liberalized divorce. Durkheim apologized for appearing to sound a reactionary note but went on to oppose divorce by mutual consent and even to question the desirability of divorce in any form. In his earlier study of suicide Durkheim claimed to have discovered a strong relation between divorce and the propensity to suicide. Other commentators had concluded from similar findings that divorce caused suicide and that divorced people were much more likely to kill themselves than married ones. But Durkheim saw things as more complicated and more ominous. By looking closely at the data for regions with high divorce rates he found that the increase in suicides came not from divorced people but from married ones. Paris, in other words, exhibited a higher suicide rate than the provinces because far more married people in the capital killed themselves than did those outside it. Single people in the city, by contrast, were only slightly more likely to kill themselves than were single people in the country. He explained this observation by suggesting that divorce was dangerous not simply in its effect on individuals but also in its effect on marriage as an institution. The purpose of marriage, Durkheim maintained, was to promote order and security, stability and instinctual restraint. When it did so, marriage created "for both spouses a moral constitution that is sui generis," one that shielded them from suicide. What made divorce so pernicious, he wrote, was its ability to weaken *all* marriages whether they broke up or not. The possibility of divorce encouraged partners to envision a new and better marriage to replace the existing one, judged always in relation to an imaginary marital ideal. Such thinking engendered a longing for novelty and variation that rendered happiness in marriage all but impossible. In extreme cases the misery that resulted could lead to suicide.[88]

To this argument Durkheim appended a revealing discussion of differences between the sexes. When he classified his statistics by gender, he discovered that the relation between high rates of divorce and suicide held true only for married men, not married women. In comparing married and single men Durkheim noticed that suicides among the former were two to three times more frequent in regions of high than of low rates of divorce, whereas among single men suicides were no more likely in regions of high rates than of low ones. The prevalence of divorce thus affected married men in particular, multiplying their suicide rate as much as three times. For women, the effect of a high rate of divorce was altogether different. Living in Paris (high rate) as opposed to the provinces (low rate) did not make married women more prone to suicide than single ones. Thus the availability of divorce hurt married men but did not raise the number of suicides for women. From this the sociologist asserted that secure marriage protected men from suicide but not women. He refused in this *Revue bleue* article to go so far as to repeat his earlier contention in *Suicide* (1897) that "the effect of divorce was to slightly increase wives' immunity [to suicide.]"[89] But his later piece left the impression nonetheless that marital stability shielded men from suicide while divorce shielded women. This conclusion, of course, is not the one he intended to make, since his purpose was to show that divorce was bad in general. But some readers, especially feminist ones, might have deduced from Durkheim's article that divorce could be a good thing for women.

Why in Durkheim's view did divorce figure significantly in men's suicide rates while it affected women's so little? His answer rested on the commonly held belief that men alone possessed restless instincts that had to be tamed. Unlike women, whose "moral constitution" remained unchanged by marriage, men needed the institution to produce a set of rules "to which the passions must submit." By directing masculine desire to a single object, "certain, defined, and in principle invariable, [marriage] prevents the heart from becoming agitated, from tormenting itself in a futile quest for goals always new and always changing." Marriage alone makes possible "the emotional peace, the inner equilibrium, that comprise the essential conditions of happiness and of healthy morals." But marriage worked this way, Durkheim was quick to add, only when its rules enjoyed universal respect. "To the extent that the bonds of marriage become fragile, or that they can be broken at will, marriage ceases to be itself and thus to yield the same virtues." Divorce saps marriage of its force and subverts the rules men need to contain their instincts, instincts that promise pleasure and produce only pain. This is why, Durkheim wrote, "the proposed liberalization of divorce will lead inevitably to higher rates of suicide." The measure purports "to alleviate the moral misery of husband and wife, but its result will be to demoralize them and to detach them all the more from life itself."[90]

This conclusion overlooked the distinctions he had just made between men and women, distinctions that implied—contrary to received opinion—that marriage benefited men more than women. That Durkheim stopped short of saying so directly suggests an uneasiness about such a judgment. Men commonly believed that marriage compromised their freedom and that by agreeing to it they made a sacrifice for which women owed them eternal gratitude. The notion, therefore, that men needed marriage more than women did threatened one of the main assumptions on which the "strong sex" based its power, or at the very least its sense of superiority.

It was one thing for highbrow publications like *La Revue* and the *Revue bleue* to run such pieces, quite another for a large-circulation women's magazine like *Fémina*.[91] Beginning in September 1904 and continuing for three straight months *Fémina* conducted an *enquête* that took the unusual tack of inviting ordinary readers to write in. Some three thousand letters were received, a narrow majority of which sided with Paul Bourget's belief in indissoluble marriage over the Marguerittes' quest for divorce on demand.[92]

Fémina's survey opened with a debate between Bourget and the brothers Margueritte, who each had recently published a *roman à thèse* to dramatize their views on divorce. The Marguerittes' novel, *Les Deux vies* (1902), told the sad story of a virtuous young woman married to a cad who refuses to grant her a divorce. The judge sides with him, giving her no choice but to leave home penniless and without her children. The moral hardly needed to be stated: just and fair divorce laws are required to free women from cruel and all-powerful husbands. Bourget's work, *Un Divorce* (1904), took the opposite stance. The heroine is a divorced woman whose remarriage brings her nothing but grief. Even though the first husband had been hideous and the second is loving, her actions estrange her from her children, from the church she values, and eventually from the second husband she once admired so much. The moral: divorce always causes more problems than it solves, with disastrous consequences to individuals as well as families.[93]

Both novels created a huge stir in the early years of the new century, and it is significant not only that thousands of readers wrote in but that Bourget's uncompromising position against divorce received the majority's support. In part the results reflected a readership of middle-class women dependent on marriage for economic reasons. But they also mirrored the middle class's caution on matters of morality and family. Those who opposed divorce in *Fémina*'s study commonly did so on patriotic grounds, viewing the family as basic to the existence of the *patrie*. In the words of one writer, the "fatherland is none other than *le plus grand foyer*."[94] By implication, then, when the *famille* was in trouble so was the *patrie*. Or as the conservative reformer Emile Cheysson put it elsewhere, "Tant vaut la famille, tant vaut la nation."[95]

By the autumn of 1904 when *Fémina*'s survey appeared, France's debate over divorce had entered its fifth year. The nation seemed almost obsessed with a problem that had captured perhaps more attention from ordinary citizens than the parallel struggle among religious and political leaders over the separation of Church and state. It may be that conservatives outside the Church found it more fruitful to attack what they took to be republican mores than to defend the Church and the religious orders directly. Or simply that the health and viability of families, and of the nation as the consummate family, were matters that directly concerned the vast majority of French men and women. But whatever the reasons, the debate over divorce raged on. Novels devoted to the issue rolled off the presses, as did doctoral dissertations, psychological studies, pieces of theater, journalistic diatribes, and above all the *enquêtes*.[96] It was almost as if the French press, increasingly alert to ways of shaping public opinion, wanted readers to talk back, if only to gauge journalism's success. After *Fémina*, surveys appeared in *Gil Blas*, the *Revue socialiste*, the *Revue hebdomadaire*, *La Française*, and *Le Matin*, to name a few. This last had particular importance because of the paper's enormous daily circulation (about 650,000) and because numerous readers responded.[97] *Le Matin* conducted its survey, "The Crisis of Divorce," from early January to late February 1908, amassing more than six thousand responses.[98] Virtually every day the front page featured excerpts of letters from ordinary readers, and the survey proved so popular that beginning in March the paper devoted a feuilleton to the subject. This was an issue that knew no bounds.

On 8 February 1908, for example, survey responses filled the three middle columns of *Le Matin*'s front page, displacing news of a coup d'état in Portugal as well as the armed struggle in Morocco.

International affairs gave way to the most domestic of affairs, and *Le Matin*'s editors exploited an insatiable interest in divorce with banner headlines: "Divorce: confession générale d'une époque" (9 February 1908); "Les douleurs du divorce" (12 February); "La crise du mariage et du divorce est portée devant le Sénat" (22 February). The paper made a token effort to give equal space to all sides of the issue, with one column reserved for advocates of divorce, one for opponents, and one for partisans of the *union libre*. But since the latter implied divorce on demand, survey director Hugues Le Roux ensured that individualist views would enjoy the most attention.

Little in the letters' content was new. Readers condemned divorce for destroying *famille* and *patrie* and they supported it for relieving the pain of familial strife. Conservatives vilified the *union libre* while individualists sang its praises. But despite the stale content, journalists found something novel in its form. Many letters contained narratives of personal trauma and individual redemption, accounts offering the same mix of titillation and moralism that made the *fait divers*, or crime brief, so popular with newspaper readers. By printing such personal confessions, *Le Matin*'s editors could assimilate a key issue of public debate to the *fait divers* without sacrificing their aura of journalistic respectability. They could, in other words, promote domestic dramas to the front page by disguising them as philosophical argument. It was a technique that enabled *Le Matin* to fuse public and private in a reportage whose guiding principle was the *fait divers*.[99]

The letters themselves could almost have been plot outlines for the era's innumerable social novels. One writer recounted how he had sacrificed the loving free union of his student days for a bourgeois marriage that would soon end in divorce. The prose was simple and direct; "I knew the happiness of a *union libre* in my student life. I got married. And now I am in the process of divorce." The writer confessed that a mindless attachment to "bourgeois respectability" had ruined his life and destroyed his love. "At the age of twenty-six, I left my mistress with whom I lived quite happily. These old [bourgeois] ideas had got the better of me, and I married a woman with a mentality entirely different from my own. And now to free myself, I am condemned to expose all my conjugal misery before a judge. . . . I am, therefore, a partisan of the *union libre*."[100]

Another letter came from the former wife of a cabinet minister who had used his power and connections to gain custody of their child. The minister, she wrote, having over the years turned the child against her, had made it almost impossible for her to visit her daughter. Here was a pure personal narrative, one that argued neither for nor against divorce but simply recounted its ravages.[101] Similarly, a third excerpt presented a *lettre d'un enfant* written by a boy who had been nine years old when his parents separated. After an extended tug of war for the child, the father simply seized custody, thanks—the boy wrote—to the police. Shortly thereafter his father forced him to compose hateful letters to his mother accusing her of every sort of heinous crime against parenthood. The letters ensured a court judgment against his mother and permanent custody for his father. The mother's failure to appear at the divorce trial convinced the boy that she had died and that his letters had caused her death. There followed a list of more horrors by the father and always the child's nagging guilt: "I think about only one thing, what they made me do to my mother. My beloved mother. They took me away from her, and I have never stopped crying for her." The letter ended with a threat, one that promised to turn a small *fait divers* into one of larger proportions. "When I'm all grown up, if I find out that my mother died because of the letters they made me write, I will be a great criminal, because I will have my revenge. I will avenge my mother; I will kill my father."[102] In this letter, like the last, there remains no hint of political exchange, only a tale of domestic woe laced with oedipal fantasies jolted to consciousness.

After two months of relentless publicity *Le Matin* closed its survey with a flair of journalistic sensation. The letters, wrote Le Roux, revealed "all the ravages of our ravaged era, an era in which paternal authority weakens from one day to the next, the conjugal bond dissolves almost to nothing. We have seen the birth of women's rights, at the cost of a thousand dramas, and we have watched the family fade away, with our children split up between mothers and fathers."[103] The journalist may have meant this as the final word, as the moral summation of his times, but for almost everyone else it represented just one more rehearsal of an unending spectacle, a collective fixation upon divorce.

It was a spectacle that remained compelling in the years before 1914 as conservatives and reformers rehearsed the debate over divorce again and again. Only, the closer France came to war, the more the conservatives seemed destined to win. Those who responded to a 1910 *enquête* in the feminist daily *La Française* expressed serious reservations about divorce, even though women still requested it more often than men. A 1912 Catholic congress held in Bordeaux evoked considerable sympathy in the press for the traditionalist position. And two years later a survey of well-educated women aged eighteen to twenty-five indicated a general agreement that divorce "painfully mutilated a woman's life" and that people should resort to it only in extreme cases, especially when children were involved.[104]

With all this ferment over marriage, divorce, and the family in the waning years of the Belle Epoque, it is no wonder that moral issues figured so prominently in the trial of Madame Caillaux. Conservatives had linked the health of *famille* to the strength of *patrie* and in doing so had encouraged French women and men to see themselves as members of a national family rather than as equal citizens of an egalitarian republic. The new conception had resonated widely in the years before 1914, permitting conservatives to attack the Caillaux for crimes against the family and against the nation forged in its image. In the *Cour d'assises*, members of the jury would doubtless take these moral considerations into account as they deliberated over Henriette Caillaux's fate, weighing them against the extent to which they considered her a passionate heroine whose transgressions could be excused.

As for Joseph Caillaux, challenges to his record in government had failed to topple him in a country in which party affiliations changed little. But the shifts registered at the level of culture and morality had made him far more vulnerable. By judging him against these stricter standards conservative commentators would ultimately achieve what parliamentary and electoral tactics had been unable to do: place his political future in doubt.

Judge Albanel
Masculinity, Honor, and the Duel

By the fifth day of the trial, 24 July 1914, the case of Madame Caillaux had monopolized the news for nearly a week. And though the French public paid little heed, it was a week during which Europe had lurched ominously toward war. As Chenu and Labori made their last-minute preparations for the testimony of the fifth session, Austria and Serbia were already preparing to fight.

The fixation of press and public on a courtroom drama that focused readers' attention inward and away from the impending European confrontation did not mean, however, that French men and women had managed to shelter themselves emotionally from the threat of war. The rhetoric and symbolism of the trial and of the commentary surrounding it: all recapitulated the moral uncertainty, the national longing, the wounded feelings of personal and national pride that had helped, in this era, to create a climate favorable to war. In particular, the almost obsessive concern with honor and masculinity revealed throughout the proceedings and emphasized on the fifth and the sixth days suggests a connection between an anxious attention to masculine pride, expressed in an upsurge of dueling, and the nationalistic devotion to patriotic honor so prevalent during the years prior to World War I.

France of the Belle Epoque—and especially the world of the Parisian male elite—possessed a culture of honor, a preoccupation with personal reputation that counted the appearance of strength in men, and of sexual virtue in women, above all else.[1] This culture had been shaped by the anxieties and insecurities stemming from the persistence of aristocratic values in an increasingly democratic society and from the consequences of France's humiliating defeat in the Franco-Prussian War. Unlike the nobility of the ancien régime, the Belle Epoque's Parisian elite existed at the top of an increasingly democratic society in which anyone with sufficient wealth, power, or intellectual and artistic accomplishment could aspire to aristocratic status. The Parisian world, therefore, was at once aristocratic and democratic, hierarchic yet porous, a situation that imbued all but the highest-born members of the elite with a certain insecurity over their social position.[2]

Heightening their insecurities were mounting fears about the emasculating tendencies of modern existence that males experienced and reexperienced in the decades following 1870. France's defeat had been so severe that, according to certain influential commentators, French men had returned from the war in 1870 feeling dishonored and lacking in the virtues of strength, action, and will so central to long-standing notions of masculinity: they had returned, it was said, to women who saw them as something less than men.[3]

There had been similar commentary, writes Bertram Wyatt-Brown, just five years earlier in another honor-bound culture, the American South. At the close of the Civil War, defeated Confederate soldiers admitted openly to being loath to return home for fear their wives and mothers considered them unmanly.[4] Although American veterans may have been more forthright about their damaged masculine pride than their French counterparts were, nonetheless the latter appeared, during the years following the Franco-Prussian War, to devote considerable effort to recapturing at home the virility they had lost at war. They did so through allegiance to a culture of honor that required them to fight surrogate wars in the form of the duel. Dueling became the emblem, during this period, of a masculine revival destined to restore the national will through a new spirit of combat. The duel, for many commentators of the Belle Epoque, was the highest form of sport, a sport so potent it fortified men for war. Others believed it was not so much the *practice* but the *ethic* of dueling that prepared men for war. Such in particular, was the view of Charles Péguy, the iconoclastic poet of national honor. Péguy wrote that France's allegiance to the philosophy and morality expressed in the duel, to the duel's chivalric ethic of honor, promised French soldiers the means to survive against a German enemy utterly ruthless in combat and indifferent to the French ideals of liberty and justice.

All these themes emerged more or less overtly throughout the

14. Judge Louis Albanel presides over the Paris *Cour d'assises* (*L'Illustration*, 25 July 1914).

trial of Madame Caillaux, but on the fifth and sixth days they moved to the very center of the case when a bizarre courtroom incident nearly led to a duel involving the Président of the *Cour d'assises*, Judge Albanel himself (figure 14). Referring to the proceedings of the fifth day, Albanel opened the following session with a statement about his courtroom judgment that ended with a resounding defense of his honor: "More than anyone else in this room I take care to defend my own honor and the honor of the magistrature— despite what anyone may have said."[5] This was, to say the least, a curious preface to a session of the *Cour d'assises*, referring as it did to a courtroom incident of which virtually everyone was unaware. The incident itself, which occurred on 24 July, was not widely reported in the Parisian press until two days later, but once it came before the public at large, it led to a series of events unprecedented in the annals of French republican justice.

When the court convened for the fifth session on 24 July, the disposition of the now famous *lettres intimes* was still unresolved. After having pulled the letters dramatically from her handbag, Berthe Gueydan had ended her testimony the day before without revealing their contents. Instead she had placed a packet of eight documents in the hands of defense lawyer Fernand Labori, who at the beginning of the fifth session wanted to exclude five he considered irrelevant to the case at hand. His efforts to do so produced a courtroom dispute between him and Berthe Gueydan, punctuated by interventions from Maître Chenu, that dragged on for more than two hours. Even though Berthe Gueydan had given Labori permission "to do with the letters what he wanted" the defense attorney declared himself unwilling to exclude five of the eight letters without her assent. Though he did not say so, he undoubtedly sought Gueydan's agreement over the disposition of the letters to remove any impression that he might be hiding something. Ever suspicious of a trap, Gueydan refused, declaring that as far as she was concerned no distinctions among the letters could be made and that all eight should be introduced as evidence in the case. Perhaps sensing an opening, Labori now told her that since she would not agree to his wishes she should take the letters back and recover sole responsibility for their use.

"Here are your letters," Labori exclaimed to Berthe Gueydan, pushing them toward her. "Do what you want with them. As for me, I regain my complete independence."

"But you have already accepted them," Gueydan responded, refusing to grasp the handwritten sheets held before her.

"Then I can do what I want with them," retorted Labori, hoping again to gain her assent for excluding five of the documents.

"Yes," she replied. "Read all or none."

"Well then, Madam, I will read none."

To read none of the letters was not a solution Labori really desired, for he needed the jury to see precisely why Henriette Caillaux had so feared their publication. Labori wanted them read, but he wanted as well to heighten the jury's expectation of them as sensitive and embarrassing by appearing reluctant to reveal them himself. Chenu, too, wanted them read to the court; he hoped they would help indict the Caillaux morally and thereby bolster his case.

"Would Madame Gueydan agree," Chenu now asked, "to entrust the letters to the *partie civile* [that is, to himself] and to the attorney general?"

"Certainly."

"But Madame Gueydan has no right to do this," Labori declared, "because she has refused to take them back from me."

Labori's statement prompted yet another intervention from Chenu, creating a cacophony of voices all shouting at once. And at this point Judge Albanel abruptly suspended the session, calling a recess before the disposition of the letters had been resolved. The trial transcript notes "Noise at the back of the room" in response to Albanel's move; otherwise nothing in the record of the courtroom proceedings betrays the bizarre but highly significant drama of honor that was to follow.

During the hour-long recess, a courtroom spectator related to a journalist from *Le Figaro* an incident that had escaped the notice of most members of the audience. *Le Figaro*'s informant reported that he had heard Louis Dagoury, one of the assistant judges sitting in the *Cour d'assises*, mutter the following words to Judge Albanel just after the recess had been declared. "Monsieur, you dishonor us."[6] Apparently none of the judges realized that anyone else had heard the remark, and Albanel and his assistant justices retired to the magistrates' chambers to discuss Dagoury's challenge to the courtroom hierarchy. According to a confidential report subsequently submitted to Albanel's immediate superior, once in camera the presiding judge demanded an apology and Dagoury complied. The two men apparently shook hands and the incident appeared to be closed.[7]

But not for long. The next day *Le Figaro* revealed the entire episode along with a statement from Dagoury claiming he had nothing to apologize for. Judge Albanel, he now told the public at large, had shown undue preference for the Caillaux by suspending the courtroom session when he did, and the assistant judge saw no reason to revise that opinion. Dagoury further told *Le Figaro* that he believed Albanel was wrong not to have seized the letters from Maître Labori so as to make them part of the court record. To permit Henriette Caillaux's defense attorney to retain exclusive control of the letters, Dagoury claimed, was to show extreme partiality to her side and thus to dishonor the magistrature as a whole.

Shortly after reading Dagoury's interview with *Le Figaro*, Albanel drafted a letter to the Premier Président of the Paris Court of Appeals in which he now characterized the dispute with his assistant magistrate as a "conflict of honor." Because Dagoury had made the whole matter public, Albanel told his superior he could no longer accept the "lukewarm excuses [Dagoury] had murmured" the day before. These excuses, Albanel wrote, "cannot satisfy me, especially now that today's *Figaro* has reported the incident incorrectly and incompletely, accompanied by a scandalously biased commentary." The judge added that "it is absolutely impossible for me to sit with a colleague who has insulted me so outrageously with the words I have just reported to you ['You dishonor us; you are a scoundrel'] until I have received the reparation that is owed me, reparation commensurate with the gravity of the offense."[8]

Suddenly, an incident that Albanel had apparently considered closed with apologies and a gentlemanly handshake the day before now became for him an affair of honor, a matter requiring reparation consonant with the "gravity of the offense." Why this transformation, why this appeal to honor complete with all the traditional rhetoric of the duel: "insult," "offense," "satisfaction," "reparation"? The crucial factor seems to have been exposure in the press, the fact that a major newspaper had seen fit to place the matter before the public. Kept strictly private, the differences could be easily resolved. Albanel, after all, apparently mollified by Dagoury's apology, had returned to the bench following the recess—with Dagoury at his side—and proceeded as if nothing had happened. It was only after *Le Figaro* had publicized the event that Albanel felt the need to take action.

Now, with the incident before the public, he could be shamed, his reputation sullied, unless he sought satisfaction. Albanel had to act to preserve his standing in a Parisian society still governed by an aristocratic preoccupation with social rank but devoid, thanks to the progress of democracy and capitalism, of the aristocracy's traditional—and largely fixed—criteria of status. In this context, public *perceptions* of one's place in the social ranking became all important. During the Belle Epoque those perceptions crystallized in a renewed concept of honor.

So striking was the Parisian elite's commitment to an impassioned culture of honor that an enormous number of writers and commentators undertook, during the years from 1890 to 1914, to explain the origins and meaning of this remarkable phenomenon.[9] Perhaps the most illuminating of these contributions came from Gabriel Tarde, the distinguished sociologist and professor at the august Collège de France. Tarde considered the Belle Epoque's culture of honor and the duels it engendered to be the pernicious product of France's newly ascendent penny press, a medium he called "a steam engine for the fabrication and the destruction of reputations on an immense scale."[10]

In Tarde's view, members of the modern Parisian elite were obsessed with their personal standing and reputation because they no longer enjoyed a fixed estate of honor determined, in large part, by birth. What they possessed instead was a mobile capital of honor that fluctuated in worth as stocks and bonds did. In the case of honor, however, it was not the economic marketplace that set its value but the marketplace of opinion controlled by the press. The more extensive and favorable the publicity given an individual, the greater his stock of honor, and vice versa. Thus, just as capitalism had deprived wealth of its once solid grounding in land and other fixed assets, so had the press stripped honor of its traditional relation to birth and social rank. "The solid, narrow, and massive honor of the past, limited to the boundaries of a small city or to a suburb, is as distant from the vast, superficial, and unstable honor of the present as the landed patrimonies of our ancestors are from the assets in government bonds or industrial shares we possess today."[11] Like wealth, Tarde suggested, honor could now be created or destroyed almost overnight, leaving society devoid of any stable hierarchy. Thanks to the press, therefore, honor now suffered the same disease of modernity epitomized by capitalism itself: "All that is solid melts into air."

Although Tarde underestimated the importance of the republic's new democratic mores in unsettling established hierarchies and therefore in shaping the culture of honor, he did capture the extent to which members of the Belle Epoque's elite tended to judge themselves according to the opinions of others. An individual's self-image had come largely to conform to the image the Parisian society had formed of him, an impression shaped by the Belle Epoque's mass-circulation penny press. Reputations once safe from popular scrutiny were now routinely exposed to the public view, and one person's challenge to another's standing could be transformed literally overnight into a public event, threatening the social position and self-images of the individuals involved. In this environment, French men—and women too—felt the need to preserve their reputations at all cost.

Unhappily, neither sex could seek redress through the law, for the Napoleonic Code provided no sanctions against affronts to personal reputation. And with the advent of the Third Republic the problem became far more serious, for the regime created two new forums of unfettered speech—the democratic parliament and the free press—without adjusting the laws of libel and defamation accordingly. The French revolutionary traditions inherited by the Third Republic had made essentially impossible the imposition of restraints on political speech, no matter how defamatory, giving French politicians and journalists virtually unlimited license to insult one another in public. As a result, men who felt themselves defamed or dishonored had no choice but to look beyond the law for redress. Increasingly after 1870 they turned to the duel. The *code napoléon* gave way to the code of the duel, republican law to aristocratic custom, as French men fought more often than at any time since the heyday of dueling in the seventeenth century.[12]

Women, in contrast, prohibited by law from filing paternity suits and by custom from dueling, could rely on neither the culture of law nor the culture of honor. Often the only means women possessed to defend reputations that turned on the appearance of chastity before marriage—and fidelity thereafter—was to commit acts of retribution against the men who had shamed them. Their inability to find satisfaction either in the law or in the duel thus helps explain why female crimes of passion loomed so large in this honor-bound society.

As for individuals accused of crimes in connection with affairs of honor, whether duels or crimes of passion, they enjoyed the sympathy of a public opinion weighted heavily in their favor. The law itself, however, made no exceptions for crimes committed in the name of honor. The statutes of France's criminal code treated a duelist who killed his opponent or a woman who killed her errant husband as murderers no different from any others. Public opinion and official justice were therefore radically at odds in France of the Belle Epoque, whose juries regularly—and sometimes defiantly—acquitted the victors of duels and the vanquished of love.[13]

It is in terms of these cultural meanings and requirements of honor that Albanel's words and actions in the wake of *Le Figaro*'s report can best be understood. Once the incident with Dagoury had come before the public, Judge Albanel had no choice but to seek reparation not just to maintain his standing in society but ultimately to preserve his own self-esteem. Indeed, a rumor began to circulate that Albanel had sent his seconds to Dagoury to demand satisfaction through a duel. And though the rumor was untrue, the judge did take a number of other steps that demonstrate the extent to which even this highly placed justice, a man sworn to uphold the country's laws against violent acts, had been imbued with the culture of honor. First, he wrote to his superior, the first president of the Paris Court of Appeals, expressing his complaint not in the language of law and bureaucratic regulation but in the words and images of honor and the duel: he sought not justice but satisfaction, not punishment for Dagoury but reparation.

Having taken this step, Albanel went on to do something that seems—at least from the perspective of the late twentieth century—more extraordinary still. He met in his chambers with Emile Bruneau de Laborie, France's premier authority on the duel and author of a widely read handbook entitled *Les lois du duel* (1906). Bruneau was an adventurer and sportsman, having hunted big game in Africa, founded the National Fencing Society, and written extensively about sport, dueling, and the rules of honor for *Le Figaro* and other prominent journals.[14] It is striking that when confronted with a matter implicating his honor, one of the leading members of the Third Republic's judicial establishment* chose to consult in person not with his professional superiors but with an expert on dueling. Albanel's actions suggest once again that when it came to a question of personal reputation, the culture of honor counted more for him than the culture of laws—or at the very least that he wanted to give the appearance that such was the case. And even if he was motivated purely by appearance, this in itself is evidence of the Belle Epoque's powerful culture of honor and of its hold upon a high-ranking judge.[15]

In his meeting with Albanel, Bruneau counseled caution, telling

---

* Albanel had risen rapidly within the ranks of the French magistrature, becoming a *juge d'instruction* in Paris at the relatively youthful age of forty-two and a member of the nation's most prominent court, the Paris Court of Appeals, only a few years later. He wrote widely about criminal justice and the sociology of crime and frequently represented the government at international conferences on law and criminality. The *Dictionnaire national des contemporains* (Paris: Office général d'édition, 1906), 4:354, called him a "magistrate of great urbanity and perfect tact who doubles as a psychologist and philanthropist of considerable intelligence."

the judge that "from the moment the incident was placed for settlement before the judicial chain of command, you have by this act alone—according to common practice in matters such as this—excluded the possibility of asking to settle it on the terrain of the point of honor [i.e., the duel]."[16] Even this advice, however, did not cool Albanel's ardor for personal satisfaction. In an interview with *Le Matin* on 26 July, the Président of the *Cour d'assises* refused to reject the possibility of an eventual duel. "I fully intend," Albanel declared, "to demand of Monsieur Dagoury an oral apology and a written retraction. As for a duel (*réparation par les armes*), I cannot, according to Monsieur Bruneau de Laborie, insist on it at present . . . but in the event that Monsieur Dagoury refuses to offer the apology to which I am entitled, I reserve my complete freedom of action. In such a case, the matter before us would become nothing more than a dispute between two men, and I would send my seconds to M. Dagoury."[17]

The incident did not end here, for a few days later Dagoury himself wrote to the first president of the Court of Appeals rejecting Albanel's demand for an apology. Dagoury explained that he had consulted two friends, both attorneys, about the matter; both had advised him to send his seconds to Albanel immediately. Both men agreed with him that Albanel's demand represented an unacceptable challenge and that "for me to remain silent any longer could be interpreted as a sort of tacit acquiescence to the unacceptable claims advanced by Monsieur Albanel." Dagoury had to respond to Albanel's statements because they represented "a veritable provocation *made public*," something that left him no choice, he explained to his superior, but to challenge Albanel to a confrontation on the field of honor.[18] Shortly thereafter, Dagoury sent his rival a telegram announcing that his seconds would be calling within the next forty-eight hours.

Although the outbreak of war appears to have prevented Albanel and Dagoury from going through with their duel, the frequent duels of other high-ranking individuals suggest that the two judges were far from atypical members of the Belle Epoque's social, political, and intellectual elite in allegiance to an ethic of honor. Hardly a day went by when the boulevards were not abuzz with tales of the latest encounter on the field of honor, for at a time when the duel had become largely extinct in England it reached its modern zenith in France.[19] The novelist Octave Mirbeau had fought eleven times by 1900, often with the writer Jean Joseph-Renard, himself an excellent duelist, present to chronicle the event. And Mirbeau was far from alone among men of the pen who turned to the sword. Paul Adam, Paul Bourget, Maurice Barrès, Robert de Montesquiou, Jules Lemaître all fought duels during the period, as did Marcel Proust himself, who sent his seconds in response to Jean Lorrain's derisive label for Proust, "the angel of Saint-Germain."[20] When Belle Epoque writers were not fighting duels they were quite often depicting them in their fiction. In particular Guy de Maupassant seemed almost obsessed with the duel, producing a series of stories on the feelings of men about to face the duel and on others who fought and won against difficult odds.[21]

In these stories and in the newspaper accounts of actual confrontations, the duel of the Belle Epoque appears as a highly stylized and ritualized event rigorously governed by rules and conventions elaborated in guidebooks like that of Bruneau de Laborie.[22] Duels could be fought either with swords or pistols, with the choice left to the seconds—or representatives—of the two combatants. The task of the seconds was to deliver a challenge or receive one and then, in the case of a minor affront, to attempt to resolve the differences between the two principals without resort to a duel. Failing that, the seconds chose the weapons to be used, established the time and location of the duel, and ensured the presence of one doctor for each side. After the duel, it was the seconds' responsibility to draft an account of the event to be sent to appropriate newspapers for publication.

Duels fought with swords were required to continue until one of the combatants drew blood from his opponent. Even a small amount of blood sufficed, and for this reason most wounds were minor. Nonetheless, some duels resulted in serious injury to one or even both combatants, especially when neither was expert in the art of swordfighting. For obvious reasons, duels fought with pistols were potentially more dangerous, but because the two combatants could be placed as far as thirty meters apart they often missed each other, sometimes deliberately. In theory, when both bullets missed their mark the duelists were expected to fight once again with swords, but in reality most duels ended after the two shots had been fired.

No official statistics on the results of dueling were compiled, though the writer Edouard Dujardin did maintain unofficial records for the decade of the 1880s, which he published under the pseudonym Ferréus as *L'annuaire du duel*.[23] Ferréus's figures were far from complete, for he neglected the many duels fought within the military and between those too obscure to have their seconds' reports published in leading newspapers, the exclusive source of his information. But they do provide some indication of the results of these confrontations. Of the 598 duels he registered for the period 1880 to 1889, 16 (3 percent) resulted in death and another 40 (7 percent) in serious injury.[24] Thus, on the basis of Ferréus's admittedly partial information, we can surmise that most duelists were likely to emerge from their confrontations unharmed. They nonetheless faced a small, though hardly negligible, risk of requiring a doctor— or even a priest. The duel was just dangerous enough to make those who fought feel proudly virile without being so dangerous as to ensure that only the truly courageous or extremely foolhardy would be willing to take part.

One final aspect of dueling that bears mention is its extremely high cost. At a time when the entire monthly budget of a Parisian working-class family seldom exceeded 200 francs, each combatant spent a minimum of that sum—not including the cost of fencing or shooting lessons—on a single duel.[25] Carriages or automobiles had to be hired, attire bought, doctors retained, meeting rooms rented, swords or pistols purchased. These costs excluded nearly all members of the working and modest middle classes. But for those even slightly more affluent, dueling often seemed a necessary expense, especially for journalists and politicians whose reputations had become matters of great public interest.

By most accounts, journalists appear to have fought even more often than other writers; as one English commentator wrote, "the journalist must make up his mind to a duel as one of the requirements of his profession."[26] The notoriously anti-Semitic editor Edouard Drumont fought constantly, as did the Bonapartist newspaperman Paul de Cassagnac. So too did journalists of the political left like Victor Méric, who elaborately justified his combat in an issue of his radical weekly, *Les hommes du jour*.[27] Of course journalism overlapped extensively with politics, and perhaps the most ardent duelists of all were the politicians of the Third Republic. Georges Clemenceau ranked first with twenty-two duels, but close behind were other controversial political figures such as Paul Déroulède and Léon Gambetta. Even Jean Jaurès himself stepped onto the field of honor, and though Joseph Caillaux neglected to challenge Gaston Calmette, declaring the editor unworthy of him, he dueled shortly thereafter with his electoral opponent, Louis d'Aillières. Commenting on this duel, one right-wing paper complained that d'Aillières should have known better than to give Caillaux such a "certificate of honorability."[28]

It is perhaps understandable that true members of the Parisian aristocracy and others almost as elite adhered to a culture of honor and its attendant requirements of the duel. But it is less clear why so many middle-class journalists, writers, lawyers, judges, and politicians embraced this culture as well. Why, in other words, did aristocratic values and aristocratic conceptions of status retain so much influence among members of the Parisian middle and upper middle classes? Several commentators of the era attempted to answer this question and in doing so tended more often to display that middle-class allegiance to aristocratic values than to explain it. Bourgeois writers such as the journalist-philosopher Lucien Prévost-Paradol and the critic Emile Faguet extolled the culture of honor as a bulwark of social order and aristocratic mores in the midst of the very changes often associated with middle-class life: religious decline, egalitarian politics, and capitalist growth.

In a study first published in 1868 but regularly reprinted and cited thereafter, Prévost-Paradol maintained that France had been able to avoid the social chaos of a modern world deprived of hereditary rule and religious authority only because it had turned to honor as a substitute system of belief. The ethic of honor, argued the former *normalien* known for an "aristocratic character" notwithstanding his middle-class birth, had succeeded Catholicism as the moral basis of French life.[29] "Honor, or better, the point of honor is the final and most powerful bulwark of our older societies, and especially of French society," wrote Prévost-Paradol. "Today, our country presents the spectacle, virtually unique in the world, of a society in which the point of honor has become the principal guarantee of social order, one that enables us to achieve the bulk of the needs and the sacrifices that religion and patriotism have lost the power to ensure." If France's laws continued to be generally respected in this society devoid of religion and duty, if the youthful soldier remained faithful to his flag, if citizens continued to fulfill their duties to the state and to one another, Prévost-Paradol concluded, it was solely out of "fear of being publicly humiliated by an action considered shameful." Alone among all the possible agents of social order, the fear of being dishonored, of being denigrated in the eyes of the community, "maintains within us the desire to act properly."[30]

Faguet too saw honor as crucial to social order in an increasingly democratic society. But for him order was guaranteed by a hierarchy of aristocratic breeding and cultivated intellect, by an elite whose culture of honor could resist the egalitarian mediocrity and capitalist materialism with which he stigmatized France's republican regime. The aim of honor, wrote Emile Faguet, himself an alumnus of the Ecole normale supérieure and a member of the Académie française, was to maintain hierarchy by moving us to "struggle . . . to distinguish ourselves" from all those considered beneath us, to convince ourselves that we are in possession of "a character far from common." For Faguet, "honor is in essence an aristocratic sentiment." It was the very "idea of the elite," the force that "enslaves us to our dignity, to our nobility, *to that which distinguishes us from beings we consider inferior to us.*" Honor, in sum, was "the aspiration to feel satisfied with myself as a result of my superiority over others."[31]

What raised one individual over others and thereby maintained the hierarchy essential to social order, Faguet suggested, was his rejection of capitalist culture, his refusal to "make mercantile calculations concerning the things that can be saved, economized, put aside today so as to bring me a good and solid profit in the future." The morality of honor "commands me," Faguet concluded, "to despise the basely utilitarian ethic of the ant and the bee . . . to oppose an egoism that is wily, fearful and stingy."[32] An unintended irony shadows Faguet's rhetoric, for as the author of some thirty books and two hundred volumes of newspaper and journal articles he clearly conducted his own life with the "ant and bee" discipline he so deplored.[33] But notwithstanding his own quasi-capitalist output, Faguet looked to honor and aristocratic values in general for an alternative to the morality of the counting house he associated with egalitarianism, the republic, and the industrial middle class.

Faguet did not make clear whether he believed a middle-class allegiance to the culture of honor could be attributed to a widespread French suspicion of the values of the marketplace. But the prevalence of aristocratic attitudes such as his can be explained in large part by the bourgeoisie's inability, throughout much of the nineteenth century, to establish itself as France's dominant political and cultural force. Although France has often been seen as the home of bourgeois revolution—first in 1789, then in 1830, and again in 1848—it nonetheless had difficulty in the nineteenth century accepting the political and cultural hegemony of an industrial middle class. Between 1800 and 1850 France was under the sway not of a modern bourgeoisie but of a group of ruling *notables*, mostly large landowners who resembled the nobility of the old regime more than they did any commercial or industrial middle class.[34] Even as France began to industrialize after the midcentury, French voters, among them the bulk of the bourgeoisie, turned not to the agents of that industrialization for political guidance but to a dictator named Louis-Napoleon Bonaparte, the nephew of Napoleon Bonaparte who called himself a prince.[35]

To be sure, many members of the propertied middle class soon became so disillusioned with the authoritarianism of Napoleon III's Second Empire (1852–1870) that they turned to republicanism in the 1860s.[36] Still, a republican regime became possible after Louis-Napoleon's military defeat at the hands of Prussia only because large sectors of the peasantry and the lower middle classes had come to support it. Once firmly in place, the Third Republic was as much a regime of these groups—people the great republican fighter Léon Gambetta called the "nouvelles couches sociales"—as of a capitalist bourgeoisie.[37]

Although the old notables found themselves too weak and too divided after 1870 to restore the monarchy, they were able nonetheless to ensure that three of the country's key institutions—the army, the Church, and the foreign service—would remain bastions of aristocratic exclusivity.[38] Moreover, by the 1890s the old conservative elites would achieve considerable influence over the republican regime itself by forming an alliance with middle-class republicans increasingly fearful of a resurgent socialist left. Much of the aristocracy "rallied" to the Republic, but only because the regime's leaders had turned to it and to its allies in the Church for ideological support.[39]

Within this new republican order, perhaps no group sought to pattern itself after the aristocracy more closely than those professional politicians who hailed from Gambetta's *nouvelles couches sociales*. For the most part these officials earned their livelihoods from the state or the practice of law, professions that separated them from the world of business and commerce and opened them to the enticements of an aristocracy they saw as preferring honor to the values of the marketplace. In identifying with French aristocrats, these new men of government imagined they could ascend the social heights by demonstrating a penchant for dueling and the accoutrements of upper-class life. As one left-wing deputy wrote, "the easiest way to appear to possess good blood lines . . . is to endanger one's own blood and to spill the blood of others."[40] French politicians may also have adopted such affectations in an effort to acquire legitimacy in the eyes of a population unaccustomed to being governed by individuals from the middle and lower-middle ranks—and to impress other European leaders and parliamentarians who remained largely upper class.[41]

Despite their contributions to the cult of aristocracy, however, France's republican politicians seldom gained access to the high society they sought to emulate. But rather than turn them against the very idea of hierarchy and privilege, this exclusion moved France's nascent noblemen from the *classes moyennes* to create a hierarchy of their own. The leaders of the Third Republic relied heavily on graduates of the *grandes écoles*, small elite institutions of higher learning created during the French Revolution, to staff many of the highest positions in government, education, and business.[42] These schools, the most important of which were the Ecole normale supérieure for future educators and intellectuals and the Ecole polytechnique for engineers, took a few dozen applicants each year from the thousands who applied. The idea was to identify the country's most promising students through a series of rigorous examinations and then to give them the best training the country could provide. France's *grandes écoles* often succeeded in this undertaking, but in doing so they helped establish an aristocracy of mind and talent divorced from the everyday realities of business and commerce. Its members disdained the values of the marketplace at least as much as the old aristocracy did, especially the *normaliens* who came under the influence of socialism in the 1890s.[43] Emile

Faguet, who graduated from the Ecole normale supérieure in the early years of the Third Republic, typifies the elitist and anticapitalist spirit of many of the Belle Epoque's leading men of letters and intellectual luminaries.

Even those Frenchmen who earned their (substantial) livings from industry and finance often sought to distance themselves from the marketplace culture that had made them what they were. They bought châteaux, aspired to marry into the nobility, and generally adopted the style and manner of their aristocratic countrymen.[44] Few members of the elite wanted to be viewed as strictly middle class; those who set France's cultural and political tone throughout the nineteenth century came not from a ruling bourgeoisie but from a nouveau aristocracy of land, money, and social distinction.

This persistent prestige of an aristocratic elite and of the culture and values associated with it were nowhere so pronounced during the Belle Epoque as in the city of Paris. Many of France's wealthiest and most venerable noble families possessed *hôtels particuliers* in Paris's faubourg Saint-Germain. And in this exclusive Parisian quarter, urban aristocrats presided over a snobbish society of taste, fashion, and refinement that seemed to fascinate the city as a whole.[45] Here was a society in which one needed to be seen—at the most fashionable salons, the most prestigious art openings, the elite race tracks at Longchamp and Auteuil, the most lavish high-society weddings, and the most exclusive dinner parties.[46] Above all, one must be invited to those salons led, as under the ancien régime, by women whose wit, wealth, and elegance enabled them to attract to their drawing rooms the counts, marquis, barons who formed the cream, or *gratin*, of Parisian society. One did not have to possess a title of nobility to attend, but good birth was essential, except in the case of those with the best intellectual and artistic pedigrees.

What distinguished the *grand monde* of the Belle Epoque from its equivalents in earlier periods was the extent to which its members were visible not merely to one another but to Paris as a whole. Thanks in large part to France's new mass-circulation press, and especially to its emergent illustrated and photographic gazettes, the activities of the Parisian *gratin* became fully public events. *Le Figaro, Le Gaulois, L'Illustration, Fémina,* and several other journals, some satirical in character, described the movements of the rich and illustrious, noting who was seen at what event and speculating on the reasons for any apparent changes in status.[47] During the Belle Epoque, therefore, members of the aristocracy—along with certain high government officials, intellectual and cultural figures, popular actors and dancers—all became grist for a vast mill of journalistic publicity. Its purpose, in large part, was to provide vicarious pleasures for those whose increasingly routinized work doubtless encouraged an interest in individuals made to appear extraordinary. As most Parisians sank into the anonymity of a mass urban existence, more and more they found themselves exposed to the lives of certain elite or otherwise prominent individuals. As a result, the elite itself lost much of the privacy that wealth had once made possible. By the late nineteenth century, the *Tout-Paris* lived largely in the public eye, before journalists who observed its every move.

Such exposure did much to maintain, even enhance, the stature and the cultural influence of the Parisian aristocracy. But at the same time the new mass-circulation press, as the Albanel-Dagoury incident made abundantly clear, had powerfully raised the stakes of its existence. For now, exclusion from a crucial social event, placement at the wrong end of a fashionable dinner table, and especially an insult received in public, threatened an individual's social standing not merely in the eyes of the *gratin* itself but before the Parisian public at large.

Gabriel Tarde, it has been noted, was particularly critical of the press for provoking so many duels, but he believed it possessed the power to do so not just because of its wide penetration but because of what he considered to be the frivolity and impressionability of its most avid readers, namely women. "Women," the sociologist wrote, "are sponges of ancient prejudices." Far more than men did, "they live for others, and for the opinion of others, which explains the intensity of their resentments."[48] Thus, when one man challenged another man's honor and the press magnified the affront, the women involved questioned his honor all the more, which explained why men, particularly prominent men, felt the need to fight so many duels.

On the surface, Tarde's broadside against the female sex expressed the contempt of a male who believed himself and most of his brethren superior to females in all respects. But in placing on women much of the blame for the press's power to determine honor, the sociologist unwittingly voiced the male fear of women's growing strength and influence so characteristic of his era. If women were really weak and impressionable, how could they mold male behavior unless men were even feebler and more impressionable?

The misogynistic comments of an esteemed sociologist thus suggest what was perhaps the most crucial reason for a fin-de-siècle discourse of honor that affected elite and middle-class men alike: the effort to recover a masculinity widely believed to be ebbing away. At the end of the nineteenth century, the rise of a women's movement, moderate as it was, overtly challenged long-standing male prerogatives already under siege after the Franco-Prussian War by what many took to be the emasculating effects of modern life. French men of the fin de siècle, especially those of the middle and upper classes, had constantly before them the myth of the real man of earlier times: the proud warrior, the adventurous merchant, the patriarch of a family of yeoman farmers or skilled artisans, whom they saw as firmly in charge of his clan, dependent only on himself, fashioning his livelihood with his own hands.[49] Such a vision of manhood persisted into the late nineteenth century but without the reality, however mythologized, that had once accompanied it. In the novel *Les Déracinés* (1897), Maurice Barrès celebrated the mythic man who "strides through the high grass with his rifle in his hands, side by side with his comrades, enveloped on all sides by danger." But he did so having admitted to the omnipresence of bureaucratic "semi-males." Likewise Emile Zola made the hero of *Fécondité* (1899) "the chief, the patriarch" of a family farm; but the character staked out this manly existence in the midst of a France "in which virility is fading away." Faguet, meanwhile, found it "revolting to see a [male] colossus performing the passive functions of a petty functionary."[50]

Confronted with images such as these, how many men of the late nineteenth century, bureaucratic, industrialized, urbanized as it was, could feel genuinely virile, genuinely confident of their manly abilities to shape the world? To many of these men, obscurely or consciously troubled about their manhood, the culture of honor must have seemed an ideal solution. It alone appeared to embody within it a golden chivalric age when sex roles were accepted without question and when one could be a man simply by adhering to the culture's clear-cut set of rules.

So much was honor associated with masculinity that journalists and moralists of the Belle Epoque commonly attributed the very source of honor to what, in their view, was the essence of manhood itself: the effort to win desirable females through sexual prowess and valor in combat. These impulses were said to originate far down on the evolutionary scale, as did the sentiment of honor they created. "It is the rivalry among males with respect to females," wrote the moral philosopher L. Jeudon, "that gives rise in animals to honor along with all its attendant feelings." Darwin was enormously influential in this as in so many other realms of late nineteenth-century thought. For as Jeudon read him, Darwin found in the animal kingdom precisely the same conflicts over honor, all originating in male sexuality, that existed in contemporary Europe. Jeudon quoted Darwin as suggesting that dueling had evolved directly from the phallic contests of male insects and birds: "It is said that praying mantises maneuver their anterior members as hussars wield their swords." The point of such contests, Jeudon added, was to win female admiration. Certain male birds, he wrote, did a kind of war dance before their females, who "observe this spectacle tirelessly, and when the male returns [in victory] his mate lets out a cry, *a form of applause.*"[51]

These origins of honor in manly prowess and success in battle explained, Jeudon claimed, how honor had come to be associated with aristocracy. In a particularly imaginative leap from human society to animal and back again, Jeudon argued that animal societies came to view members that regularly achieved victory in battle as superior to those that did not, creating the link between honor and supremacy humans would apply to themselves. Thus by the medieval era, he argued, honor—still defined as valor and victory for the favor of females—would be seen as the essential attribute of aristocracy. For what was the joust, Jeudon asked, but the battle of aristocratic males for their females? The applause of one's women, like that of the female birds, "was the victor's best recompense."[52]

If the medieval man could impress his women through valor and victory in knightly combat, the modern man could do so, Jeudon maintained, through the duel. By risking his life in a duel, a man of the Belle Epoque could even "rekindle a woman's love and esteem."[53] Tarde, for his part, made much the same point by asserting that "the tiniest scratch received in a duel suddenly renders a man interesting to the average woman, [even] produces the spontaneous generation, *ex abrupto*, of a violent love."[54] Beyond the disdain of women that such a statement reveals, it is extraordinary for its wishful thinking, for the idea that a man, no matter how unappealing, needed only step onto the field of honor to render himself sexually desirable.

Tarde's view was nonetheless far from novel for male writers of the Belle Epoque, many of whom came to see dueling as a condition of masculinity itself. The German commentator Alfred von Bogulawski went so far as to claim that the custom of dueling itself originated in one man's challenge to another's virility. In medieval Scandinavia, Bogulawski wrote, two men were obliged to fight a duel when one declared, "You do not have the heart of a man," and the other responded, "I am as much a man as you."[55] In France the idea that the duel made the man became such a central and enduring feature of the national culture, argued the criminologist Emmanuel Lasserre, that most men and women of the Belle Epoque still believed that "the individual who suffers an affront without seeking satisfaction is not a man."[56] Even the left-wing journalist Victor Méric, who considered the duel "idiotic and useless," decided to fight one anyway after his opponent declared in a published letter, "I had expected to find you a man . . . instead I find you a miserable coward." Méric wrote that he preferred to violate his own principles than to be accused of "lacking physical courage."[57]

All these cultural associations of honor with aristocracy, masculinity with successful combat, virility with the duel only reinforced the humiliation French men already felt as a result of the war with Prussia. In a national duel with the Prussians, French soldiers had lost their very manhood and an entire generation of men was "demoralized," as *Le Gaulois* put it, "by the acceptance of defeat."[58] Even so, many social commentators viewed the war more as symptom than cause of this decline. The problem's deeper origins were said to lie in France's overly intellectualized culture, in the enervation and overstimulation of modern urban life, and in the excessive comforts of an aristocratic existence. The antidote to this degenerative masculine disease, it was often suggested, could be found in the culture of honor and in the cult of sport.

A work entitled *Soyez des hommes: à la conquête de la virilité* (1909) by the moralist F. A. Vuillermet began by stating bluntly and simply, "There are no longer any men." It went on to argue that French males no longer acted decisively, no longer demonstrated will and masculine energy, because they had been enervated by a culture that paid too much attention to their minds and too little to their bodies. "The present generation, born of enervated parents, is wilting before our very eyes. No longer is there any equilibrium between [men's] muscles and their nerves. The nerves are overexcited, the muscles languid. Neurasthenia and neurosis and all the other maladies of our time affect the great mass of our young men, whose intellectual faculties have been completely overwrought." Vuillermet exhorted his male readers to recover their masculinity, and with it the will to fight, by turning to physical exercise and especially to sports. "Sports give rise to the spirit of combat and struggle that creates valiant men."[59]

French men of the middle and upper classes seemed to take this advice to heart, especially after the turn of the century, showing an interest in sports as never before. So strong was their engagement—and the quest for virility it implied—that French men turned the duel itself into a sport, even a spectator sport, wrote the journalist G. Letainturier-Fradin, commenting on all the publicity attending the duel.[60] Perhaps the duel's mounting popularity during this period stems from its ability to enhance the combatants' virility even more than traditional sports. Not only was the duel a form of physical exercise, it promised a taste of the danger associated with real combat while enabling both participants (and their seconds) to strengthen their quotients of masculine honor. That accounts of the duel might impress particular women or the mass of newspaper readers only added to the benefits it was said to provide.

Thus the resurgence of dueling, notable from the 1870s on, may have played an even more prominent role in the attempt to revive masculine will and the "spirit of combat" than did competitive games and other forms of physical activity. Gabriel Tarde wrote that "the duel, echo of a time when courage was everything, says and is right to say to the softened and enervated man of our century: you must be brave."[61] Dueling restored to men the elemental masculinity associated with combat, violence, and physical courage. For this reason, wrote one pamphleteer, dueling ought to be encouraged within the French army and especially among officers for whom the point of honor would "restore a combative virility, something that is indispensable in this [troubled] time."[62] The French nationalist Paul Déroulède could not have agreed more, intent as he was on maintaining the army as France's repository of "male sentiments" and "habits of virility."[63]

One interesting variation on the association of dueling, honor, and gender identity came with respect to religion. Prévost-Paradol argued that honor had replaced Christianity as the foundation of France's moral system, but many of those who followed him added that this was true only for men. Christianity, they suggested, was the faith of women; honor, the new religion of men. Perhaps the first to articulate this gendered notion of religion and honor was Alfred de Vigny, a writer preoccupied as early as the 1830s with the problem of how an age without religious belief could sustain morality. Vigny's answer resembled that of Prévost-Paradol: "The Religion of honor has often been powerful enough to replace Christian faith in the hearts of men." But unlike Prévost-Paradol, Vigny stressed the manly and virile aspects of this morality of honor. His fictional work, *Servitude et grandeur militaire* (1833–1835), concludes with a lyrical "profession de foi" that defines honor as a "virile purity" (*pudeur virile*), a morality unique to men. The locus of this *pudeur virile*, its "tabernacle," as Vigny put it, was the army; because this was so, the army did more to keep honor alive than any other institution of the early nineteenth century. Thanks to the military, Vigny wrote, the morality of honor had become a "magic magnet" that "attracted and attached itself to hearts of steel, to the hearts of the strong."[64]

Honor for Vigny is the religion of the gallant and virile man. That Christianity is the religion of the weak and passive woman he implied but never stated explicitly. It would be up to commentators of the Belle Epoque to take this step. In his work on the morality of honor, Jeudon contrasted the manly "chivalric spirit" with an essentially feminine ethic of Christianity. The first represented "the revolt of the Germanic and especially the Celtic spirit against Christian morality, the revenge of the Occident against the Orient," the male values of "pride and love" against the female attributes of "humility and chastity." He quoted Ernest Renan who formulated the same opposition even more explicitly: "I know of nothing more curious,"

Renan wrote in his *Essais de critique et de morale*, "than the spectacle of this revolt of the male sentiments of heroism against the feminine sentiments that formed the very essence of the new religion [of Christianity]."[65] For Jeudon, the male sentiments included not just heroism but "will, activity, and mastery." The female sentiments he defined as "the predominance of the idea, of intelligence, in short of passive principles."[66] Honor, therefore, was a masculine religion because it encouraged action, strength, will, and accomplishment. Christianity was feminine because it inspired charity, humility, contemplation, and self-sacrifice. This notion of a gendered religious divide, it should be noted, paralleled the overall nineteenth-century masculine effort to separate male from female spheres, to distinguish an amoral masculine marketplace of action and will from a feminine home-sweet-home of selflessness and virtue.[67]

It is interesting that this belief in the superiority of honor over Christianity, masculine will over feminine humility, action over intelligence, cut across nineteenth-century France's otherwise rigid ideological divide. In general, to be conservative was to endorse Christianity; to be progressive was to reject it. Yet when it came to the definitions of masculinity and femininity, to the efforts of men to fortify themselves with a reassuring ideal of maleness, gender identity could take precedence over religious loyalty. The romantic conservative Alfred de Vigny could anticipate the anticlerical Dreyfusard Jeudon in preferring a masculine religion of honor to a feminine religion of Christ.[68] Both sought to achieve social order through a male ethic of honor; Vigny hoped to do so through a literature of virility, Jeudon through a secular republic governed by men of action and will.

Such in theory was the tie between honor and masculinity. The religion of honor provided a system of belief and action that would reclaim the nineteenth century's softened and enervated man, the feminized man, to true masculinity. But would it in truth? French men, especially of the middle and upper classes, had been forced by the end of the century to contend with such serious blows to this masculine ideal of honor that to restore it would have been an extremely difficult task. Despite all the duels and all the exhortations to devote oneself to sport and the spirit of combat, French writings of the period betray more the sense of manhood lost than the confidence in any ability to recapture it.

Perhaps the most influential of all these works, the handbook on dueling by Bruneau de Laborie, unwittingly expressed the very anxieties about masculinity that books such as his were intended to allay. Parts of Bruneau de Laborie's *Lois du duel* first appeared in *Le Figaro* where they were serialized in September 1903 as "La théorie du duel." The larger work, which complemented theory with praxis, was published prominently three years later. It was a "how to" book for the cultured classes (which perhaps explains why Judge Albanel would consult its author), including everything from how to dress for a duel to how to phrase the requisite letters of challenge and response. It discussed, among other things, when a duel was permissible and when it was obligatory, who was permitted to fight (gentlemen) and who was not (working-class men and all women). While many other handbooks of the period contained such practical information, though none so elaborately detailed, what is remarkable about Bruneau's work is the tortured and contradictory terms in which it expressed the connection between masculinity and the duel. Bruneau began his work by asserting that men of high social standing engaged in the duel as a demonstration of their courage, as an expression of their refusal to be slighted in the eyes of society despite the physical danger they might have to face. The man of honor was a man of bravery. His willingness to submit to the laws of the duel proved that he had the three qualities indispensable to a social elite: steadfastness, independence, and courage.[69] Yet no sooner did Bruneau make this statement than he appeared to contradict himself at the level of language and imagery, a level whose implications the author seems not to have consciously perceived. A crucial part of his argument constituted an attempt to justify the class bias in dueling, to explain why upper-class men need not duel with those beneath them. But in making this argument Bruneau undermined his view of elite men as manly and brave by characterizing them in words and images that the Belle Epoque usually reserved for women.

In a republican society such as France's, Bruneau argued, the ability to duel had to be the exclusive preserve of gentlemen of the social elite not because they were more honorable than members of the lower classes but because they were more fragile and more vulnerable—and therefore more easily affronted—than those beneath them. "Artificial conditions of life"—namely, intellectual work untempered by physical activity—Bruneau wrote, "had created an elite distinguished by an overdeveloped nervous sensitivity among its members." This elite alone required recourse to the duel because only its members were so highly strung, their feelings so delicately balanced, that even the most minor affront was intolerable. A rugged working man could easily ignore an insult, even a serious one, because he was not nearly so fragile. For this reason, to require a gentleman to fight a duel with an individual much "less sensitive" than he would be not unlike "placing a man, stripped of all his clothes, into close quarters with a robust being, outfitted with a solid suit of armor covered with spikes, whose movements were all the more harmful in that he was invulnerable to the movements of the other man."[70]

Bruneau clearly intended this argument as a justification of social hierarchy and social distinction on the basis of psychological difference. But embedded in the words and images he chose was a portrait of elite men that contradicted quite dramatically the effort he had made at the beginning of his work to depict them as brave and strong. By characterizing men of high standing as tense, fragile, overly sensitive, and ruled by their nerves, Bruneau gave them the qualities commonly attributed to women. Unconsciously, Bruneau echoed Vuillermet and the gendered commentary already noted in connection with other aspects of the *affaire Caillaux* in expressing the fear that modern society had made men—especially elite men—effeminate. Only the still robust working-class male seemed exempt from the decline of French manhood, which explains in part why members of the middle and upper classes found it difficult to make concessions, however timid, to the mounting demands of a labor movement clamoring for social justice.[71] And, of course, what concerned French commentators even more was the questionable ability of those at the top of their society, the feminized and overly refined social elite, to face up to the blood and iron of a German empire they regarded as quintessentially male.

The contradictory images of France's male elite woven into Bruneau de Laborie's work may represent a subliminal perception on his part of the remarkable artistic shift from the masculine to the feminine that had accompanied and reinforced the renewal of aristocratic prestige at the fin de siècle. As Debora Silverman shows, the profoundly different emphases of the Paris International Exhibitions of 1889 and 1900 revealed a widespread rejection, at the close of the century, of the modern technological forms, the bourgeois and masculine culture, that the Eiffel Tower had exemplified at the earlier of the two events. By 1900 many of France's leading artists, writers, and intellectuals had turned to forms of art and design far more feminine—and aristocratic—in character.[72]

Eiffel's monument and its accompanying *galérie des machines*, constructed entirely of iron and glass, had explicitly celebrated the accomplishments of France's republican fathers in the male sphere of industrialism, science, and public life. They had been designed, wrote a leading official of 1889, to "show our sons what their fathers have accomplished in the space of a century through progress in knowledge, love of work, and respect for liberty." The exhibition of 1900, by contrast, shrouded the iron and glass structures of 1889 beneath traditional stone facades of the old regime while directing visitors toward exhibits of an intimate, aristocratic, and highly feminine interior design. All but forgotten were the soaring heights of the Eiffel Tower, "metaphor for the spectacular ascent of man."[73] Instead, visitors focused on a pair of more diminutive structures at the tower's base—the Palace of Woman and the Pavilion of the Decorative Arts. Inside these two buildings, the male world of industrial technology gave way to the female realm of interior design, to an art nouveau reminiscent of the eighteenth-century woman's aristocratic taste. Likewise, the two permanent buildings constructed for the 1900 World's Fair, the Petit and Grand Palais, eschewed the industrial symbolism of the nineteenth century in favor of the female and aristocratic design of the eighteenth: the architect of the two palaces modeled his structures after Versailles's Petit and Grand Trianon, so admired by Marie Antoinette.[74]

This cultural shift stemmed both from a reaction against the era's ubiquitous, if highly exaggerated, image of the New Woman and from the elite's growing disillusionment with the results of Baron Haussmann's redevelopment of Paris.[75] The supposedly mannish woman emancipated by feminism and loosed upon the boulevards of Haussmann's new metropolis was to be restored to her proper role as soothing guardian of the home by the countervailing cultural image of the real woman of the domestic interior.[76] Just as the aristocratic lady of the eighteenth century had created a nest of elegance for her lord, so would the bourgeois wife of the nineteenth design a refuge of beauty for her husband. The purpose of this refuge would be to shield the harried male from the intensity and overstimulation for which Haussmann's Paris of crowded sidewalks and teeming traffic was widely condemned.[77]

These efforts to protect Parisian men from the putative overstimulation of their urban world added luster to the culture of grace and refinement, the unhurried and pleasurable life that many Parisians believed to characterize the aristocracy of the Belle Epoque. At the same time, the shift in architectural focus from monumental exteriors to intimate interiors appeared to affirm the value of the domestic woman and of the aristocratic lady widely presented as her model. It also associated aristocracy with femininity more closely than at any time since the latter decades of the eighteenth century. This time, however, there was no significant male republican reaction against the newly feminized aristocratic taste. The *gratin's* prestige had grown so great that the feminized art with which it had become associated, dedicated as that art was to the real woman, seemed reassuring rather than threatening to male commentators of the bourgeoisie.[78] Thus, when middle-class men joined aristocratic men in an effort to reinforce their virility, there was nothing to prevent either group from embracing the very upper-class culture that had become so tinged with feminine traits. Both categories of men could attempt to renew their masculinity by turning to aristocratic conceptions of honor and to the manly contest of the duel. But given the sexual ambiguity of the aristocratic ethos, their efforts were bound to produce paradoxical results.

Bruneau de Laborie had registered this paradox without acknowledging it explicitly. Another work on dueling, published two years later by a Count Estève, was to make Bruneau's largely unconscious worries concerning masculinity central to its argument. Dueling, the count maintained, had once been the symbol of noble independence and bravery in those who refused to submit to the king's bureaucratic system of justice. It had degenerated by the late nineteenth century, he claimed, into a sign of weakness, not virility, susceptibility to the passions, not the manly ability to control them. "Nothing but weakness is revealed in this exaggerated sensitivity that makes us take certain minor offenses with undue seriousness." The essence of strength, Estève added, was to "maintain one's equilibrium, to be independent and calm, to resist the influence of external stimuli, to remain, in other words, indifferent to the passions that can sap our force." That so few men demonstrated such strength was a "sign of the degeneracy that invariably results from all our unhealthy overstimulation." As for the current rash of dueling, Estève found it the logical result of an "extreme touchiness that comes from the softening of character" in those "whose nervous systems are exhausted and therefore have become physically and morally impressionable."[79]

Estève's critique of the emotional origins of the duel is striking in its similarity to the explanation commonly given for the crime of passion, which was seen as stemming from a nervous system overly sensitive to the feelings of the moment. Women, as we have seen, were deemed especially susceptible to such blind passions, to such nervous stimuli; this susceptibility, psychologists claimed, often turned the normal emotions of anger, grief, and jealousy into the sources of violent crime. Estève found the feminized men of the Belle Epoque equally prone to emotional upset, only they expressed their passions through the violence of the duel. Emile Faguet, though more favorable to the duel than Count Estève, described the emotional sources of the duel in terms even closer to those generally applied to the crime of passion. Honor, Faguet wrote, "inflames us, it is a passion, a passion ardent and invincible," that when combined with duty impels a man to action "in the same way as do the most elemental of passions—as do love, jealousy, drunkenness, or libertinage. The duty of honor has become a passion that is intoxicating and even mortal." Men, Faguet explained, using the psychological terminology common to so many of these discussions, would face the danger of a duel, would even face certain death, because honor was an "imperative impulsion," a "blind passion that itself becomes a nervous excitation that alters the health of the soul."[80]

Faguet, like Bruneau de Laborie, attempted to justify the duel by claiming that it imposed a calming structure of decorum and civility on individuals overwrought by "an unaccustomed shock to the nervous system followed by an exceptional expenditure of energy." But such a justification only confirmed Estève's point. Men of the elite, feminized, oversensitive, emotionally fragile, and buffeted by even the mildest of passions, resorted to the duel for many of the same reasons that drove women to crimes of passion. Both the *crime passionnel* and the duel were said to provide a "nervous détente," as Bruneau put it, for individuals at the mercy of emotions beyond their control.[81] Far from an act of virility that affirmed manly strength and determination, the duel had become to some observers little more than a disguised and socially acceptable crime of passion for the effeminate men of a neurasthenic Belle Epoque.

Such an implicit association of the duel and the crime of passion, consonant with what some writers saw as the hermaphroditic culture of the Belle Epoque, puts Madame Caillaux's act into a new perspective.[82] Although Henriette Caillaux portrayed her assassination of Calmette primarily as a *crime passionnel*, she explained it immediately after the event itself in the language of the duel. In her pretrial interviews with the *juge d'instruction*, held in April 1914, Henriette claimed she had been so terrified that Joseph would kill Calmette in a duel fought to defend her honor that she decided to challenge the editor herself. "The idea came into my head," she told the judge, "to take my husband's place, to go myself to *demand satisfaction* from the editor in chief of *Le Figaro*."[83] A note Henriette wrote to her husband shortly before going to see Calmette on 16 March gives her statement to the *juge d'instruction* considerable credibility. In it she declared: "I don't want you to sacrifice yourself. France and the Republic need you. It is I who will act in your place."[84] It may be that the tendency of Belle Epoque commentators to explain—even to justify—the duel and the *crime passionnel* in a nearly identical vocabulary of fragile nerves and neurasthenic oversensitivity ultimately led Henriette to merge the two in her mind. The act of violence Madame Caillaux would mostly present at the trial as a crime of passion, she may well have imagined on 16 March, much more positively, as a duel for her honor.

Whatever her conscious—or unconscious—motivations, Henriette appears to have been genuinely concerned about the threat Calmette posed to her honor, for to publish her *lettres intimes*, she maintained at the trial, would have been "to strip me of my honor as a woman."[85] As the Belle Epoque debate over the real woman had so clearly shown (see chapter 3), honor for a woman depended not so much on actual chastity before marriage and fidelity thereafter but rather on the sustained appearance of these virtues before the public at large. Just as men were dishonored only when insults reached the penny press, so women suffered that fate only when their sexual transgressions became widely known. Thus Henriette presented her honor as endangered not because she had behaved immorally but because Calmette had threatened to make that immorality public. Honor was the product not of her own actions but of the way others construed them. "Society remained merciless," wrote the historian Jacques Chastenet, "toward the imprudent woman who allowed herself to slide [into moral ruin] . . . but people especially refused to pardon her for having betrayed the image of her that society wished to maintain."[86]

Throughout her testimony Henriette sought to evoke the court's sympathy by recalling again and again the extent to which her honor had been compromised. During Calmette's campaign against her husband she had been "obliged to leave [a session of parliament] in shame"; she believed that Berthe Gueydan had given the letters to Calmette to "dishonor her"; she feared being shamed in the presence of the queen of England, whom she was soon to meet.[87] Her supporters went even further, justifying her actions in the language of honor and shame. The Radical newspaper *La Lanterne* declared that it would be a gross injustice to "qualify as a crime" Madame Caillaux's effort "to raise her hand in defense of her hearth and her honor."[88] What is more, the paper continued, there would never have been a drama at *Le Figaro* were it not for the "outrages against the honor of Monsieur Caillaux."[89] Similarly, Gustave Hervé's revolutionary *Guerre sociale* asked rhetorically: "When the laws are powerless to defend the honor of women in a country that calls itself civilized, do these violated women have the right to take justice into their own hands or not?" Hervé's answer in the case of Madame Caillaux was an emphatic yes.[90]

Perhaps no one used the language of honor more vehemently in the defense of Henriette Caillaux than Joseph himself, who sought to defend his own honor as well. In his testimony Joseph Caillaux portrayed Calmette's press campaign against him as having been designed to "get at me politically through my honor, my honorableness, and at the same time to get at my wife through her honor, because it was our household itself that he was after." Calmette had made an unacceptable "incursion into my intimacy" in which "our honor, together, as a couple" was called into question.[91] Like Henriette, Joseph characterized his honor as something that could be compromised not by his own dishonorable behavior but only by Calmette's efforts to make that behavior public. By "dishonoring" the Caillaux in this way, Calmette had exceeded the bounds of normal political discourse and created a situation, Joseph suggested, in which it would not be unreasonable to seek satisfaction.

In fact, other testimony at the trial revealed that Caillaux had indeed threatened to challenge Calmette to a duel. August Avril, one of Calmette's lieutenants at *Le Figaro*, told the court that Joseph had taken him aside in a corridor of the Palais Bourbon just as the paper's anti-Caillaux campaign was about to begin in earnest. Caillaux wanted to know whether "Calmette plans to continue these attacks," and when Avril answered that he did not know, Caillaux gave the following response: "I have had enough, you know, and if this continues, I will send him my seconds." Avril remembered Caillaux as having added, "I shoot well. I go every day to Gastinne-Renette [to practice] and every shot hits the target." When asked at the trial whether he had made such comments, Caillaux replied: "I could indeed have said something of the sort."[92] Caillaux's comments about his marksmanship were more than an idle boast, for an employee of Gastinne-Renette apparently confirmed to a journalist that not only did the Radical leader practice regularly, but he fired so well that everyone in the shop stopped to watch.[93] It is interesting to note that Henriette herself practiced on the firing range at Gastinne-Renette, further suggesting that, like her husband, she too was preparing for some species of duel with Calmette.

According to *Le Figaro*, Calmette fully expected Joseph Caillaux to challenge him to a duel, for the editors quoted him the day before he was shot as being "astonished that Caillaux does not send his seconds."[94] Caillaux must have considered doing so very seriously, for his memoirs include an elaborate explanation for why he did not. In essence, the reason he gave was that Calmette possessed too little honor to be worthy of a challenge. "I do not give people like *him*," Caillaux wrote, "the honor of engaging them on a plane of equality." Caillaux added that he had not been aware in 1914 of all the dishonorable things Calmette had done, "but I knew enough to see him for what he was: a libertine bandit."[95] Thus, according to Caillaux, his opponent was too ill-bred and low born to grant him the equal standing a duel implied. There could be no question of cowardice in his refusal to challenge Calmette, Caillaux suggested, because he did not hesitate to duel with the aristocratic Louis d'Allières shortly thereafter.

At the trial of his wife Joseph elaborated on his claim that Calmette had no honor, contrasting what he said was his own disinterested career in public service with Calmette's supposed history of venality and corruption at *Le Figaro*. Armed with a copy of Calmette's will, illicitly obtained, Caillaux revealed that the editor, once a man of modest means, had left an estate of some thirteen million francs accrued in the short space of a dozen years. As for Caillaux himself, he claimed he was no wealthier now than when he entered public life. "I was born of parents . . . who were millionaires, and when I suffered the pain of losing them I inherited about one million two hundred thousand francs. I could show you that my fortune is no higher today."[96] The statement was astute, for Joseph presented himself as too wealthy to be dependent on politics for his living and not wealthy enough to have profited from it financially. Implicitly, he claimed to belong to a civic republican elite, to a latter-day *noblesse de robe*, whose members sought in political office not personal gain but the honor of public service.[97] Caillaux was the honorable one, Calmette the mercenary, for as commentators like Faguet had made clear, the culture of honor made the preoccupation with making money the very badge of dishonor.

The persistence of this culture of honor and Caillaux's apparent acceptance of its values make it highly unlikely that he could have conspired with Henriette, as Chenu claimed he had, to kill Calmette. Nothing could be worse for a man who sought honor than to have his wife fight a duel in his place, which is why Caillaux's enemies accused him of having done precisely that. Shortly after the assassination of Calmette, the right-wing deputy Jules Delahaye declared before the Chamber: "In the past, ministers caught doing wrong killed each other; nowadays they send their wives to kill those who denounce them." Likewise the journalist Lucien Descaves wrote that in better times the wife "never established herself as the one who defended the family honor." Instead she says to her husband, "Go and fight!" Now, in March 1914, he says to her, "Go strike him down."[98]

Such statements may have made for powerful polemics, but they provided no more believable an explanation for Caillaux's failure to challenge Calmette than that of the Radical leader himself. In reality, Caillaux declined to duel not because he wished to send his wife in his stead nor because he considered Calmette unworthy of him but rather to maintain the fantasy of invulnerability so central to his personality. To challenge Calmette to a duel would have been to admit that the editor's attacks had done him harm; such a step Caillaux was emotionally unequipped to take. In this case, as in so many others, Caillaux's troubled psyche created difficulties he might easily have avoided. Had Caillaux challenged Calmette to a duel and then fired to the side, as he was to do with d'Allières, he might well have made it difficult for the editor, himself imbued with the culture of honor, to continue his journalistic offensive.[99] Such, at least, was the view of one of the editor's closest friends, the playwright Henry Bernstein, who testified that "Gaston Calmette was honor itself" and that he awaited a challenge from Caillaux "to bring his press campaign to an end."[100]

By dueling with Calmette, Caillaux might also have gained a measure of grudging respect from his enemies on the right, causing them to moderate their attacks, at least momentarily. Some allies on the left would perhaps have wondered publicly whether he was truly a man of peace, but secretly they might have been overjoyed to see such an important leader acquit himself with honor. For her part, Madame Caillaux, who assumed that her husband "could not defend himself because of his high position in government," need not have felt that "it was up to me to avenge on his behalf the insults raining down on both of us."[101] Had Joseph fought the duel, certainly Henriette would not have felt impelled to attempt one herself, and Calmette's life—and Caillaux's political career—would have been spared. An act of largely symbolic violence would have left Joseph Caillaux in a position to lead his country into the very real violence that lay ahead.

But because Caillaux chose not to duel with Calmette, questions concerning his honor surfaced again and again during the trial of Henriette. The most dramatic of these moments came when Henry Bernstein pushed his way into the packed courtroom on the seventh day to challenge something Caillaux had said about him earlier in the session. In his youth Bernstein had deserted from the army, and Caillaux, in an attack on the playwright, referred to "certain events" in the author's past when he had failed "to fulfill his duty vis-à-vis the fatherland."[102] Bernstein was not present in the court-room at the time, but friends alerted him by telephone as to Cail-laux's comments, and he hurried to the Palais de Justice at once.

"Are you there, Caillaux?" yelled Bernstein from the spectators' gallery, unconcerned about interrupting the courtroom proceedings.

Judge Albanel, apparently helpless to impose any judicial order, was reduced almost to the level of observer in his own courtroom. "Speak about something precise," was all Albanel could say.

"Let me speak my piece," Bernstein responded. "I speak to defend my honor, Monsieur le Président. You have spoken about your own [honor] through the voice of the press, and I have my [honor] too." Bernstein had a point. Albanel himself had made the defense of his own honor so much a part of the courtroom proceedings that he was hardly in a position to deny others the right to do the same. Albanel objected no more, and Bernstein began a long defense of his honor that had nothing to do with the legal matters at hand.

"In my youth," the playwright began, "I committed an idiocy that I have regretted publicly. Not because of the odious persecution I suffered at that time, but because my regrets were long-standing, profound, and sincere. I adore my country passionately, and I did more than apologize." During the Agadir affair, he went on, "a time of diplomatic crisis almost equal to the one we are witnessing today, I asked to be reenlisted in the army. During my first period of military service, I had been assigned to a unit that did not fight." In 1911, "despite a deplorable state of health I asked to be assigned to an armed unit, and I was accepted. [Now] I am part of a fighting force. I am an artilleryman. I am slated to leave on the fourth day of the mobilization, and the mobilization is perhaps for tomorrow. I don't know what day Caillaux leaves. But I must warn him that in war you cannot have a woman take your place. You have to fire yourself." The last two sentences created such an uproar with cries of "Bravo! Bravo, Bernstein!" that Albanel, unable to master the tumult, was forced to clear the courtroom and call a recess.[103]

In *Le Figaro*'s commentary on the seventh day of the trial, the editors applauded Bernstein for defending his honor with courage and eloquence—and for the "male energy [that] shone on his face."[104] The paper had already made clear that it considered Caillaux less than a man for having failed to challenge Calmette himself, an idea that Bernstein's testimony strongly reinforced. But the playwright did something more in his testimony than merely reiterate the anti-Caillaux polemics that had come before. In his response to Caillaux, Bernstein proved himself willing to make explicit what virtually all the trial's other participants were managing to repress: the likelihood of war. Bernstein brought the impending war into the equation of masculinity, honor, and the duel by "warning" Caillaux that he could not send his wife to fight the Germans in his place. The war was on the horizon, Bernstein declared, and real men, honorable men, would be needed to fight it. Because Caillaux had failed to confront Calmette like a man, failed to defend the honor of his wife, he could not be trusted to defend the honor of the fatherland itself. The duel was war in miniature; it prepared men for combat writ large.

As Bernstein was making these connections in public, Charles Péguy was doing so in private with a sustained philosophical discussion of the duel. For Péguy, France's long-standing attachment to the duel provided the inspiration and the confidence for the looming war with Germany, a confrontation he saw as the ultimate—and necessary—duel for the future of humanity. In his *Note conjointe sur M. Descartes et la philosophie cartésienne*, a fascinating work written during the height of the Caillaux Affair,* Péguy sought to show that France's chivalric traditions, its belief in the duel, gave it the means to survive the inevitable conflict with a German empire more ruthless in war and stronger in its material resources. Péguy argued that there existed in European history two opposing kinds of combat corresponding to the opposing systems of law, morality, and religion respectively embodied in the French and German "races." In the first system, the one native to France, the battle was everything—more important than victory, more important even than life itself. "This system," Péguy wrote, "is the system of heroism. It is the system of honor. It is contained in its entirety in the code of the duel." The other system, the German, sought not the

---

* This was literally the case, as Péguy was known to have worked on it during the last week of July 1914, interrupting his essay in midsentence to volunteer for frontline combat duty on 1 August. Péguy was killed in battle on 5 September 1914, and the *Note conjointe* was published posthumously in 1917 (see Hans A. Schmitt, *Charles Péguy* [Baton Rouge: Louisiana State University Press, 1967], pp. 33–34).

honor and beauty of combat as ends in themselves but pursued only victory and, through victory, domination. The German system was "everything there could possibly be that is most foreign to the duel, to the code of the duel, to honor itself." Success, for the Germans, justified everything; "the idea does not even exist that any victory, no matter how it is won, could be dishonorable." What counted for the French, by contrast, "is solely that the duel take place, and naturally that it take place in due form. Once this is the case, that there are a victor and a vanquished has no importance whatever."[105]

Here Péguy implied what others said outright, namely that one reason for the valorization of the duel, for the desire to fight Germany regardless of the consequences, was that the duel equalized the two combatants. It placed both on the same plane of honor, for when one man agreed to fight another he signified that the other was worthy of him and that he was his equal before the laws of honor.[106] Thus for Péguy the ability to vanquish Germany was less important than the willingness to fight it, because simply by joining battle with its adversary France would overcome the stigma of its prior defeat. France would become equal with the German empire once again. The traditions of dueling, therefore, help explain some of the nationalist ardor, after 1905, for war with Germany. The fight itself was what counted; God would do the rest. From the nationalist perspective, to pursue peace and reconciliation, as Caillaux did, was to acquiesce forever in France's subordination to the Germans. The only way to restore equality was to fight them once again. For conservatives and for nationalists, Caillaux's failure to challenge Calmette was all too consistent with his apparent unwillingness to stand up to the Germans, to elevate the fatherland by defending the national honor in a duel with the enemy.

So strong was Péguy's belief in the duel that he found in its ethic of honor the origins of the French commitment to liberty itself. Should France lose in a war with Germany, he proclaimed, "an entire world would perish with us, and it would be the world of liberty. It would be the world of grace." But France's attachment to the laws of the duel, he admitted, raised a troubling question. How was it that France, with its commitment to honor and decorum, could continue to survive in the face of a German empire long moved only by the desire to dominate? Was it not true that "the force [chivalric France] employs for taking the measure of itself, it no longer possesses for domination; the force it employs for the sake of pure combat, it no longer possesses for victory; the force it employs for being just, it no longer possesses for being strong?" France had not been exterminated, Péguy replied, for one simple reason: "France is the last of the elected peoples." It was the modern beneficiary of a divine grace that had extended from "Jerusalem all the way to Paris, by way of Athens, Rome, and Florence." France had survived against all the odds because "there must be in liberty, in justice (and perhaps in truth), a secret of force, a unique vigor, a flash of hope, in essence a form of grace."[107] God, in effect, had bestowed his grace upon France because of the liberty and justice born in its commitment to honor and to the duel.

France, Péguy suggested, could thus achieve both honor and survival—though he did not add victory. Even Charles Péguy, mystical nationalist that he was, could not ignore the extent of France's defeat in September 1870. But Péguy did not want to see any lasting consequences in that defeat. He did not want his compatriots to conclude that it would be futile to pursue France's struggle with the Germans. The essential point of his essay on the duel was that France need not be discouraged by all the material advantages that seemed to weigh in Germany's favor. Even though "a powerful movement, utterly opposed to [France's] genius, has sprung up next to her and even inside of her. [Even though] this materialistic movement benefits a brutal and disciplined people, ruled by machines and regulations," France resisted the force of this movement, because "she carries within herself the sacred charge."[108] As long as she remained loyal to the ethic of the duel, God would protect her.

It is significant that Péguy's ode to the duel shared with Bruneau de Laborie's *Lois du duel* the unacknowledged recognition that such combat might be a sign of honor and moral stature but that it was not necessarily a sign of strength. Because France's chivalric commitment to the duel had compelled it to sacrifice force for justice, might for right, what military prowess the French possessed came not from within their culture, Péguy suggested, but from the appreciation their culture inspired in God. The French could enter into war with Germany full of hope and confidence not because the duel had prepared them for successful combat but because it had made them an honorable people worthy of God's grace. Such indeed was the spirit with which France ultimately went to war. For despite inferior weapons, a smaller army, declining demographics, and weaker natural resources, France joined the war confidently, even jubilantly, expecting victory in a matter of months. Its generals pursued a perilous offensive strategy, oblivious to the material reasons favoring a more cautious approach. And its soldiers went off to war convinced that honor and bravery would see them through.

The French eagerness to fight—the deluded confidence that spurred them on—stemmed in part, therefore, from the ethic of honor so central to the culture of the Belle Epoque. For some commentators of the era, the duelists' field of honor was a training ground for the coming international conflict, a place where feminized French males could reclaim the status of true men. Others were less certain of the duel's masculinizing effects, fearing that the obsessive sensitivity underlying the duel signified weakness instead of strength, femininity rather than virility. Still, most writers wished, with Péguy, to see in the duel the emblem of France's moral superiority, a superiority that would enable it to survive, the ungallant likes of Joseph Caillaux notwithstanding, the inevitable confrontation with Germany.

6

Gaston Calmette
The Power and Venality of the Press

It was not until the sixth day of the trial that the famous *lettres intimes*, at long last, were read to the court. Rumors concerning their contents had been circulating since the assassination of Calmette, and Gueydan, Chenu, and Labori had been arguing over them since the fourth day. Meanwhile, Judge Albanel had made them the centerpiece of an affair of honor that seemed destined to result in a duel. Finally, just before the opening of the sixth session, Chenu and Labori had come to an agreement over which documents to present in open court. Labori would read two of the three letters that, in his view, were most relevant to the case, ones that Henriette Caillaux claimed had precipitated her violent act.

Madame Caillaux maintained that she had been moved in March 1914 solely by the desire to prevent these letters from seeing print. But now, on 26 July, she had no choice but to agree that they be read aloud, an act that would place them on the front pages of virtually every newspaper in the land. If she was to demonstrate that Calmette would have compromised her honor by publishing the correspondence, the jury had to be shown why. Thus Maître Labori, early in the sixth session, turned to a pair of documents addressed to "Ma chère petite Riri" and began to read aloud.[1] The letters were long, especially the first one, and they could not have been more explicit about the adulterous love Joseph and Henriette had once shared. "When I met you, my love," Joseph had written Henriette on 19 September 1909, "I threw myself toward you with passionate fervor." Joseph went on to detail the strategy he had been plotting for ridding himself of Berthe Gueydan, telling Henriette that they would have to take the utmost care to keep their affair secret until the next election was over. Joseph realized that the duplicity and the patience this effort required would be painful, especially for Henriette, but he assured his "dearest love, that I love you above everything and beyond everything, that I feel happiness with you, that I long for that happiness, that I hope to have it and that I live entirely in the hope of its realization."

The longer Labori went on the paler Henriette Caillaux became, and when her attorney arrived at the closing to Joseph's second letter, "A thousand million kisses all over your adored little body," she fainted dead away.

Earlier in the trial, Madame Caillaux had maintained that the "Ton Jo" letter had made her fear the publication of other, more compromising, letters. She was afraid that Gaston Calmette would use his powerful and respected *Figaro* to reveal to all the world an intimate correspondence intended for her eyes only. Henriette believed herself at the mercy of the French press, of an editor determined to use the power of his medium to ruin her reputation—and thus her honor—for all time.

Madame Caillaux had good reason for such fears, for during the Belle Epoque the press had achieved a relative level of power and influence that no single medium of communication would ever enjoy again. By the eve of World War I, the four largest Paris papers—*Le Petit parisien, Le Petit journal, Le Journal,* and *Le Matin*—together were printing some 4.5 million copies a day.[2] Given a French population of approximately forty million, if only two or three adults saw each issue of the four leading journals in circulation, the *quatre grands* alone would have reached perhaps half the French adult population. Taking all the other daily papers into account, we might reasonably imagine that almost every French adult—literacy was essentially universal by this time—was exposed to at least one newspaper nearly every day. Such unprecedented penetration, and corresponding influence, had succeeded in giving the press a virtual monopoly over the dissemination of information, entertainment, taste, values, fears, and anxieties to the masses. After the First World War, radio and cinema would compete powerfully with the press for France's mass audience, as would television after World War II. But before 1914 print journalism stood alone, and those like Gaston Calmette who controlled it enjoyed what may well have been a historically unique power to shape popular culture and public opinion.

In recent years much has been made of Michel Foucault's discourses on knowledge and power, on the importance in the modern age of knowledge as an essential form of power.[3] It is not just presidents, legislators, generals, and police chiefs who exercise power; so too do professionals, writers, and intellectuals. The latter groups exercise power, Foucault writes, by possessing learning that others do not, by using their learning to shape the public discussion of issues and ideas in such a way as to confer authority and legitimacy on themselves and on their way of organizing and controlling public and private life. Foucault focuses his study on certain key institutions—namely, prisons, hospitals, and schools—whose central endeavor since the late eighteenth century has been to collect the kinds of information about people that lead to ever more sophisticated means of exercising control over them.[4] Thus, prison officials and penologists exercised power over inmates not simply by the act of incarcerating them but by organizing the incarceration according to a new penal theory that stressed surveillance. By the early nineteenth century, prisoners were no longer herded together into towers or dungeons but housed in individual cells open in front and built around a central court from which they could be perpetually observed. Such examination gave prison officials a detailed knowledge of the inmate who, once known, could be "rehabilitated" in a way that suited the penologists and prison officials who were watching him. Knowledge, therefore, produced the institutions and the practices that led to new knowledge and new and increasingly potent modes of control. Foucault may, in this work, underestimate the extent to which inmates themselves could achieve knowledge that would enable them to resist these methods of control, but some of his later work seems to rectify the assessment.[5] What he does not consider, primarily because his work focuses on the early and midnineteenth century, is the question of the mass media and its unprecedented ability to exercise power through the dissemination of knowledge. Foucault's "disciplines" may once have been the centers of knowledge-power, but by the latter years of the nineteenth century they were eclipsed by the penny press, whose influence they only reinforced. No other institution at the fin de siècle could have plausibly boasted the omniscience engraved onto *Le Matin*'s masthead itself: "*Le Matin* voit tout, sait tout, dit tout" (*Le Matin* sees everything, knows everything, says everything).

Like Foucault's disciplines, the mass-circulation press of the Belle Epoque exercised its formidable power not so much at the level of overt political persuasion, of party allegiance and parliamentary politics, but at the level of culture and values. In an effort to alienate as few readers as possible, the *quatre grands* presented themselves as politically neutral; though they often subtly supported whatever government was in power, they rarely argued in favor of a particular party or political program. They adopted instead the much more powerful technique of influencing readers by appealing to deeply embedded attitudes about religion, nationality, and sexuality, all of which in conducive circumstances could make certain cultural proclivities profoundly political. The controversies over the crime of passion, the nature of the real woman, of marriage and divorce, of honor and patriotism—all became matters of public concern during the Belle Epoque in large part because of their treatment in the press. The *enquête* was nothing if not an attempt to arouse French men and women over some of the most divisive cultural matters of the era: divorce, feminism, women's suffrage, national defense, the jury system, and capital punishment.[6] By choosing the issues to place before the public and by interpreting the results of their surveys, newspaper editors made themselves central to the political and cultural life of pre-1914 France.

But editors were not forced to rely primarily on devices like the *enquête* to exercise cultural power; far more important was the rhetorical style the journalists used and their ability to determine which events and stories ought to see print. And what the penny press deemed particularly worthy of attention was the *fait divers*, the true-crime story narrated in a colorful prose designed to stimulate a welter of contradictory emotions: horror over the crime combined with a certain fascination for the criminal himself; a sympathetic identification with the victim tempered by a secret relief that the victim was someone else.

Mirroring the true *faits divers* were fictional tales of murder, suspense, love, and adventure delivered by the penny press in daily installments and known as *romans-feuilletons*. Newspaper readers were particularly drawn to detective stories and romances, and to the adventures of men whose strength, will, and talent made them larger than life.[7] The writing style of these fictional feuilletons was virtually identical to that of the factual *faits divers*; the two blended together and nourished each other with references and images. It is not unlikely that readers of the penny press saw the fictional pieces as only slightly less real than the "true" ones, the true stories at least as suspenseful and exciting as the novels.[8] And because fact and fiction in the penny press took similar literary forms, newspapers appeared to require some external device to separate them. The task was neatly accomplished by the fold in the journal, which divided the front page into top and bottom halves. The top was reserved for *l'actualité*—the news of the day, whether it was crime, natural disaster, or scandal—the bottom for the *roman-feuilleton*. It was common for newspapers such as the *Petit journal* and the *Petit parisien* to gain ten or twenty thousand readers with the beginning of a new serial novel, the inspiration for which tended more often than not to come from the *faits divers* featured above the fold.[9]

Whether they were intended to or not, these *faits divers* and installment novels undoubtedly gave readers an exaggerated sense of the prevalence of crime and of its potential danger to them. Readers took refuge, as a result, in a desire to maintain capital punishment, as a survey sponsored by the *Petit parisien* demonstrated in 1907. But their indulgence for the crime of passion clearly showed that they did not necessarily seek retribution against all species of criminal.[10] It remains clear, nonetheless, that the general cultural tone of the Belle Epoque's mass-circulation press was conservative, for the *quatre grands* in particular appealed in both fact and fiction to traditional family values, to an elemental nationalism that stereotyped Germans as the cultural "other," and to an ideal of "Frenchness" that excluded Jews.[11]

In making this appeal, the French press powerfully shaped the nature and quality of Belle Epoque life, though perhaps not as extensively as most commentators imagined. Virtually everyone who wrote about the press during the years from 1890 to 1914 saw it as possessing almost unlimited powers, which writers frequently characterized in demonic terms; the analysis of the press was often as unsophisticated as the journalism it deplored. Socialists claimed that mainstream newspapers almost singlehandedly kept the capitalist system afloat, while anti-Semites believed the Jews' supposed dominance of the press had made them the masters of France.[12] Others saw the press as undermining religious values, as destroying the family and encouraging crime.[13] The latter was a particularly common complaint, for commentators—often with impeccable academic or medical credentials—regularly claimed newspaper accounts of crimes were so emotionally vivid that readers, particularly women readers, were moved to imitate them. "Each time a popular newspaper recounts a sensational crime," wrote Dr. Séverin Icard in the respected journal *La nouvelle revue*, "a similar crime inevitably takes place shortly thereafter."[14] Or as Gabriel Tarde put it, "because of the contagion of murder and rapes, reports of criminal events, in themselves, have caused [a great many] crimes to be committed."[15] Crimes of passion, Icard added, were particularly contagious, as were suicides. He told of one incident in which an elaborate press account of a young woman's suicide led a few days later to the suicide of another woman of approximately the same age. As a macabre suicide note, the second victim left the newspaper whose tale she had copied open to the article in question.

Icard explained the press's seemingly hypnotic hold over its readers, its ability to drive them to murder and suicide, by portraying the brain as a kind of movie camera capable of recording images to be used as a script for future action. "The brain," he wrote, "is a perfect recording machine. Every sensation it perceives, weak or strong, conscious or unconscious, leaves an imprint as on a photographic plate. These cerebral imprints are indelible, *they are acts about to be realized, acts in a latent state.* A minor incident or event is enough to transform these acts from a latent to an active state." When this occurs, he concluded, "publicity accomplishes its evil work, stimulating a powerful instinct of imitation so easily awakened."[16]

The cinematic imagery Icard employed suggests the influence of the prominent psychologist Hippolyte Bernheim, who argued that "visual images" unmediated by rational thought routinely penetrated people's minds and imprinted themselves on the brain.[17] Such images were the product of what Bernheim called "suggestions," namely words, gestures, pictures, or events from the environment that lodged themselves in an individual's brain before being projected back outward as actions imitating the original suggestion. This process occurred, Bernheim maintained, beneath the level of the individual's awareness, for under the influence of these imagistic suggestions people behaved as if under a hypnotic trance; they could be hypnotized, many of his followers came to believe, by environmental stimuli alone.

By the late nineteenth century Bernheim's ideas had found a wide readership among medical doctors, criminologists, and journalists, and they appear to have affected the disposition of more than a few legal cases.[18] Indeed, Henriette Caillaux's testimony may itself have been shaped by the idea of suggestibility, of cinematic images imprinting themselves on the brain for later enactment. On the first day of the trial she had explained her irrational impulse to confront Calmette as having been produced by the vision of "a cinematographic film [that] flashed before my eyes," a film in which she saw her husband, "skillful shooter that he was, killing M. Calmette." Somehow, Henriette went on, she found herself re-enacting this filmic image of the brain, making herself, rather than her husband, protagonist of its drama: "the idea of substituting myself for him took over my mind."[19]

Dr. Icard did not testify for Henriette Caillaux, but ideas such as his were useful to her cause. Icard maintained that few women possessed the strength of character, the intellectual and moral force, required to control the instinct of imitation that could impel them to commit violent crimes. Echoing Gabriel Tarde and many others, Icard claimed that women "by their very nature possess a predisposition" to emulate what they see and read. Since large numbers of women existed on the "edge of madness," Icard added, "we can understand how an especially powerful newspaper article might dislodge the rational faculties of certain women and place them momentarily in the realm of mental illness." Even women who were not particularly unbalanced, he maintained, could be moved to crime or suicide if they read a particularly gripping *fait divers* during their menstrual cycle or while temporarily "agitated or depressed."[20] Henriette Caillaux, it should be noted, had made a point of testifying to her "agitated and depressed" state the previous March, and to her regular reading of *Le Figaro* and other daily newspapers, all of which were full of emotion-ridden stories of violent crime.

While most of the era's commentaries were as alarmist and misogynistic as Dr. Icard's, one influential writer took a more subtle approach, criticizing the press not for driving readers to crime and madness but for diverting their attention from the mundane realities of everyday life to an imaginary world of danger and excitement. Henry du Roure, a leading liberal Catholic associated with *Le*

Sillon, explained that the press had achieved extraordinary power because it gave readers what their "own lives did not provide them . . . a life of romance . . . of incredible adventures and overwhelming sentiments, of blood, sex, and death."[21] No longer, wrote Roure, was the journalist a sharp analyst of key social and political events. Instead, he had become "the *metteur en scène* (film director) of a daily spectacle of magic designed to embellish real life for the greatest satisfaction of workers and bourgeois alike."[22]

The cinematic metaphor is notable once again, but in this case it suggests the influence not only of Bernheim but of Henri Bergson, perhaps the most prominent philosopher of the fin de siècle. Like Bernheim, Bergson believed in the power of environmental suggestions to accomplish what was to be the cinema's very essence: the transformation of ideas into images. Bergson, too, held that suggestions imprinted themselves on the unconscious mind, directly bypassing consciousness itself. To consider the role suggestions played in shaping mental phenomena Bergson turned in particular to art, to the ways in which artists achieved their effects: painters, musicians, and writers reached their audiences not by appealing to the conscious mind but by "putting reason to sleep," by employing an almost hypnotic power of suggestion "to trigger emotional states."[23] It was this latter notion that distinguished Bergson's views from those of Bernheim, who believed that suggestion triggered not only emotional states but physical action as well. Bergson, by contrast, held that images from the environment shaped the mind while doing little to propel the body.

It is in light of Bergson's ideas that Roure's commentary can best be understood. Unlike Tarde and Icard, he saw journalism more as a form of art than an agent of psychological impulsion, as a medium that moved readers to tears, not to action. The penny press, for Roure, possessed the same capacity to evoke images of pleasure and pain, of desire, melancholy, and fear, that critics would later attribute to film itself. But journalism, no more than the cinema, did not lure people into a world of crime. What the press did—still considerably better than the early cinema—was to enable its audience to experience that world vicariously, to feel it without having to live it.

Newspaper readers, Roure's account suggests, could enjoy the safe pleasures of the voyeur, the distanced delights of the spectator titillated by the action but spared the risks and dangers it posed. Individuals dulled by bureaucratic work and by the routines of family life, their emotions carefully controlled lest they anger an employer or alienate a relative, could turn to the daily paper for the experience, however vicarious, of forbidden passions. Opening the paper to a pithy *fait divers*, the reader, according to Roure, "licks his chops. He believes himself to experience one by one—and with what transports of joy!—the emotions of an unfortunate woman attacked at night and cut into pieces with successive blows of a sword; then, in trying to enter into the character of the assassin, he tastes the incomparable psychological pleasures which he, as a practical man, has never experienced directly."[24] Through these accounts of the *fait divers* the reader could first identify with the criminal's pleasure of aggression unleashed and later, in seconding the condemnation of the evildoer, safely express the anger and fantasies of vengeance that necessarily arose in the course of a relatively powerless existence.

For many of the same reasons, Roure suggested, the press devoted considerable attention to the private affairs of France's most public men. By revealing the financial and sexual exploits of famous politicians, journalists opened a window onto worlds of excitement and luxury in which most of their readers could never directly indulge. In doing so, the press fulfilled a complex psychological function, for it allowed readers both the thrill of identifying with those who ruled them and the pleasure of venting an anger born of envy against them. And when members of the elite were punished for their scandalous behavior, readers could feel confirmed in the justice of their own straight and narrow lives.

The emotional effects on readers of these journalistic accounts of crime and mayhem were extremely important. As more recent commentators on the press have pointed out, virtually all the articles published in the Belle Epoque's penny press, not just those devoted to crime and scandal, were cast in the rhetorical and stylistic mold of the *fait divers*.[25] Thus, articles concerning national politics and international affairs, social problems and intellectual dilemmas, took on an anecdotal narrative form. Events and issues were no longer analyzed in detail but recounted in a style designed to engage the reader, to stimulate his emotions and pique his curiosity. Discussions of Caillaux's proposed income tax, for example, sought not to determine its equitability by comparing the existing tax structure with the proposed new one or to consider how much revenue the new system might produce. Instead, they told the story of the parliamentary effort to pass or to block the new tax legislation, creating suspense over the outcome wherever possible. They considered the political biographies of the leaders of both camps, condemning or applauding the bill in terms of the personalities on either side. Stories such as these engaged readers more than did overtly analytical accounts; but in narrating politics as if it were a sporting event or a tale of drama and suspense, newspapers created a certain emotional satisfaction at the expense of intellectual substance.

This *"fait diversification* of the political sphere," as Jacques Kayser calls it, seemed to turn the world into a spectacle with the newspaper its stage and the readership its audience almost unlimited in number. By presenting political and social life as an unfolding drama of heroes and villains, the popular press swept its readers into a vast theater of the real, into a realm of emotional engagement all the more compelling because the characters and events it portrayed really existed.[26] Because this drama, unlike the drama of theater or literature, had no trajectory or conclusion fixed in print, readers could imagine themselves not only as participants but as creators, as individuals whose vote or voice could affect the outcome of the narrative. Male readers could vote a scandalous politician out of office, and women could join them in lending support to a leader unjustly misunderstood. These possibilities could give men and women alike a sense, however briefly it lasted, that their lives were not so insignificant after all.

In this theatrical world of mass journalism, nothing could have provided a more fitting subject than the Caillaux Affair. It possessed all the elements of an ideal newspaper narrative: murder, romance, sex, and political intrigue, set in the palpably engaging context of the real. The trial transcript itself contained far more drama than the average play and for that reason appeared verbatim in all the major Paris papers—some of which produced special supplements to contain the extra pages required.[27] Like the popular novels newspapers regularly published, the transcript came out in daily installments, a format dictated, to be sure, by the structure of the trial but which conveniently left readers hungering to know what would transpire the following day. By perusing the transcript each morning, readers became part of a courtroom audience that extended to the whole of the country, bringing modern France the closest to the civic theater of the Greeks it could ever come.

The trial of Madame Caillaux was so perfect a vehicle for the "*fait diversification* of the political sphere," so ideal a means of turning public events into theatrical spectacle, that for eight days at the end of July 1914 the French press paid attention to little else. As Jean-Jacques Becker shows in a detailed analysis of six major French dailies—four from Paris and two from the provinces—France's newspapers devoted the bulk of their space to the trial of Henriette Caillaux even after the dire diplomatic events of late July should by rights have displaced it.[28] Between 21 July, when the trial began, and 25 July, when news of Austria's ultimatum to Serbia was a full day old, virtually every major Paris newspaper devoted half or more of its front page to the *affaire Caillaux*. Conservative papers such as *L'Echo de Paris, La Presse*, and, unsurprisingly, *Le Figaro* devoted their *entire* first pages (save occasionally for the bottom corner of the right-hand column) to the event. Only the staid *Journal des débats* kept its front-page Caillaux coverage to a minimum. As for the overall surface area of the journals in question, the *Echo de Paris* of 24 July held the record with nearly 60 percent of the entire paper consumed by the affair. The quasi-official *Le Temps* gave the trial 51 percent of its overall space on 22 July, while the *Petit parisien* allowed it 48 percent the same day. On 29 July, just two days before France was to order its general mobilization for war, *Le Petit parisien, L'Echo de Paris*, and *Le Temps* all allotted more space to the trial than to the European crisis. *Le Figaro*, for its part, gave the trial five of its six front-page columns on 29 July and three of six a day later. Virtually no newspaper banished the case from its headlines until the general mobilization had actually been declared. As for the diplomatic situation itself, none of the six papers Becker studies gave the crisis more than 30 percent of its overall space until 30 July, and only one of Becker's four Parisian papers, the socialist *L'Humanité*, paid more attention to the crisis than to the trial before that same day.[29]

Beyond the trial's narrative and dramatic appeal, it commanded such front-page attention because it was powerfully photogenic. Only in the four or five years preceding the affair had the French press improved its photographic reproduction enough to produce relatively clear images on newsprint.[30] Once it had, large front-page photographs became de rigueur. Editors sought to cover stories that would photograph well, and in July 1914 the Caillaux Affair proved an infinitely better subject than a nebulous diplomatic crisis occurring abroad and involving individuals unknown to most French newspaper readers. How much more satisfying it was to produce photographic images of the attractive Madame Caillaux and the elegant men who surrounded her.

This fixation on the Caillaux Affair was so powerful that the press made its own obsession—and that of its readers—part of the story. Such had been the case at the time of Calmette's assassination four months earlier, and such would be the case when the trial began. Several days after the shooting, *L'Illustration* declared that "rarely have people snatched up newspapers with such feverous interest, and rarely have we seen the dailies devote, as they have in the past few days, virtually the entirety of their pages to the same subject." By the trial's opening day the fever, according to *La Presse,* had only increased. "The trial," its editors proclaimed, "will most likely stir public opinion much more than the infinitely more important questions on which the future of the country depends. Fascination with this *fait divers* will reduce the alliance with Russia to a matter of minor concern."[31] And as if to confirm that fear, the paper asserted on 25 July that "the trial of Madame Caillaux has made us forget altogether Monsieur Poincaré's state visit to Russia." The editors might have added that they were in large part to blame, for on that very day they had plastered their front page with the event whose monopoly over the news they so deplored. Twenty-four hours later, the Catholic *La Croix,* a paper that had hardly ignored the affair, was equally dismayed. The editors found it deplorable that "one could easily imagine that there is no longer anything in France but Madame Caillaux!" All Russia, the editors went on, had acclaimed the visit of President Poincaré, while the French barely knew he was abroad.[32]

Thus, with Europe facing the risk of a general war, France was preoccupied with a journalistic drama that reduced its peripheral vision almost to nothing. It was not that the French had been rendered oblivious to the looming conflict, but that in the crisis atmosphere of July 1914, they spoke its language and experienced its warning signs through the seemingly safe remove of a national *fait divers.* Just as readers had indulged the fear and exhilaration of crime from the safe position of the voyeur, so they experienced the prelude to war through journalistic accounts of a trial whose characters could speak only in the figurative language of the duel. The European crisis could be apprehended only through the lens of French national politics. And thanks to the "fait diversification de la politique," largely through the personalities of its elite, including the one member whose death had turned ordinary politics into an affair of symbolic significance.

Gaston Calmette had been so central to the culminating campaign of France's prewar struggle between nationalists and antinationalists, between enemies and friends of Joseph Caillaux, that the trial of Henriette Caillaux could hardly avoid reiterating that battle. Throughout the trial, and especially during the sixth and seventh sessions, the two sides clashed over the question of whether Calmette and his journal were responsible, at least in part, for the violent events of 16 March 1914. Calmette's allies portrayed him as a gentle patriot martyred in a noble journalistic quest to protect the nation from the evil designs of Joseph Caillaux. Calmette's enemies, and especially Caillaux, pictured him as an editorial saboteur intent on using the vast power of the press to defame and dishonor a man who sought nothing more than peace and fiscal justice for his country—albeit against the interests of *Le Figaro*'s privileged elite. Both sides saw the press as crucial to these struggles and took Calmette as the emblem of its influence (figure 15).

Calmette had joined *Le Figaro*, one of France's oldest newspapers, in 1883. The fledgling reporter was then twenty-five years old, having chosen journalism after briefly attending the military officers' training school at Saint-Cyr and then studying law.[33] His family background was quite modest. Calmette had lost his mother at an early age, and his father had been a provincial bureaucrat, reaching the level of subprefect in midcareer but going no higher. Calmette's first position at *Le Figaro* was as assistant to the editor of a section called "échos," a sort of literary gossip column, and there he published his first signed article in 1885. A short time later, he took over as the "échos" editor. According to Raymond Recouly, a longtime journalist at *Le Figaro*, Calmette attracted the attention of the paper's editor in chief, Francis Magnard, by the way he celebrated his promotion from a position as writer paid by the piece to salaried

15. Gaston Calmette, editor of *Le Figaro,* at the height of his power (*L'Illustration,* 21 March 1914).

editor. Calmette spent his entire first month's income on an elegant dinner party, a gesture, according to Recouly, that "deeply impressed" Magnard. The next day the director made a point of telling Calmette that what he had done showed class. "Not everyone," Magnard effused, "would have had such an idea."[34] Magnard was so impressed with Calmette's talents as a Parisian host that he took him under his wing, making him his editorial assistant in 1892. In this capacity Calmette wrote a series of major articles on the Panama scandal of the early 1890s, a sordid episode that tainted French parliamentary government for years to come.

Calmette possessed considerable journalistic ability but owed his rapid advancement at the paper to his even greater social skills. After Magnard's death in 1894 deprived Calmette of a protector, the young journalist acquainted himself with the daughter of Georges Prestat, the man who dominated *Le Figaro*'s board of directors and controlled the paper financially. In 1896 Prestat's daughter became Calmette's wife. Six years later, with the paper in deep financial crisis and its readership plummeting, Prestat ousted both the editor in chief, Fernand de Rodays, and the managing editor, Antonin Périvier, to give Calmette both positions. It is unclear why Prestat discharged both of *Le Figaro*'s top editors, although political dissension stemming from the Dreyfus affair and the declining readership undoubtedly contributed. But perhaps even more important was the board of directors' desire to restructure the paper's capital base. To do so, Prestat counted on the loyalty of his son-in-law, Gaston Calmette. Thus, as the very young age of forty-three, Calmette found himself in the enviable position of directing both *Le Figaro*'s editorial policy as well as its day-to-day financial affairs.[35]

Under Calmette's leadership, *Le Figaro* deemphasized party and parliamentary politics to devote even more attention than before to the glittering literary and social life of Paris. The new director apparently succeeded quite well in this endeavor, for the paper's circulation more than doubled between 1902 and 1912.[36] At a meeting of shareholders in 1905 Calmette boasted that the paper "had reconquered sympathies that a period of torment [i.e., the Dreyfus affair] had lost to us." The proof, he maintained, "is in our list of subscribers that grows from month to month and that constitutes a Who's Who of the aristocracy, the wealthiest part of the bourgeoisie, and the leading representatives of commerce, industry, the army, as well as the most elegant of the foreigners living within our midst." With such an "admirable clientele," the editor concluded, "the path to follow on the terrain of politics—and of social life—is laid out before us."[37] Thus, under Calmette's direction, *Le Figaro* was to be conservative rather than reactionary, intelligent but not intellectual. It was to appeal to the unadventurous literary tastes and careful politics of its high-society readers. "The power of *Le Figaro*," writes the popular historian Arthur Conte, "lay in its ability to be at once a journal of information and a journal of ideas, a journal for political engagement and for escapist reading."[38]

Calmette, from all descriptions, was perfectly suited to direct such a journal, addressed as it was to a social elite with literary pretensions. Conte calls him "the Parisian who had more social contacts than anyone else."[39] He was widely known for his affability, his charm, his easy and gracious manner. Recouly wrote that "never before has a man been able to lead a major newspaper with such good grace, such courtesy, such powers of seduction." Calmette owed his success in the rarified world of Parisian high society, Recouly added, to a "certain attractive charm born of a nature and sensitivity feminine in essence." Echoing Bruneau de Laborie and countless others, Recouly thus described this intellectually inclined man of the elite in explicitly female terms. Calmette, he wrote, "embellished the ordinary events of everyday life with an infinite number of gentle touches, with an exquisite delicacy of manner." And beyond these feminine traits, the editor always "did his best to please, for he was attentive and obliging, doing everything in his power to soothe and smooth relations between men that have become too rough and too harsh."[40] In this description Calmette sounds much like the accomplished society wife, the one who has learned the lessons of the marriage manuals to perfection.

Given all of these amiable personality traits, it is not readily apparent what moved him to undertake such a violent and mendacious campaign against Joseph Caillaux. Until then, Calmette had been unaccustomed to the dark underworld of political combat, maintaining a dignified journalistic tone that left harsh rhetoric and character assassination to papers further to the right. Poincaré wrote in his memoirs that Calmette's "aggression conforms neither to the general tone of [*Le Figaro*] nor to the habitual style of M. Calmette, who until now has been the most courteous of journalists."[41] Likewise, Francis Charmes, the political columnist for the *Revue des deux mondes*, noted that Calmette, who in the past had always been "amiable, courteous, and benevolent," appeared with his press campaign "in an entirely new light . . . energetic, ardent, vigorous in his attack."[42] It is true that Calmette, like Caillaux's rivals Barthou, Briand, and Poincaré, opposed the income tax and supported the three-year draft, yet the editor had been anything but an extreme nationalist. His paper had even supported Caillaux's negotiations with the Germans during the Agadir crisis.[43] Calmette appears, however, to have been genuinely upset when Caillaux overturned Barthou's right-of-center government in December 1913, feeling, in the words of Alain Decaux, "the fall of Barthou as if it were his own."[44] Yet similar political setbacks had not in the past provoked from Calmette such a vigorous response.

Why then did Calmette agree to lend his talents and his journal to the effort to unseat Caillaux? According to Recouly, Calmette's willingness to pursue Caillaux so ardently was consistent with a personality more complex than most people realized. "Hidden beneath the sunniest and most pleasing surface," the journalist maintained, "was an utterly passionate temperament, a simmering sensitivity." Calmette, in sum, "was impetuous in his hatreds and even more so in his friendships."[45] Here again, the editor is made to resemble the typical woman of the Belle Epoque, especially the one likely to commit a crime of passion, the one whose animal feelings lurked just beneath a seductive exterior of beauty and charm. If Calmette's ferocious campaign against Caillaux was a crime, Recouly implied, then it was a crime of passion. Still, this portrait of his personality does not explain why he had never reacted so violently in the past, why his "simmering sensitivity" had spilled over into a persecutory zeal only against Caillaux and only in the winter of 1914.

Perhaps the editor hoped that by attacking Caillaux he would increase *Le Figaro*'s circulation, still less than half of what it had been fifteen years earlier.[46] This possibility cannot be excluded, although no evidence exists to suggest that Calmette had in fact made such a calculation. Nor does the campaign against Caillaux appear to have improved the paper's sales, since the mass-circulation journals rehearsed all Calmette's accusations as soon as he made them. Was there, then, a personal rivalry between Calmette and Caillaux?

Jean-Claude Allain suggests that such may well have been the case, although the evidence is far from complete. The Swiss ambassador to France sent a dispatch to his government the day after Calmette's assassination in which he declared that "from the very beginning of Calmette's campaign in *Le Figaro* against M. Caillaux, everyone in Parisian high society has been saying the campaign owed its origins to an *histoire de femme*." According to this high-society gossip, Caillaux had been planning to divorce Henriette in order to marry a writer whom he was urging to divorce her husband. But rumor had it, wrote the ambassador, that Calmette "was equally interested in this lady." The Swiss diplomat considered these notions unfounded, even "slanderous"; nonetheless, he suggested that Henriette Caillaux may have taken them seriously. "Perhaps the unfortunate Madame Caillaux," he wrote, "ultimately found out about this slanderous gossip against her husband and then lost her head."[47] Why she would have wanted to eliminate her husband's rival for possession of this other woman the ambassador did not say.

Chenu alluded to this hearsay at the trial, declaring, "Some rumors have circulated, but I will leave them aside." The rumors, Chenu's son later wrote, held that "Madame Caillaux feared in 1914 that she would undergo the same fate as had Madame Gueydan [namely, that her husband would summarily divorce her]."[48] Even though these reports would have compromised Joseph Caillaux, Chenu chose not to bring them to bear in the trial because in doing so he would have undermined his entire courtroom strategy. Throughout the trial, Chenu endeavored to present Joseph and Henriette as solidly united, as working in tandem to fulfill a single-minded desire to preserve his career. Henriette, Chenu maintained, had killed Calmette purely to protect Joseph from the revelations of the *document Fabre*. To present the Caillaux as being on the verge of divorce might have made jurors skeptical of Chenu's argument.

If personal rivalry does not explain why Calmette had been willing to go to such lengths in leading the campaign against Caillaux, then what can? Perhaps the editor believed, with Raymond Poincaré, that Caillaux's success in overturning Barthou's government in December 1913 had "broken the charm and shattered the national movement"?[49] Although the majority of France's voters did not turn sharply to the nationalist right after 1912, many members of the social and political elite did, especially writers and journalists. It may be that Calmette and his *Figaro* were so integral to this elite shift to the right that he felt impelled to lead the charge against the politician Maurice Barrès had labeled the "most hated man in France." It also seems likely that Calmette understood Caillaux's support in parliament and among the voters to be so secure that only an extraparliamentary effort of uncommon force could succeed in dislodging him. That force had to come from the press. No other institution or medium of communication could reach so many people, could equal the press's ability to sway public opinion and shape public perception. In the winter of 1913–14 Gaston Calmette, editor of *Le Figaro,* decided to undertake what no politician or political party possessed the power to do: banish Joseph Caillaux from the center of French public life.

The press had not long enjoyed such power. In 1850 French newspapers consisted of two or four pages of closely lettered newsprint devoid of drawings, pictures, or even headlines. Papers were seldom sold by the issue but almost entirely by quarterly or yearly subscription. And subscriptions were expensive, so expensive that only those with comfortable middle-class incomes could afford them. Literate working people sometimes pooled their resources to share the cost of an *abonnement,* and those unable to do this could read various newspapers at a local café or in makeshift popular libraries known as *cabinets de lecture.* Individuals who went to such lengths to read the press during the first half of the nineteenth century tended to be highly politicized since newspapers were, above all, the organs of groups desiring to convey a political message. Newspapers contained opinions, arguments, and doctrines; they were not yet the chronicle of spectacular events and the compendia of information they were to become.[50]

Emile de Girardin is generally credited with having founded the modern French newspaper with the appearance of *La Presse* in 1836. Girardin's innovation was to cut the subscription price in half by introducing paid advertisements into the journal. He also decided to broaden the paper's appeal by reducing its overtly political content and by publishing in daily installments the works of popular novelists such as Eugène Sue.[51] The formula appeared to succeed, for by 1848 Girardin achieved a circulation (about 30,000) many times that of the traditional papers. Still, *La Presse* never surpassed this figure, quite modest by late nineteenth-century standards, nor did it change the basic character of French journalism. The older *presse d'opinion*, highly political and difficult to read, continued to dominate French journalism until the mid-1860s. Only then did new technology and growing literacy make possible a wholly new kind of publication.

In 1800 most French men and women could not read; by 1900 nearly everyone could.[52] Such a dramatic advance of literacy created a potential market of newspaper readers that included the entire adult population. But just as the English textile industry could not meet a potentially unlimited market before the technological advances of the late eighteenth century, so the French press could not reach out to a rapidly growing literate population until it developed new industrial methods. As late as 1860, newspaper production remained an artisanal endeavor: unit costs were high and circulation low. At best, printing presses could turn out each day only a few tens of thousands of issues that seldom exceeded four pages. Making matters worse was a tax imposed by Napoleon III's government on any journal that published articles treating political and economic questions. The tax made French newspapers even more costly than they already were; its purpose was to render them too expensive for working-class readers, believed to be dangerously and easily aroused by political reportage.[53]

The French press was prevented, therefore, from exploiting the potential of the country's newly literate populace by a wide array of political, economic, and technological obstacles. Newspapers were too expensive to capture a genuinely popular readership, and production remained too artisanal to lower unit costs. Innovations were desperately needed. Thanks to a veteran newspaperman named Moses Millaud, they were not long in coming. In 1863 Millaud launched *Le Petit journal*, a newspaper destined to transform journalism into a commodity for mass consumption.[54] Millaud's main innovation was to sell his paper for one sou (five centimes) an issue at a time when most journals cost two or three sous each. One sou put a daily paper easily within reach of France's working classes, for five centimes represented only about a hundredth of a Parisian worker's daily wage and about twice that fraction of a provincial worker's income. Relative to other articles of consumption, moreover, the newspaper at one sou was considerably less expensive than the daily journal would be nearly a century later. During the Belle Epoque one sou represented about one-tenth the price of a kilogram of bread, whereas in 1980 the average daily paper cost more than half the price of a kilo-sized loaf. In 1900, the newspaper at one sou amounted to less than one-fifth the price of a liter of milk but more than four-fifths eighty years later; one-third the cost of a metro ride in 1900 and almost its full equivalent in 1980.[55]

Thus in setting his price at one sou—half or even a third of what his competitors had been charging—Millaud had truly created a newspaper accessible to the masses. But having made his journal so inexpensive, Millaud had to compensate by selling a large number of copies. To achieve this goal he made significant innovations in all aspects of newspaper publishing: advertising, content, distribution, and technique.

Millaud was particularly innovative in the realm of advertising. Not only did he open his paper to those who wished to publicize their products, he advertised his paper itself. He prefaced the appearance of *Le Petit journal* on 1 February 1863 with a massive monthlong advertising campaign whose ubiquitous posters heralded the coming of *"le journal à un sou."*[56] By the end of January the Parisians' curiosity had been aroused; initial sales were high and they climbed steadily for three decades, reaching the remarkable figure of a million copies a day by 1890.[57]

Millaud had been able to set such a low price for his journal in part because he decided not to treat politics and economic life at all, thereby avoiding Napoleon III's six-centime-per-issue tax. Instead of politics, *Le Petit journal* devoted itself to the facts and events of everyday life. Like a certain social history of the midtwentieth century, *Le Petit journal* intended to describe the world of ordinary people with the politics left out. It included the practical information about agriculture, medicine, and the weather that had long been the hallmark of the almanacs popular in rural France since the seventeenth century.[58] But its innovation was to feature above the fold on page one a *chronique* devoted to what its writer, the remarkable journalist Léo Lespes, called *"L'actualité"*—everything that is happening now. Lespes described his column, written under the pen name Timothée Trimm, as a chronicle of "the recent event, the *actualité* still in progress, the latest anecdote, the summary of a play to be performed the next day, the polite but convincing review of a book published the day before."[59]

Day in and day out Lespes filled most of *Le Petit journal's* front page with a kind of common man's "Talk of the Town." Often funny but seldom ironic, his was an impressive mélange of advice, comment, humor, pedagogy, and reportage that eschewed the sophistication, the inside jokes, the literary references, that had long characterized France's more elite publications. Working people alienated by highbrow papers such as *Le Journal des débats* or by the *haut monde* refinement of *Le Figaro* found *Le Petit journal* accessible and edifying. "Timothée Trimm," wrote a shop foreman named Urbain Desvaux, "knows how to broaden the horizons of us working men." Not necessarily a great man of letters, Trimm "makes us understand things we never understood before; he sheds light on what is good to observe; he gives us advice that is good to follow. His advice helps always to make us good citizens, good Frenchmen, good comrades, good sons, good husbands, and good fathers."[60] Thanks in large part to the talent of Léo Lespes, Millaud did much to transform French journalism from a forum for politics and polemics into a medium of instruction and diversion for working men and their families.

The *Petit journal* diverted its readers not just with the chronicle of Timothée Trimm but with the *faits divers* and *romans-feuilletons* soon to become as central to the industrialized penny press as they had been to the popular literature of centuries past. Nor did Timothée Trimm monopolize the reporting of "*L'actualité.*" Much of what the *Petit journal* took as news in the repressively depoliticized world of Napoleon III was the story of spectacular crime, the *fait divers*.[61] In 1869 the *Petit journal* saw its circulation rise from 350,000 to almost 600,000—a figure no one would have dreamed possible just ten years earlier—as it told the story, the "roman vrai" as the paper called it, of the *affaire Troppmann*. On 23 September 1869 the *Petit journal* devoted the entire first two pages to a hideous crime that had occurred the day before. A mechanic named Jean-Baptiste Troppmann had brutally murdered the parents and six children of a family from the modest Paris suburb of Pantin. As details of the crime became known and the criminal himself began to talk, the *Petit journal* devoted an ever-increasing portion of its space to the affair. By the end of September the entire paper spoke of little else but

Troppmann; the more space the affair received, the higher the *Petit journal*'s circulation climbed. It reached the peak on 15 January 1870 when it published an elaborate description of the murderer's execution. All along, the journal's reporters had conducted their own inquiry independent of the police investigation, weighing evidence and speculating about the killer's motives. So close were journalists to the events they reported that according to a widely believed rumor, one of the *Petit journal*'s writers, a "fanatic of capital punishment," actually served as aide to Troppmann's executioner.[62]

Given the widespread appeal of dramatic reportage and of the daily doses of novelistic suspense, we can see how the *Petit journal* and papers like it could attract an audience of newly literate readers. Still, circulation figures as high as those the *Petit journal* enjoyed could never have been attained, no matter how appealing the writing, without certain fundamentally important technological advances in printing that Millaud and his colleagues had helped pioneer. Between 1863 and 1872 French newspapers—led by the *Petit journal* and a few others—developed the technology to transform themselves into true mass media.

This transformation began slowly in the eary 1860s, rapidly gaining momentum after 1866 when Millaud's competitor Emile de Girardin, still harboring his dream of a paper for the masses, joined forces with the printer-inventor Hippolyte Marinoni to produce a new kind of printing press. Girardin had been following the printing developments taking place in the United States and realized that the only way to compete effectively with Millaud was to adapt the new American technology to the French market. He had Marinoni produce for him a pair of fully mechanized rotary printing presses each capable of turning out ten thousand four-page papers an hour. Marinoni's machine marked an enormous advance over the manual and partially mechanized models that could produce, at best, fifteen hundred copies per hour.[63] It also gave the French a technological advantage over the British, Germans, and Americans that they enjoyed in virtually no other industrial field. Marinoni's machine was smaller, lighter, more efficient, and less costly than the rotary presses used in those other countries.[64]

In 1872 Marinoni, encouraged by the fall of Napoleon III's repressive regime, unveiled a machine capable of printing twenty thousand newspapers an hour, adding an automatic paper folder six years later. The latter was the first of a series of gradual improvements that by 1902 resulted in a rotary press destined, with only small modifications, to remain in service until the 1970s.[65]

Thus by 1880 the French rotary press had already reached a speed and efficiency that the industry would take almost a century to surpass. What slowed progress in the late nineteenth century was the artisanal nature of typesetting. European and American inventors had experimented with typesetting machines since the 1820s, but none was put to use until 1872 when the *London Times* bought a half-dozen still primitive contraptions. A more efficient device appeared in 1884 when Ottmar Mergenthaler, a German who had emigrated to the United States, produced an apparatus soon to be known as a linotype, a machine that produced lines of type. Rather than laying out metal letters one by one as in manual typesetting, the linotype created an entire line not of metal letters but of a mold of those letters. A typewriter-style keyboard that hammered the impressions of letters into a matrix of plaster formed the mold. The linotype then poured into the mold a liquid lead alloy that, after drying, formed a solid metal line of raised letters. The machine justified the lines by inserting blank spaces of appropriate width. Each linotype was costly, about three thousand 1890 dollars, but one linotype operator could do the work of six artisan typesetters. The innovation quickly paid for itself, though not without some protest from the workers affected. A few Parisian papers had installed linotype machines by the early 1890s, but they did not come into widespread use until 1900. At that point typesetting finally reached mechanized speeds consonant with those the rotary presses had achieved three decades earlier. Not only could mass-circulation newspapers circulate more copies but they could now produce papers of six, eight, and even twelve pages instead of the four pages standard until the turn of the century.[66]

With technology in place and the content oriented to a mass readership, the penny press possessed the potential to market its wares not just in Paris but throughout the whole of the nation. All that remained was to devise an efficient means of distribution. Traditionally, newspapers had been sold by subscription and dispersed through the mails. This system suited the small-circulation elite press of the preindustrial age, but it could not accommodate the intentions of Moses Millaud; the readers he hoped to capture could not afford to pay for several months of a paper all at once. They could buy only one issue at a time, and to reach them Millaud employed a small army of ambulant newsboys to sell his journal—and only his journal—in the streets of Paris. To secure provincial readers, the *Petit journal* imitated the methods pioneered some fifteen years earlier by the left-wing press of the Second Republic. In an effort to reach rural voters, the democratic-socialist press of 1848 had sent packets of newspapers to train stations newly built in population centers throughout the country. From these stations provincial peddlers, or *colporteurs*, took the papers deep into the countryside where they offered them to peasants and rural artisans hungry for political news.[67]

After 1863 Millaud would do much the same thing, only on a considerably larger scale. He established depots at most of France's growing number of train stations and engaged scores of ambulant news sellers to market them in the surrounding towns and villages. Millaud's strategy proved a brilliant success, and by 1880 *Le Petit journal* had achieved a circulation of nearly 600,000—having grown from 220,000 in 1872. In the course of this rapid and unprecedented expansion, the paper captured more than 25 percent of the entire Paris market for daily newspapers. It demonstrated even greater success in the provinces, so much so that by 1911 it was selling 80 percent of its 800,000 daily issues outside the nation's capital.[68] The figures were similar for the paper's nearest rival, the *Petit parisien*, which by 1910 possessed 13,500 sales depots around the country and marketed 75 percent of its copies in the provinces.[69]

It is interesting that Millaud's journal, as well as France's other mass-circulation newspapers, earned most of its revenue not from advertising, as contemporary American newspapers do, but from single-copy sales. In 1905, with the *Petit journal*'s circulation at about 850,000, the paper received 75 percent of its income from news-stand or ambulant sales. Only 3 percent came from subscriptions and 20 percent from advertising. As for the *Petit parisien*, it earned 85 percent of its gross receipts in 1905 from sales of individual news-papers and only 14 percent from advertising. These percentages were typical for both newspapers during the entire period from 1880 to 1914.[70] Such overwhelming dependence on single-copy sales for the newspapers' revenue required the mass-circulation dailies to double and redouble their efforts to peddle newspapers.

Sensationalist reportage and suspenseful *romans-feuilletons* were not enough; newspapers like the *Petit journal* and the *Petit parisien* deemed it necessary to set up elaborate advertising campaigns to attract readers and sponsor contests in which individuals could win fantastic prizes.

In 1903 the *Petit parisien* invited its readers to guess the number of grains of wheat contained in an empty wine bottle. A drawing of the bottle, whose label read "Une fortune dans une bouteille," appeared daily in the paper during the three-week competition. Individuals had to write their name, address, and estimate on a form printed in the paper and send it to the *Petit parisien*'s headquarters. First prize was the substantial sum of 25,000 francs in cash. Second was a house twenty minutes' drive from Paris worth 15,000 francs, third a summer cottage at the beach valued at 12,000 francs, fourth and fifth were new automobiles worth 4,900 and 4,100 francs respectively. Other prizes, all listed individually and said to be valued at 200,000 francs, ranged from thirteen motorized cycles to a piano, perfume, rugs, jewelry, and dinnerware, all selected from the "elegant" catalogue of the Parisian department store the *Grands magasins du Louvre*.[71] Of all the prizes, only the vehicles—the two cars and the mopeds—were pictured, emphasizing the element of modernist technological fantasy to which the contest appealed. In 1903 a car, much more than a house or cash, was an item so new and so fantastic as to lie beyond even the imagination of the overwhelming majority of the *Petit parisien*'s readers.* In sponsoring such a contest the newspaper not only enticed new readers, it dispensed fantasy. Like articles of *actualité* and installments of fiction, the contest offered the possibility of escape from the mundane world of the everyday. But for all its element of fantasy, the contest held out one thing that journalism itself could not: the possibility of changing one's life. Stories of fact and fiction could lift readers out of their everyday lives only emotionally and mentally; the contest could make them rich.

These promotions attracted great interest during the years from

---

* Other Parisian newspapers quickly imitated the *Petit parisien*'s idea of mobilizing readers through contests and promotions. Some attracted attention by sponsoring sporting events; others organized the events themselves, as *Le Matin* did with its Tour de France automobile race of 1899 and its air show of 1910. Newspapers sponsored referenda on capital punishment, divorce, marriage, and other pressing cultural and political issues to draw in even more readers.

1900 to 1914, but because they were often expensive to run, costing as much as 250,000 francs, only the largest and wealthiest papers could afford the financial burden they imposed. As a result the *quatre grands*, newspapers that by the eve of the war accounted for 40 percent of the nation's total daily circulation (75 percent in Paris), were able to draw increasing numbers of readers, often at the expense of other, less solvent, journals.[72] Since France's papers earned the overwhelming portion of their gross incomes from single-copy sales, the more readers the *quatre grands* attracted, the less the bulk of the others could earn. The French population hardly grew at all during the two decades prior to World War I, which meant that in most cases one journal's increase in readers was another journal's loss. Indeed, some papers lost so many readers that they could not continue in print. In 1882, when France possessed only one mass-circulation daily, the *Petit journal*, ninety different newspapers were published every day in Paris. In 1892, following the rise of the *Petit parisien*, the number had declined to 79 and by 1914, to 57. The number of provincial dailies declined more slowly, mainly because most were so local in scope that they did not compete with the major Paris journals. But the provincial papers that did compete declined precipitously in number. Lyon boasted twelve dailies in 1892 but only two in 1914, Grenoble seven in 1892 and only one on the eve of the war.[73] As a result, the *quatre grands* not only turned newspaper publishing into a virtual oligopoly but increasingly centralized the production of journalistic knowledge and mass culture in Paris. France's vaunted regional diversity may have persisted into the twentieth century, but on the eve of the Great War the nation's culture was more homogenous than ever before.

Because the *quatre grands* drew off so much of the French readership, the rest of the French press had to find other ways to compensate for stable or declining circulations. They did so by accepting payments, often from foreign governments, but also from French business and the French state, for favorable coverage of their political or financial affairs. Banks and enterprises such as the Panama Canal Company paid "subsidies" to various newspapers for the purpose, as the journalist Georges d'Avenel put it in 1901, of "creating or maintaining a favorable climate of opinion around their business ventures even when nothing newsworthy is actually going on."[74] Publicists for the enterprises often wrote articles flattering to their operations, which were inserted in the business sections of the newspapers as genuine reportage. Moreover, columns analyzing the advances and declines of the stock market tended to be little more than advertisements for the companies that subsidized the journal in question. These analyses typically singled out the companies' own stocks as excellent values and encouraged readers to buy them. Banks used such subsidized articles to promote their bond issues, as did foreign governments in hopes of raising substantial sums from French investors.

One enterprise in particular, Charles de Lesseps's Panama Canal Company, contributed an enormous amount of money—about 13 million francs between 1880 and 1888—to French newspapers in an effort to disguise from potential investors the extremely difficult technical and financial obstacles facing the canal project. Payments seemed to be made not according to the size of a paper's circulation but to the journal's perceived influence within the political and economic elite. Thus the *Petit journal* (circulation 900,000) received about 500,000 francs in subsidies, while the society-oriented *Le Figaro*, selling 80,000 copies per day, received slightly more. Meanwhile *Le Temps* (circulation 30,000), the paper branded by the Marxist leader Jules Guesde as "la bourgeoisie faite journal" (the bourgeoisie embodied in a newspaper), received some 1.8 million francs in Panama largesse.[75]

Thanks to the revelations of *L'Humanité*, which became the official organ of the French Communist party in 1920, Russia's prewar subsidies to the French press are well documented. In the early 1920s Soviet leaders gave the editors of *L'Humanité* copies of captured czarist records that they hoped would discredit both French capitalism and the Russian old regime. These documents, published in a volume indelicately titled *The Abominable Venality of the Press* (1931), demonstrated that the Russians—often with the tacit support of the French government itself—sought to use Paris newspapers to win public support for their foreign policy and for their efforts to raise money from French investors. Between 1889 and 1904 the Russians placed 5.5 billion francs of bonds on the French market, an effort that cost them a relatively modest average of 200,000 to 300,000 francs per year in subsidies to the Parisian press. By 1905, however, with French investors increasingly wary of Russian bonds in the wake of the czar's disastrous war with Japan and the revolution of 1905, the Russians felt it necessary to raise their annual subsidies to more than 2 million francs.[76] Though the effects of the Russian war and revolution on French investors had subsided by 1910, the czar's financial adviser in Paris, Arthur Raffalovitch, nonetheless considered it crucial for his government to continue to pay the French press for favorable treatment of Russian interests. "It is important," Raffalovitch wrote, "to have at our disposal a few respected organs such as the *Journal des débats* and *Le Temps*, as well as some mass-circulation journals such as the *Petit parisien, Le Journal*, and perhaps *L'Echo de Paris*."[77] Poincaré's ability, after 1911, to maintain a controversial military alliance with Russia stemmed in part from Raffalovitch's success in keeping French journals at "our disposal."*

Though Calmette does not seem to have been at anyone's financial disposal in his efforts to discredit Joseph Caillaux, the "abominable venality of the press" became part of the Caillaux Affair nonetheless. Joseph Caillaux defended himself against *Le Figaro*'s insinuations of treasonous behavior by accusing Calmette's paper of being the real agent of disloyalty to France. He denounced *Le Figaro* for maintaining a venal attachment to Krupp, the powerful German metallurgical firm and armament manufacturer, and for taking payments from the Hungarian government in exchange for favorable coverage. He accused *Le Figaro,* in other words, of aiding and abetting the enemy both by supporting its armaments industry and by championing the interests of its key ally, Hungary.[78] In his testimony on the trial's second day Caillaux referred to a claim allegedly made by the German socialist leader Karl Liebknecht that Krupp had paid *Le Figaro* a "subsidy" to print articles designed to encourage the movement for a military buildup in Germany. The implication was that *Le Figaro*'s greed had so corrupted its nationalism that the paper was willing to do almost anything to bring France and Germany to the brink of war, even if it meant forming an unholy alliance with Krupp. Caillaux referred to this supposed arrangement with Krupp only in passing and perhaps had little concrete evidence to support it, for when *Le Figaro*'s chairman of

---

* Joseph Caillaux, among others on the French left, sought above all to reduce the very Franco-German tensions that the Russian alliance exacerbated.

the board challenged these allegations the Radical leader did not persist.

Caillaux's case with respect to Hungary, however, was much better documented. He seems to have received information compromising to Calmette directly from a Hungarian national named Lipscher, who had been the intermediary in *Le Figaro*'s negotiations with Budapest.[79] As part of his testimony, Caillaux read from a translation of Hungary's congressional record in which a member of that country's parliamentary opposition condemned his government for purchasing favorable coverage from *Le Figaro*. Since the Hungarian government supported Germany while the opposition sided with France, Caillaux used this incident to suggest that Calmette was so venal as to violate basic national interests. The Hungarian opposition deputy to whom Caillaux referred had based his allegations on a copy of a contract between the Hungarian prime minister, Count Tisza, and *Le Figaro* that Lipscher had arranged in 1913. Officially, Lipscher was to serve as Calmette's correspondent in Budapest, but his contract was curious to say the least. It reversed the normal arrangement of work and payment, stipulating that he would pay *Le Figaro* for publishing his articles, instead of its paying him. Lipscher was to forward to *Le Figaro* 30,000 francs per year in cash for "rendering political services to the Hungarian government" plus an additional 10,000 francs for publicizing Hungary's tourist attractions and thermal spas. All articles destined for *Le Figaro* were to be written by members of the Hungarian government's official press office.[80]

In response to these allegations Georges Prestat, Calmette's father-in-law and *Le Figaro*'s chairman of the board, maintained that *Le Figaro* had rebuffed Krupp's efforts to place articles in their paper. As for Lipscher and the Hungarians, Prestat claimed that *Le Figaro*'s contract with them was purely to publicize certain Hungarian spas; it had nothing to do with diplomacy or foreign policy. Lipscher had indeed sent two articles to *Le Figaro*, both of which were published, but Prestat insisted that as soon as colleagues in Budapest questioned the correspondent's credentials Calmette immediately broke all relations with him. With respect to the 30,000-franc cash payment, "*Le Figaro* never received a single centime, neither directly nor indirectly, neither from Lipscher nor from anyone else."[81]

This denial was not wholly convincing, for Caillaux had quoted

Count Tisza, again from his translation of the Hungarian congressional record, as admitting some contact with Calmette's paper: "As far as *Le Figaro* is concerned," the count declared, "I believe I remember that the journal wanted to obtain a subsidy [from us]." Caillaux also cited evidence that the payment offered to *Le Figaro* could not have been purely to publicize its spas. In a letter from *Le Figaro* cited in Hungary's parliamentary transcript, the paper's publicity director referred to *two* payments from Lipscher, the one for the 30,000 francs mentioned above, plus another for 10,000 francs to finance an illustrated travel supplement featuring Hungary's "thermal bath resorts." Caillaux concluded from this evidence that the 30,000-franc payment was not for tourism but for pro-Hungarian propaganda in direct contradiction to French interests.[82] Whether or not Caillaux's allegations were true—and it appears that *Le Figaro* may well have accepted the Hungarian subsidy—he was shrewd to make them. The venality of the press was so common and so well known that jurors and newspaper readers could easily imagine that Calmette himself had been corrupt.

Their conjectures may have grown after Caillaux presented to the court a copy of Calmette's will showing that since ascending to the directorship of *Le Figaro* he had become one of the wealthiest men in France.[83]

"How, Monsieur, did you obtain [Calmette's will]?" asked Judge Albanel.

"The same way," Caillaux responded, "that Calmette obtained the 'Ton Jo' letter."

Caillaux then proceeded to read aloud sections of Calmette's testament. To do so was irregular at best: wills were confidential documents and Caillaux could have obtained a copy only by taking advantage of his former position as government minister. But the trial as a whole had been nothing if not irregular—with the recital of embarrassing intimate correspondence, the discussion of top secret diplomatic documents, the potential duel between Albanel and Dagoury—that no one even tried to prevent Caillaux from making Calmette's will public. Chenu would have been well advised, however, to stop him, for the testament made the editor's fortune appear highly suspect. Calmette's own lower-middle-class family had left him nothing; before he married Georges Prestat's daughter, Calmette possessed little beyond his modest income as a journalist.

Yet by the time of his death eighteen years later he was in a position to leave thirteen million francs to his heirs. Ten million of that sum he had inherited from two wealthy individuals "in memory of the devotion I showed them" as Calmette put it in his will. But the other three million he had acquired on his own, presumably as a result of the power and influence he owed to his position at the pinnacle of French journalism. It was a sum of money, declared Caillaux, that "our bourgeois families would need one hundred fifty years to acquire."[84] With this last comment Caillaux sought to bring Calmette's alleged avariciousness home. Legitimate fortunes, he implied, are built up over centuries; only illegitimate ones can be acquired in a mere eighteen years. Calmette had become wealthy, Caillaux wanted the court to believe, through the "abominable venality of the press," through the illicit payments he and his paper had received for propagating the interests of foreign governments.

However Calmette had acquired his three million francs—and foreign governments were only one possible source—clearly knowledge represented more than power alone for France's magnates of the press; it was money as well. Wealth brought with it yet more power, ultimately allowing Calmette to achieve a political goal that had eluded the president of the Republic himself. The editor of *Le Figaro* had indeed acquired the power to bring Caillaux down, but only at the cost of his own, prosperous, life.

Epilogue

·

On the eighth day—28 July 1914—the lawyers' summations began. Charles Chenu rehearsed virtually the whole of the trial, retouching the portrait of Henriette and Joseph Caillaux he had painted throughout. Henriette, he maintained once again, had committed her act calmly, deliberately, and with premeditation, impelled to murder Calmette by a vengeful husband whose political ambitions knew no bounds. "In this marriage," he declared, "there was an emulation of pride and of anger. Because they both agreed . . . that Calmette had to die, and because Madame shoots as well as Monsieur—and runs less risk for doing so—it was she who took on the task."[1] In portraying both Caillaux as motivated by ambition and politics alone, Chenu represented Henriette as more male than female, so unwomanly as to merit no indulgence from the court. And he rendered the Caillaux morally unsympathetic by casting them as selfish individualists for whom the sacrament of marriage meant nothing at all.

Maître Labori, for his part, dwelt on the psychology of Henriette Caillaux's captive will, on her act as a tragic result of unbridled female passions. He went so far as to introduce new evidence concerning Henriette's mental state, a memo written by "one of the most eminent specialists from the Paris faculty of medicine." The memo claimed, as we have seen, that Madame Caillaux was governed on 16 March 1914 by "a subconscious impulse that resulted in a split personality."[2] Labori questioned the motives of Berthe Gueydan, whose failure to destroy the *lettres intimes*, the defense attorney claimed, had made the entire drama possible. Without these letters there would have been no crime of passion, for Madame Caillaux would have had nothing to fear from Gaston Calmette. In making this claim, Labori emphasized once again that his client had killed not out of any masculine need for political revenge but out of a wholly, if irrationally, feminine desire to preserve her sexual reputation.

In these closing arguments both attorneys could not but refer, however obliquely, to a European military and diplomatic situation worsening by the hour. By doing so each sought to harness national sentiments to his own courtroom cause. Labori's was the more eloquent of the two patriotic pleas, for he had far more at stake. In asking the twelve jurors to acquit Madame Caillaux, the defense attorney urged the court—and his countrymen at large—not to punish his client, but to "preserve our anger for our enemies from without." Rather than condemn Henriette Caillaux, he concluded, French men and women must "proceed united as one . . . toward the perils that threaten us, the perils that we must now confront as we reach, at long last, the end of these overly long debates."[3]

Outside the courtroom, large and rapidly growing crowds were gathering to await a verdict toward which, it seemed, no one was indifferent. The journalist Geneviève Tabouis wrote that "Paris waited breathlessly for the news on the day of the verdict. All thought of war was forgotten. The Palais de Justice had become the battlefield where the political war was carried out between the Right and the Left. That morning, several self-appointed judges had fought duels over the trial."[4]

The jury retired from the chamber to begin its deliberations at 7:55 P.M. By 8:20 it returned to the courtroom—but not yet to deliver its verdict. The citizen-magistrates had two questions for Judge Albanel, both relating to the length of the sentences Madame Caillaux could receive according to the criminal code. Fortified with Albanel's responses, the panel retired once again, only to return some thirty minutes later. Now, after less than an hour of deliberations, the jurors were ready to reveal their verdict.

"Is Madame Caillaux guilty of committing, on 16 March, a voluntary homicide against Gaston Calmette?" asked Judge Albanel in the first of the two questions he was required to pose to the jury.

"On my honor and my conscience," the foreman responded, "before God and before all men, the decision of the jury is NO."

The second prescribed question now seemed superfluous, and it was barely audible amidst the bellows of anger and joy already filling the room. "Was the said homicide committed with premeditation and criminal intent?"

"No," again was the foreman's response, confirming an acquittal that the jury had voted eleven to one.[5]

At this, Madame Caillaux threw her arms around Fernand Labori, and this time she did not faint. The courtroom erupted into
howls of anger and cries of victory as, moments later, did the
swelling crowd outside.[6] Instantly, chants of "As-sas-sin! as-sas-
sin!" began to compete with shouts of "Vive Caillaux," "vive Labori!" A cordon of municipal guards immediately blocked the entrance to the Palais de Justice, attempting at the same time to keep
the two opposing sides from coming to blows. Though the crowd
seemed little concerned with the Austro-Serbian war declared earlier in the day, the outbreak of hostilities in the Balkans had doubtless exacerbated the domestic political tensions already heightened
by the trial. Members of the extreme right-wing *Action française*
attacked Caillaux's most vocal supporters in the crowd, many of
them Corsican toughs recruited specially for the occasion. And after
police dispersed the mostly young street fighters from the Ile de la
Cité, enemies and partisans of Caillaux headed toward the *grands
boulevards* where they would continue the brawl.

Meanwhile, Joseph Caillaux himself seemed in danger of physical violence, even death. Hostile crowds chanting "Death to Caillaux!" descended on the Caillaux' residence, as Joseph and Henriette received friends and supporters, and a flood of anonymous
phone calls threatened the Radical leader with assassination. After
the murder of Socialist leader Jean Jaurès on 31 July, Jean-Louis
Malvy, minister of the interior and Caillaux's loyal friend, judged
the danger so grave that he urged Caillaux to leave Paris immediately. This was sound advice, for Raoul Villain, the nationalist
fanatic who had murdered Jaurès, apparently planned to kill Caillaux as well. The assassin's confessor, Father Calvet, later wrote
that Villain had bought a pair of identical revolvers in the wake of
Calmette's death. On the grip of one he had carved the initial J; on
the other, C.[7]

Henriette Caillaux seemed virtually forgotten in the tense atmosphere of impending war that followed her acquittal, but not her
husband. Never before in his tumultuous political career had Joseph Caillaux been threatened with death.[8] Now in the aftermath of
the Caillaux Affair, a perilous moment of impending war when
leaders consecrated a "sacred union" of all the French, Caillaux had
come to symbolize what the fatherland could no longer be. At a time
when France endeavored to recreate itself as one holy family in a

union sacrée, Caillaux appeared to subvert the very family life believed to give the nation its strength. As Maurice Barrès would later write, mixing the metaphors of family and nation, Joseph Caillaux had "invented a new kind of treason: a lack of faith in his country. He is a man who believes not in the virtue of his mother. With him there is an element of parricide."[9] Revealing no allegiance to the family, to the purity of mothers or the authority of fathers, to the virtue of women or the honor of men, Caillaux could not but betray the Fatherland itself.

Before the trial President Poincaré had reportedly confided to Jean Dupuy, editor of *Le Petit parisien*, that he would have no choice but to appoint Caillaux prime minister "if his wife is acquitted."[10] But after the trial, acquittal and all, such an appointment was out of the question. Joseph Caillaux had come to represent the antithesis of the values embodied in the *union sacrée*. He was now a single symbolic enemy against whom all French patriots could unite.

Henriette Caillaux, for her part, emerged from the trial intact, even vindicated by a verdict that resulted largely from her skilled portrayal of a fragile woman driven over the emotional edge by a compromising *lettre intime*. Henriette had depicted her act as a crime of passion, as the tragic result of an effort to preserve her honor, and this had done much to sway the court to her side. Not only had female passion absolved Madame Caillaux of responsibility for her crime; it had enabled her to escape punishment for the moral consequences of divorce.

Henriette Caillaux could be forgiven these transgressions because she appeared to affirm the traditional conceptions of a gender order increasingly in doubt. The trial of Madame Caillaux had occurred at a time of growing confusion about the nature of masculinity and femininity, a time in which perceptions—especially male perceptions—of the lines separating the sexes had become increasingly blurred. And because of the unprecedented readership and influence of the penny press, this cultural confusion, with its attendant male fears, had permeated French society, affecting Parisian life most of all. In the midst of this uncertainty, men of the middle and upper classes, hoping to strengthen their masculinity through honor and the duel, found themselves disoriented even more as some commentators called dueling itself a display of feminine hypersensitivity. In the meantime, women's efforts to achieve

a measure of equality within the family and a toehold in the professions outside it increased male apprehension still more. Women's
emancipation, it was widely believed, not only subverted the authority of husbands and fathers, it weakened the nation as well.

In an effort to overcome these anxieties and restore their rightful
place, men turned in growing numbers to a set of conservative
values and beliefs concerning marriage, family, and sexuality, beliefs once enshrined in the hierarchic gender order of the Napoleonic Code. That they did so at a time when France's parliamentary
politics leaned regularly to the left only emphasized the depth of
their uneasiness over the question of gender. In this context, Madame Caillaux's ability to turn herself into the real woman of masculine myth did much to absolve her of the cultural and political
threat her husband had been made to represent.

Neither Joseph nor Henriette Caillaux would lead an easy life in the
years following her trial, but for him the decade from 1914 to 1924
would be especially cruel. The affair's damaging portrait of Caillaux's moral life followed by the outbreak of war not only prevented
him from returning to government; it began a process that would
culminate in his own imprisonment for "intelligence with the enemy," for crimes against the extended family of wartime France.
Though charged unjustly, Caillaux was nearly executed for treason
in 1918. It is true that he had unwisely consorted with some disrep-
utable—even pro-German—individuals during the war, but the
essential reasons for his persecution lay in public perceptions of his
politics and his morals that had been shaped and reinforced by
Henriette's trial. Writing in the *Action française* in 1920, Léon Daudet
doubtless expressed the views of Clemenceau and Poincaré as well
in maintaining that the wartime arrest of Caillaux had "delivered a
mortal blow against radicalism in the person of *Ton Jo.*"[11]

Even after the war and his release from prison in 1920, Joseph
Caillaux remained enormously unpopular. Noisy demonstrations
followed him almost everywhere he went. Restaurants and hotels
refused him service, and strangers insulted him on the street. Even
former friends condemned him in the columns of the press. He was
secure only in his rural home at Mamers, where he devoted himself
to the memoirs he hoped would justify his earlier life. He attacked
this project with such determination that Rudolph Binion has aptly

labeled him "a perennial defendant, reduced from making history to writing it."[12]

Caillaux was not, however, to remain at Mamers for good. When the fiercely conservative political climate of the postwar years diminished and the moderate left returned to power in 1924, Joseph returned as well, achieving a political comeback unimaginable a year or two earlier. France's economy was faltering, and the Radicals needed an experienced minister of finance who would not alienate the Socialists upon whom they depended for support: Caillaux was their only choice. His reputation as a genius of finance had remained intact, while his wartime martyrdom had earned him the Socialists' trust, almost as if his suffering at the hands of the right had absolved the sins of his capitalist past. But unfortunately for the left, and perhaps for the country as a whole, Caillaux was no longer the man he had been a decade before. Berthe Gueydan's niece Isabelle, who had not seen him for many years, wrote that "his ordeals, the nights without sleep, had marked him."[13] France's political transformations had marked him as well, for by the mid-1920s, with the emergence of a vocal Communist party and a powerful Socialist one, Joseph Caillaux was no longer a man of the left, as the Marxists soon understood. In the new political context, his opposition to "collectivism," to the nationalization of an economy he believed should remain in private hands, placed him in the center or even on the right.

French conservatives, however, never forgave him for Agadir, for the income tax, or for being *Ton Jo,* and he spent the rest of his long career consigned to a political no-man's-land of neither left nor right.[14] Still he wielded no small measure of power, albeit mostly negative, playing a major role in the fall of Léon Blum's Popular Front government in 1937. And if living long is the best revenge, he was able to take a certain pleasure in simply outlasting all his old rivals; Clemenceau, Poincaré, Barthou, and Briand—all preceded him in death.[15] Caillaux remained a member of the French Senate until the Franco-German armistice of June 1940. He died shortly after the liberation in November 1944.

As for Henriette Caillaux, though she suffered no imprisonment for her crime, she too would never escape the echoes of her past. In November 1914, having accompanied Joseph on a wartime mission to Brazil, Henriette found herself shunned by Rio's high society, as much for her divorce as for the assassination of Calmette.[16] She experienced as her husband did the indignity of being refused service in restaurants and hotels and confronted hostile demonstrations almost everywhere she traveled. On one occasion, a well-dressed woman sat down across from Henriette and, without uttering a word, laid a revolver on the table.[17] She had to endure, moreover, Joseph's fatal attractions to extramarital *liaisons élégantes*.[18]

Still, Henriette remained wealthy enough to live a comfortable life and allowed herself to enjoy the advantages she possessed. Late in life she turned to scholarship, earning a diploma from the Ecole du Louvre in 1933 with a thesis on the sculptor Aimé-Jules Dalou, a work she published in 1935.[19] Madame Caillaux's next project was a study of the painter Van Eyck; when she attempted to deliver a lecture on that work, members of the *Action française*, seldom seen on such erudite occasions, prevented her from speaking.[20] The extreme right would never allow her to forget her past, and after this event she seems to have withdrawn to the Caillaux home at Mamers and to her own property at Cheffes in the Maine-et-Loire. Her diploma and her scholarship notwithstanding, Joseph continued to view Henriette as he always had, as a bourgeois and domestic goddess. On the eve of a trip to Mamers in 1941, Joseph, seventy-eight years old, wrote that he looked forward to returning to his ancestral home and to "the Woman who is its guardian angel."[21]

Unfortunately for Berthe Gueydan, Joseph Caillaux had never used such imagery to capture her. Though the divorce settlement gave her a certain financial security, she was unable to overcome its emotional consequences. She did not remarry and, according to Isabelle Couturier de Chefdubois, lived out the rest of her years in bitterness and jealousy.[22] Berthe Gueydan had imagined life as a queen of the Third Republic; when she was humiliated and abandoned by one of its kings, she turned against the regime itself. Madame Gueydan became a political reactionary, taking her ultimate revenge by writing a right-wing history of the Republic that blamed all its putative faults on the sins of Joseph Caillaux.[23]

Thus for Berthe Gueydan—as for Henriette and Joseph Caillaux—the Caillaux Affair ensured that the Belle Epoque would live on for them as memory and motive, as the time against which they would always measure the rest of their lives. But for French society as a whole, the *affaire Caillaux* was to be this beautiful era's closing event. Many of the distinctive manners and mores that had helped give the Belle Epoque its name were banished forever in the physical and moral carnage of the Great War of 1914. In particular, the war rendered the duel virtually extinct, for during the four long years it lasted French men were forced to test their honor in ways no subsequent duel could ever reproduce. As for the Belle Epoque's peculiar mélange of public chastity and private transgression, this too largely succumbed by the 1920s to a relative sexual openness and a growing equality between the sexes in marriage. The war itself, by giving French women important responsibilities on the home front, did much to make these developments possible. Even so, France was slow to give women's economic and cultural gains their requisite political expression. It was not until 1944 that French women would win the right to vote.

In many ways, then, the trial of Madame Caillaux marked the end of a pivotal era of modern French life, an era whose embryonic efforts to forsake the culture and values of the nineteenth century only revealed how persistent those mores could be. The Caillaux Affair did not, of course, cause the era's demise; only the war could have had so profound an effect. But as a historical episode that, for one week in July 1914, probed the boundaries between private life and high politics, between the province of women and the realm of men, the Caillaux Affair gives us a Belle Epoque richer perhaps than the one we knew.

Notes

PROLOGUE

1. Marcel Proust, whose manuscript *Swann's Way* had brought him nothing but rejections from publishers, dedicated his great work to Gaston Calmette after the latter convinced Grasset to bring it out. The dedication reads:

> To Monsieur Gaston Calmette
> as a testament to my profound
> and affectionate gratitude
> Marcel Proust

2. Such, at any rate, was what Bourget quoted Calmette as having said, in testimony at Madame Caillaux's trial. Transcript—*Le Figaro*, 22 July 1914. All translations of French are my own unless otherwise noted.

3. See the account in *Gil Blas*, 7 April 1914, as well as the transcripts of the trial's first three days printed in *Le Figaro, Le Temps, Le Petit parisien*, and most other Paris dailies on 21–23 July 1914. Since all those who observed these events immediately after the gunshot—including Madame Caillaux—described them in almost exactly the same way, I have felt free to present this part of the narrative not as a "representation" of what occurred but as the pure events themselves. In this discussion as in the chapters to follow, I am indebted to several excellent narrative accounts of the Caillaux Affair. See Paulette Houdyer, *L'affaire Caillaux . . . ainsi finit la belle époque* (Les Sables-d'Olonne: Editions le cercle d'or, 1977); Benjamin F. Martin, *The Hypocrisy of Justice in the Belle Epoque* (Baton Rouge: Louisiana State University Press, 1984); John N. Raphael, *The Caillaux Drama* (London: Max Goschen, 1914); Peter Shankland, *Death of an Editor: The Caillaux Drama* (London: William Kimber, 1981); Charles-Maurice Chenu, *Le procès de Madame Caillaux* (Paris: Fayard, 1960).

4. The *Cour d'assises*, or Assize Court, was reserved for felony cases, often those involving a possible sentence of death.

5. On the ultimatum and the events leading to Austria's declaration of war on Serbia, see L. C. F. Turner, *Origins of the First World War* (London: Edward Arnold, 1970), ch. 5. See also Fritz Fischer's now-famous discussion of Germany's interest in encouraging an ultimatum Serbia would be

unable to accept, in *Germany's Aims in the First World War* (New York: Norton, 1967), pp. 61–72.

6. John F. V. Keiger, *France and the Origins of the First World War* (London: Macmillan, 1983), p. 147.

7. Roger Martin du Gard, *Les Thibault*, vol. 3, *L'été 1914* (Paris: Gallimard, 1936), p. 269.

8. Jean-Jacques Becker, *1914: comment les Français sont entrés dans la guerre* (Paris: Presses de la Fondation nationale des sciences politiques, 1977), pp. 131–35.

9. For excellent descriptions of how the *Cour d'assises* operated, see Eugène Sice, *Dictionnaire d'assises* (Paris: Librairie générale de droit et de jurisprudence, 1938); Jean Cruppi, *La cour d'assises* (Paris: Calmann-Lévy, 1898); Robert Gaston, *Le code pratique et expliqué du jury criminel* (Carhaix: Imprimerie du peuple, 1914).

10. Sice, *Dictionnaire d'assises*, pp. 230–31.

11. E. Debois, *Des fonctions du président de la cour d'assises* (Poitiers: Lévrier, 1912), pp. 80–83. Judges did more than simply oversee the action; they did much of the questioning and often did it aggressively. In effect, French defendants had to face a trio of prosecutors: the judge, the government attorney, and the private prosecutor retained by the *partie civile*.

12. On French law and judicial procedures, see Martin, *Hypocrisy of Justice*.

13. The best accounts include Chenu, *Le procès de Madame Caillaux;* René Floriot, *Deux femmes en cour d'assises* (Paris: Hachette, 1966); Houdyer, *L'affaire Caillaux;* Martin, *Hypocrisy of Justice*.

14. Perhaps the most useful recent book on the political and social history of the Belle Epoque is Madeleine Rebérioux's, *La république radicale? 1898–1914* (Paris: Seuil, 1975). Its translation by J. R. Foster, *The Third Republic from Its Origins to the Great War, 1871–1914* (Cambridge: Cambridge University Press, 1984), includes Jean-Marie Mayeur's *Les débuts de la IIIe République* (Paris: Seuil, 1973). For a view of the period considerably more optimistic than Rebérioux's, see Eugen Weber, *France: Fin de Siècle* (Cambridge, Mass.: Harvard University Press, 1986). An excellent general account of the Third Republic up to the Great War is provided by R. D. Anderson, *France, 1870–1914: Politics and Society* (London: Routledge and Kegan Paul, 1977). In *France 1815–1914* (New York: Oxford University Press, 1983), Roger Magraw devotes several useful chapters to the period, as does Theodore Zeldin in *France, 1848–1945,* vol. 1 (Oxford: Clarendon Press, 1973). Two exemplary political biographies illuminate the period, that of Pierre Sorlin, *Waldeck-Rousseau* (Paris: A. Colin, 1966); and of Harvey Goldberg, *The Life of Jean Jaurès* (Madison: University of Wisconsin Press, 1962). Still useful are Jacques Chastenet's now classic works on the period: *La belle époque* (Paris: Fayard, 1949); *La France de monsieur Faillières* (Paris: Fayard, 1949); and *Histoire de la Troisième République*, vols. 3 and 4 (Paris: Hachette, 1955). On the era's abortive attempts to achieve social reform, see Judith F. Stone, *The Search for Social Peace: Reform Legislation in France, 1890–*

1914 (Albany: State University of New York Press, 1985) and Sanford Elwitt, *The Third Republic Defended: Bourgeois Reform in France, 1880–1914* (Baton Rouge: Louisiana State University Press, 1986).

15. Emmanuel Le Roy Ladurie, *Montaillou: The Promised Land of Error,* trans. Barbara Day (New York: Penguin Books, 1978); Natalie Zemon Davis, *The Return of Martin Guerre* (Cambridge, Mass.: Harvard University Press, 1983); Carlo Ginzburg, *The Cheese and the Worms: The Cosmos of a Sixteenth-Century Miller,* trans. John and Anne Tedeschi (New York: Penguin Books, 1982). See also several important other works of "microhistory": Judith C. Brown, *Immodest Acts: The Life of a Lesbian Nun in Renaissance Italy* (New York: Oxford University Press, 1986); Gene Brucker, *Giovanni and Lusanna: Love and Marriage in Renaissance Florence* (Berkeley: University of California Press, 1986); Pietro Redondi, *Galileo Heretic-Galileo eretico* (Princeton: Princeton University Press, 1987); Joseph Shatzmiller, *Shylock Reconsidered: Jews, Moneylending, and Medieval Society* (Berkeley: University of California Press, 1990). Other works in this vein—even though they do not center on trials—include Georges Duby, *Le dimanche de Bouvines* (Paris: Gallimard, 1973); and Robert Darnton, *The Great Cat Massacre, and Other Episodes in French Cultural History* (New York: Basic Books, 1984). Many of the American microhistories have been influenced by Clifford Geertz's famous essay, "Deep Play: Notes on the Balinese Cockfight," in his *Interpretation of Cultures* (New York: Basic Books, 1973). Geertz's work, currently under attack by fellow anthropologists for being insufficiently "dialogical," nonetheless remains fundamental for cultural historians. For the critique of Geertz, see George E. Marcus and Michael M. J. Fischer, *Anthropology as Cultural Critique: An Experimental Moment in the Human Sciences* (Chicago: University of Chicago Press, 1986); Steven Webster, "Dialogue and Fiction in Ethnography," *Dialectical Anthropology* 7 (1982). See also Aletta Biersack, "Local Knowledge, Local History: Geertz and Beyond," in Lynn Hunt, ed., *The New Cultural History* (Berkeley: University of California Press, 1989). The microhistories cited above, justly praised when they first appeared, have themselves lately been the object of critical reviews. For a critique of Ginzburg, see Dominick LaCapra, *History and Criticism* (Ithaca: Cornell University Press, 1985), ch. 2. Natalie Davis's work is the subject of a lengthy attack on positivist grounds in Robert Finlay's "The Refashioning of Martin Guerre," *American Historical Review* 93, no. 3 (June 1988), a challenge Davis survives very well indeed with her response, "On the Lame," *American Historical Review* 93, no. 3 (June 1988). Finally, Thomas Kuehn, in "Reading Microhistory: The Example of Giovanni and Lusanna," *Journal of Modern History* 61, no. 3 (September 1989), provides a useful and instructive critique of Gene Brucker's work and of microhistory in general.

16. The original stenographic transcripts are no longer available.

17. "Thick description" is, of course, an interpretive approach associated with the work of Clifford Geertz, from his essay "Thick Description: Toward an Interpretive Theory of Culture," in *Interpretation of Cultures.* For an exemplary effort to understand murder cases involving women in the

social and cultural context of their times, see Mary S. Hartman, *Victorian Murderesses* (New York: Schocken Books, 1977).

18. These scholars will be identified throughout the notes. Here I would like to acknowledge in particular my debt to the work of Jean-Claude Allain, Jean-Jacques Becker, Claude Bellanger, Jean-Denis Bredin, Ruth Harris, Steven C. Hause, Paulette Houdyer, Gerd Krumeich, Joan B. Landes, Benjamin F. Martin, Anne Martin-Fugier, Annelise Maugue, Arno J. Mayer, Claire Goldberg Moses, Robert A. Nye, Karen Offen, Michael B. Palmer, Michelle Perrot, Joan W. Scott, Debora L. Silverman, Bonnie G. Smith, Judith F. Stone, and Bertram Wyatt-Brown.

19. See Robert F. Berkhofer, "The Challenge of Poetics to (Normal) Historical Practice," *Poetics Today* 9, no. 2 (1988), for an argument, based on Roland Barthes's *S/Z* (New York: Farrar, Straus, and Giroux, 1974), that gives up too easily on the possibility that historical evidence and historical writing can refer to a past reality. For similar misunderstandings, see David Harlan, "Intellectual History and the Return of Literature," *American Historical Review* 94, no. 3 (June 1989). A theoretically sound and brilliant corrective to views such as Berkhofer's and Harlan's is Lionel Gossman, "Towards a Rational Historiography," *Transactions of the American Philosophical Society* 79, no. 3 (1989).

20. For an uncritical discussion of Jacques Derrida's notion that there is no "outside-the-text," see E. M. Henning, "Archaeology, Deconstruction, and Intellectual History," in Dominick LaCapra and Steven L. Kaplan, eds., *Modern European Intellectual History* (Ithaca: Cornell University Press, 1982). For an interesting treatment of the problems of text and context, see Dominick LaCapra, "Rethinking Intellectual History and Reading Texts," in *Modern European Intellectual History;* Dominick LaCapra, *Rethinking Intellectual History: Texts, Contexts, Language* (Ithaca: Cornell University Press, 1983), pp. 26–27, 84–117; LaCapra, *History and Criticism*, pp. 81–86. LaCapra's sense of the relations between text and context is so complex that one easily wonders, with John F. Toews, whether "the theory of the linguistic density and complexity of texts, contexts, and their apparently circular relationships outruns its possible utility as either a clarification of, or guide for, historiographical practice." See John F. Toews, "Intellectual History after the Linguistic Turn: The Autonomy of Meaning and the Irreducibility of Experience," *American Historical Review* 92, no. 4 (October 1987): 886.

21. Here I follow Gossman's "Towards a Rational Historiography." Unlike many recent critics of historians and historical practice, especially those influenced by French literary theory, Gossman grounds his discussion in a solid sense of what historians *actually do*, not just when they write their narratives but when they perform their research, integrate and evaluate the work of others, revise and reconceptualize their scholarship in the face of new evidence and critical scrutiny. See also James T. Kloppenberg's interesting argument for assessing historical inquiry on the basis of what he calls a "pragmatic hermeneutics": "Objectivity and Historicism: A Century of

American Historical Writing," *American Historical Review* 94, no. 4 (October 1989).

22. Joan W. Scott enunciates its value in a recent and justly influential essay entitled "Gender: A Useful Category of Historical Analysis." See her *Gender and the Politics of History* (New York: Columbia University Press, 1988), ch. 2.

23. Scott, "Gender," p. 49. There is by now an extensive literature on gender and society in nineteenth-century France. Those from which I have benefited the most include Steven C. Hause, *Women's Suffrage and Social Politics in the French Third Republic* (Princeton: Princeton University Press, 1984); Anne Martin-Fugier, *La bourgeoise: femme au temps de Paul Bourget* (Paris: Grasset, 1983); Annelise Maugue, *L'identité masculine en crise* (Paris: Rivages, 1987); Claire Goldberg Moses, *French Feminism in the Nineteenth Century* (Albany: State University of New York Press, 1984); Karen Offen, "Depopulation, Nationalism, and Feminism in Fin-de-siècle France," *American Historical Review* 89, no. 3 (June 1984); Michelle Perrot, ed., *Une histoire des femmes est-elle possible?* (Paris: Rivages, 1984); Bonnie G. Smith, *Ladies of the Leisure Class* (Princeton: Princeton University Press, 1981).

CHAPTER 1

1. *Le Petit parisien*, 20 July 1914; Jean-Claude Allain, *Joseph Caillaux, Le défi victorieux, 1863–1914* (Paris: Imprimerie nationale, 1978), 1:79–85.

2. *Le Petit parisien*, 20 July 1914.

3. Ibid.; Allain, *Caillaux*, 1:47. For a sense of the Caillaux' privileged position on France's increasingly hierarchic pyramid of wealth, see Adelaine Daumard, Félix-Paul Codaccioni, Georges Dupeux, Jacqueline Herpin, Jacques Godechot, and Jean Sentou, *Les fortunes françaises au XIXe siècle* (Paris: Mouton, 1973).

4. *Mercure de France*, 16 July 1914, review of John N. Raphael, *The Caillaux Drama* (London: Max Goschen, 1914).

5. Raphael, *Caillaux Drama*, pp. 289 ff. French courts possessed the right to forbid jurors from talking about cases outside the courtroom or from receiving information about them but in practice rarely exercised that right. See Eugène Sice, *Dictionnaire d'assises* (Paris: Librairie générale de droit et de jurisprudence, 1938), p. 178.

6. Jean Cruppi, *La cour d'assises* (Paris: Calmann-Lévy, 1898), pp. 21–28. A typical list of 1,500 prospective jurors for the *Cour d'assises* of the Seine (Paris) included, Cruppi found, 849 (56 percent of the total) small tradesmen, artisans, sales representatives, and salaried commercial employees; 281 (19 percent) individuals who lived on rental income or on investments; 174 (12 percent) members of the liberal professions plus civil servants and engineers; 64 (4 percent) retired persons; 57 (4 percent) architects; 53 (3 percent) doctors, veterinarians, and pharmacists; and 22 (1 percent) artists. This list of prospective jurors included no wealthy or elite individuals and no factory workers. The jury for the Caillaux trial mirrored the typical list,

casting doubt on *Le Figaro*'s claim (17–18, 22 May 1914) that government officials had tampered with it on Caillaux's behalf. The twelve Caillaux jurors included seven (58 percent) tradesmen and artisans; two (17 percent) individuals living on investments; two (17 percent) civil servants; and one (8 percent) architect. The list of jurors for the Caillaux trial was published in the *Journal des débats*, 21 July 1914.

7. *Le Petit parisien*, 21 July 1914.

8. On the French law and the possible punishments for murder see Benjamin F. Martin, *The Hypocrisy of Justice in the Belle Epoque* (Baton Rouge: Louisiana State University Press, 1984), p. 205; Peter Shankland, *Death of an Editor: The Caillaux Drama* (London: William Kimber, 1981), p. 149.

9. On the crime of passion defense as romantic melodrama, see Ruth Harris, *Murder and Madness: Medicine, Law, and Society in the Fin de Siècle* (Oxford: Clarendon Press, 1989), pp. 213–28. On the melodramatic mode of discourse itself, see Peter Brooks, *The Melodramatic Imagination: Balzac, Henry James, Melodrama and the Mode of Excess* (New Haven: Yale University Press, 1976). In a recent article on the famous pre-Revolutionary case of the comte de Sanois, Sara Maza underscores the extent to which Sanois's defense attorney Pierre Louis de Lacretelle composed his published brief in the melodramatic mode—a style of writing that excelled in "hyperbolic language, strong emotions, and moral polarization," a "democratic" style designed to convey meanings immediately accessible to even the most unschooled spectators. See Sara Maza, "Domestic Melodrama as Political Ideology: The Case of the Comte de Sanois," *American Historical Review* 94, no. 5 (December 1989): 1257–59.

10. *L'Illustration*, 25 July 1914.

11. *Le Matin*, 21 July 1914.

12. On consumption, shopgirls, and department stores see Rosalind Williams, *Dream Worlds: Mass Consumption in Late Nineteenth-Century France* (Berkeley: University of California Press, 1982); Michael Miller, *The Bon Marché, Bourgeois Culture and the Department Store, 1869–1920* (Princeton: Princeton University Press, 1981).

13. *Le Figaro*, 21 July 1914.

14. *Le Petit journal*, 21 July 1914.

15. *L'Echo de Paris*, 21 July 1914.

16. These theories do not, of course, mean that the criminologists' questions about personal responsibility made them argue in general against the desirability of punishment. As Robert A. Nye and others show, late nineteenth-century theories found justification for punishment in social defense, in the need to protect society from the harm criminals did it and to encourage law-abiding citizens to remain so. Still, as will be clear below, the experts' deterministic explanations of criminal responsibility made the laymen who served as jurors reluctant to convict certain kinds of criminals, especially those who claimed passion as their motive. See Robert A. Nye, *Crime, Madness, and Politics in Modern France* (Princeton: Princeton University Press, 1984). Michel Foucault's *Discipline and Punish*, trans. Alan Sher-

idan (New York: Pantheon, 1977), has sparked interest in the history of crime and criminology in nineteenth-century France; the literature, generally excellent, is large and growing. In addition to Nye's brilliant and pathbreaking study, see Ruth Harris's equally important works, *Murder and Madness* and "Murder under hypnosis in the case of Gabrielle Bompard: psychiatry in the courtroom in Belle Epoque Paris," in W. F. Bynum, Roy Porter, and Michael Shepherd, eds., *The Anatomy of Madness* (London: Tavistock Publications, 1985); Michelle Perrot, ed., *L'impossible prison: recherches sur le système pénitentiaire au XIXe siècle* (Paris: Seuil, 1980); Patricia O'Brien, *The Promise of Punishment* (Princeton: Princeton University Press, 1982); Thomas J. Duesterberg, "Criminology and the Social Order in Nineteenth-century France," Ph.D. diss., Indiana University, 1979.

17. One of these medical experts, Maurice de Fleury, wrote: "Anyone who dares to descend into the depths of himself . . . is obliged to admit that at certain atrocious times he has seen himself, with terror, capable of evil, of some hideous action toward himself or someone else. At certain moments he has had in his mouth the horrible taste of crime." Fleury is quoted in Edouard Toulouse, *Les conflits intersexuels et sociaux* (Paris: Bibliothèque Charpentier, 1904), p. 296. On the question of crime, psychology, and personal responsibility see Harris, "Murder under hypnosis."

18. Transcript—*Le Petit parisien*, 21 July 1914.

19. Ibid.

20. Ibid.

21. Transcript—*Le Temps*, 29 July 1914.

22. *Le Figaro*, 13 March 1914.

23. Transcript—*Le Temps*, 21 July 1914.

24. See *Le Figaro*, 29 July 1914.

25. *Le Temps*, 21 July 1914; *Gil Blas*, 7 April 1914.

26. Transcript—*Le Temps*, 21 July 1914. Harris shows that the tales of suicidal longings were almost formulaic parts of crime-of-passion defenses during the fin-de-siècle period. See Harris, *Murder and Madness*, pp. 213–28.

27. Transcript—*Le Temps*, 21 July 1914.

28. Ibid. According to Harris, society women like Madame Caillaux commonly claimed that their motive for committing a crime of passion was to defend their reputations or to "defend their honor as a woman." They turned to violence, Harris suggests, "in much the same spirit as men engaging in a duel." Harris, *Murder and Madness*, p. 213. For further discussion of women, the crime of passion, and the duel see chapter 5 below.

29. Joseph's testimony, *Le Temps*, 22 July 1914.

30. Transcript—*Le Temps*, 21 July 1914.

31. *Le Petit parisien*, 26 March 1914. This testimony comes from the pretrial *instruction*. It is important to note that Henriette did not repeat it during the trial. Clearly, it implies premeditation.

32. *Le Petit parisien*, 25 March 1914.

33. Transcript—*Le Temps*, 21 July 1914.

34. Cited by Jules Herbaux, the public prosecutor. Transcript—*Le Temps*, 29 July 1914.

35. *L'Autorité*, 17 March 1914, quoted in *La Guerre sociale*, 16–24 March 1914.

36. Chenu quoted these lines in his summation on the eighth and final day. Transcript—*Le Temps*, 29 July 1914.

37. Joseph Caillaux, *Mes mémoires* (Paris: Plon, 1947), 3:83–84.

38. Georges Suarez, *Briand* (Paris: Plon, 1938), 2:481.

39. For these rumors of an extramarital affair, see Rudolph Binion, *Defeated Leaders: The Political Fate of Caillaux, Jouvenel, and Tardieu* (New York: Columbia University Press, 1960), p. 69; Allain, *Caillaux*, 1:423.

40. Transcript—*Le Figaro*, 22 July 1914.

41. See chapters 2 and 4 for a detailed analysis of this conservative attack.

42. Louise Weiss, *Mémoires d'une européenne* (1893–1919) (Paris: Payot, 1968), 1:175.

43. Ibid.

44. Transcript—*Le Temps*, 21 July 1914.

45. Ibid.

46. *Le Figaro*, 30 July 1914.

47. *Les Hommes du jour*, 25 July 1914.

48. *La Lanterne*, 21 and 26 July 1914.

49. *Journal des débats*, 30 July 1914.

50. Transcript—*Le Temps*, 29 July 1914; *Le Figaro*, 30 July 1914.

51. For a more detailed discussion of the "woman question" and the crime of passion see chapter 3. For recent work on women and the crime of passion in France, see Harris, *Murder and Madness*; Joëlle Guillais, *La chair de l'autre: le crime passionnel au XIXe siècle* (Paris: Olivier Orban, 1986). In *Victorian Murderesses* (New York: Schocken Books, 1977), Mary S. Hartman compares British and French murderesses; for an excellent account of the American situation, see Ann Jones, *Women Who Kill* (New York: Ballantine Books, 1988).

52. *La Guerre sociale*, 22 July 1914. Alone among the protagonists in this case, the ultranationalist *Action française* (21 July 1914) was hostile to the way psychology had helped to turn the crime of passion into an excuse for murder. In the editors' view, Caillaux's republican allies hoped to convince jurors that "this crime [had] other motives, intimate and private motives [not criminal ones]. They sought to reduce it to one of these crimes of passion about which it is so easy to confuse jurors and the public at large by drawing on certain psychological theories, theories designed to overwhelm them with that wave of humanitarian indulgence before which all feelings become sacred and equal and which represents the decay of judgment."

53. See for example the work of a leading criminologist, Louis Proal. In *La criminalité féminine* (Paris: Editions de Soye, 1900), Proal deplored the increase in crimes that "result from passions that can no longer be con-

tained" (p. 26). See also Louis Holtz, *Les crimes passionnels* (Paris: Imprimerie A. Mellottée, 1904), p. 62.

54. Louis Proal, *Passion and Criminality in France,* trans. A. R. Allinson (Paris: Charles Carrington, 1901), p. 178.

55. Harris, *Murder and Madness,* p. 210 n.3; Holtz, *Crimes passionnels,* pp. 128–34; Duesterberg, "Criminology and the Social Order," p. 394. Current work by James M. Donovan, "Female Criminality and the Juries in France, 1825–1913" (paper presented to the Western Society for French History, October 1989), confirms Harris's evidence that juries were extremely lenient toward female crimes of passion between 1900 and 1913. Beyond murder rates for Paris alone, the rates of acquittal for all French crimes, especially when broken down by sex, are noteworthy as well. For men, acquittal rates fluctuated between 19 and 25 percent from the 1850s to the 1890s and stood at 28 percent in 1900. High as it was, the male rate had at least not risen substantially. More significant were the statistics for women. During the period from 1856 to 1860, 33 percent of women accused of felonies and misdemeanors were acquitted. By 1876 or 1880 the rate had inched up to 35 percent, and by 1892 it had soared to 52 percent where it remained until 1900.

56. Hélie Courtis, *Etude médico-légale des crimes passionnels* (Toulouse: C. Dirion, 1910), pp. 10–11, 104–5.

57. Joseph Sur, *Le jury et les crimes passionnels* (Poitiers, 1908), pp. 17, 23, 29.

58. Proal, *Passion and Criminality,* p. 310.

59. Nye, *Crime, Madness, and Politics,* pp. 132–70; Duesterberg, "Criminology and the Social Order," pp. 291–356; Holtz, *Crime passionnel,* pp. 61–62, 72, 144; Debora L. Silverman, *Art Nouveau in Fin-de-Siècle France* (Berkeley: University of California Press, 1989), ch. 5.

60. Cited in Courtis, *Etude médico-légale,* pp. 57–58.

61. Ibid., pp. 69, 70, 95, 97.

62. Ibid., pp. 96–97, 69–70; Nye, *Crime, Madness, and Politics,* pp. 78–96. On Cesare Lombroso, the leader of the Italian school, see Nye, *Crime, Madness, and Politics,* ch. 4; Harris, *Murder and Madness,* pp. 81–84. For Lombroso's highly problematic views on women and crime, see Harris, *Murder and Madness,* p. 36 n.31; Jones, *Women Who Kill,* pp. 5–11.

63. Holtz, *Crimes passionnels,* pp. 10, 104.

64. *La Lanterne,* 21 July 1914. Emphasis mine.

65. *La Guerre sociale,* 22 July 1914.

66. Proal, *Passion and Criminality,* p. 292 and passim.

67. Paul Bourget, *Le démon du midi* (Paris: Plon, 1914).

68. André Gide, *Souvenirs de la cour d'assises* (Paris: Editions de la Nouvelle revue française, 1913).

69. Gide, *Souvenirs,* pp. 78–79.

70. "La réforme du jury," *Revue judiciaire,* 25 April 1914.

71. According to Pierre Prud'hon, *Le jury criminel* (Paris: Rey, 1914), p. 160, such *enquêtes* appeared in *L'Opinion, Le Journal, Gil Blas, Le Journal des*

débats, Excelsior, Le Figaro, La Revue judiciaire, Paris-Journal, L'Eclair, Les Echos parisiens, and *Le Temps,* among many others.

72. "La psychologie du jury, enquête," *L'Opinion,* 18 October 1913.

73. Ibid., 25 October 1913.

74. Sur, *Jury,* pp. 29, 32.

75. Proal, *Passion and Criminality,* p. 178.

76. On this discovery, see Henri F. Ellenberger, *The Discovery of the Unconscious: The History and Evolution of Dynamic Psychiatry* (New York: Basic Books, 1970).

77. Holtz, *Crimes passionnels,* pp. 5–6.

78. Cited in ibid., p. 67.

79. Cited in Courtis, *Etude médico-légale,* p. 70. As Courtis made clear, Ferri's work was extremely influential in France.

80. Courtis, *Etude médico-légale,* p. 102.

81. Ibid., p. 58.

82. Cited in ibid.

83. Stemming from the French Revolution, the legislation that gave birth to this code is brilliantly analyzed in Cruppi, *Cour d'assises,* pp. 31–59.

84. Sice, *Dictionnaire d'assises,* pp. 246–247. Jurors were supposed to base their judgments on "all the elements—material, moral, psychological—that emerged in each of their minds as a result of the oral arguments and discussion that took place in their presence." For an illuminating discussion of the relationship between fact and law in anthropological perspective, see Clifford Geertz, "Local Knowledge: Fact and Law in Comparative Perspective," in Geertz, *Local Knowledge* (New York: Basic Books, 1983).

85. For the revolutionaries' debates over these issues, see Emile Giraud, *L'œuvre d'organisation judiciaire de l'Assemblée nationale constituante* (Paris: Giard, 1921). Michael Fitzsimmons, *The Parisian Order of Barristers and the French Revolution* (Cambridge, Mass.: Harvard University Press, 1987), discusses the Jacobins' attack on the French legal profession.

86. Quoted in Cruppi, *Cour d'assises,* p. 35.

87. Ibid., pp. 59, 60. Harris opens her book, *Murder and Madness,* with this quote.

88. Transcript—*Le Temps,* 21 July 1914.

89. Ibid.

90. *Les Hommes du jour,* 25 July 1914.

91. Transcript—*Le Figaro,* 21 July 1914.

CHAPTER 2

1. *La Lanterne,* 22 July 1914.

2. *L'Illustration,* 25 July 1914.

3. *Le Figaro,* 22 July 1914.

4. The best recent work on the Dreyfus affair is Jean-Denis Bredin, *L'affaire* (Paris: Julliard, 1983), trans. by Jeffrey Mehlman as *The Affair: The*

Case of Alfred Dreyfus (New York: G. Braziller, 1986). On René Waldeck-Rousseau, see the exemplary biography by Pierre Sorlin, *Waldeck-Rousseau* (Paris: A. Colin, 1966).

5. On Caillaux's family and his early life, see Jean-Claude Allain, *Joseph Caillaux*, vol. 1, *Le défi victorieux, 1863–1914* (Paris: Imprimerie nationale, 1978), chs. 1–4.

6. On the *inspecteurs de finance*, see Jean-Noël Jeanneney, *L'argent caché* (Paris: Fayard, 1984), p. 111.

7. Joseph Caillaux, *Les impôts en France*, 2 vols. (Paris: Chevalier-Maresco, 1896 and 1904); John F. V. Keiger, *France and the Origins of the First World War* (London: Macmillan, 1983), p. 31.

8. Allain, *Caillaux*, vol. 1, ch. 9.

9. For this discussion of Caillaux's early political career I am indebted to Allain's *Caillaux*, esp. 1:148–67.

10. Allain, *Caillaux*, 1:160; Jean-Denis Bredin, *Joseph Caillaux* (Paris: Hachette, 1980), p. 31.

11. Alfred Fabre-Luce, *Caillaux* (Paris: Gallimard, 1933), p. 17.

12. Allain, *Caillaux*, 1:166–67.

13. Jean Morceau, "Les raisons d'une audience," *Cénomane: Nouvelle revue sarthoise*, no. 2 (Winter 1980): 4.

14. Fabre-Luce, *Caillaux*, pp. 37–39.

15. Quoted in ibid., p. 17.

16. Allain, *Caillaux*, 1:168.

17. Joseph Caillaux, *Mes mémoires*, vol. 3, *Clairvoyance et force d'âme dans les épreuves, 1912–1930* (Paris: Plon, 1947); Alexis de Tocqueville, nineteenth-century scion of one of France's venerable noble families, referred to his constituents in exactly the same way. See his *Recollections*, trans. George Lawrence (London: Macdonald, 1970).

18. Allain, *Caillaux*, 1:202.

19. For an excellent portrait of the Third Republic's political elite, see Jean Estèbe, *Les ministres de la République, 1871–1914* (Paris: Presses de la Fondation nationale des sciences politiques, 1982), pp. 79–95.

20. Quoted in Estèbe, *Ministres de la République*, p. 84.

21. On Jaurès's home life, see Harvey Goldberg, *The Life of Jean Jaurès* (Madison: University of Wisconsin Press, 1962), pp. 42, 44, 107; on Berthe Gueydan as a political spouse, see Estèbe, *Ministres de la République*, p. 83.

22. Estèbe, *Ministres de la République*, p. 83.

23. Isabelle Couturier de Chefdubois, unpublished memoir, conserved at the Fondation nationale des sciences politiques in the Emile Roche–Joseph Caillaux Archive, carton 10 (hereafter ERJC–10), dossier 2, p. 103.

24. Roger de Fleurieu, *Joseph Caillaux, au cours d'un demi-siècle d'histoire* (Paris: R. Clavreuil, 1951), p. 64.

25. Louise Weiss, *Mémoires d'une européenne* (1893–1919) (Paris: Payot, 1968), 1:175.

26. On the cultural conservatism of the Belle Epoque elite, see Jacques Chastenet, *Histoire de la Troisième République, Jours inquiets et jours sanglants*

(Paris: Hachette, 1955), 4:125–69; Madeleine Rebérioux, *La république radicale? 1898–1914* (Paris: Seuil, 1975), pp. 143–48.

27. On Raymond Poincaré, see Gordon Wright, *Raymond Poincaré and the French Presidency* (Stanford: Stanford University Press, 1942); Pierre Miquel, *Poincaré* (Paris: Fayard, 1984).

28. Estèbe, *Ministres de la République*, p. 85.

29. Caillaux, *Mes mémoires*, 3:8. Nevertheless, at the trial he took great pains to portray his marriage to Henriette as revealing a desire to conform to cultural expectations; see chapter 4.

30. *Journal officiel de la République française*, 5 July 1905.

31. Paul Vergnet, *Joseph Caillaux* (Paris: Renaissance du livre, 1918), p. 2. The first volume of Jean-Claude Allain's superb recent biography of Caillaux is subtitled *Le défi victorieux*.

32. Caillaux, *Mes mémoires*, 3:100. Caillaux quotes Jaurès as calling him "un personnage de Balzac." Paul Vergnet (*Caillaux*, p. 1) credits Jaurès with giving Caillaux the label "dandy balzacien," a label reproduced later by Jacques Chastenet, *Troisième République*, 4:83.

33. Quoted in Allain, *Caillaux*, 1:447.

34. Fleurieu, *Caillaux*, p. 175. See also Rudolph Binion, *Defeated Leaders: The Political Fate of Caillaux, Jouvenel, and Tardieu* (New York: Columbia University Press, 1960), p. 18; Bredin, *Caillaux*, pp. 8–9; Allain, *Caillaux*, 1:447–49.

35. Allain, *Caillaux*, 1:448.

36. In order, Fabre-Luce, *Caillaux*, p. 47; Allain, *Caillaux*, 1:447, 448.

37. Vergnet, *Caillaux*, p. 3; T. H. Thomas, "Caillaux," *The Atlantic Monthly* 135 (June 1925): 830.

38. *Le Bonnet rouge*, 13 December 1913, quoted in Allain, *Caillaux*, 1:466.

39. Quoted in Bredin, *Caillaux*, p. 10.

40. Vergnet, *Caillaux*, pp. 161–62.

41. Maurice Barrès, *Dans le cloaque* (Paris: Emile-Paul Frères, 1914), pp. 68, 35.

42. "Recollections set down . . ." quoted in Emile Henriot, "Les mémoires de Joseph Caillaux," in ERJC–10, dossier 2. *Ma jeunesse orgueilleuse; Mes audaces; Clairvoyance et force d'âme dans les épreuves.*

43. *La Liberté*, 30 June 1901, cited in Allain, *Caillaux*, 1:449; Pierre Bouchardon, *Souvenirs* (Paris: Albin Michel, 1953), pp. 374–75.

44. Monzie and Berl cited in Bredin, *Caillaux*, p. 11; Octave Homberg, *Les coulisses de l'histoire: souvenirs, 1898–1928* (Paris: Fayard, 1938), pp. 136–37; the German ambassador cited in Allain, *Caillaux*, 1:455.

45. On the way Caillaux's intelligence alienated those around him, see Allain, *Caillaux*, 1:452–53.

46. Ibid., 76–77.

47. Transcript—*Le Figaro*, 22 July 1914.

48. Ibid. See also Raymond Poincaré, *Au service de la France: neuf années de souvenirs, L'union sacrée* (Paris: Plon, 1927), 4:83.

49. Transcript—*Le Figaro*, 22 July 1914.

50. Joseph Caillaux, *Mes mémoires, Ma jeunesse orgueilleuse, 1863–1909* (Paris: Plon, 1942), 1:229, 83.

51. Joseph Caillaux, *Mes mémoires, Mes audaces—Agadir, 1909–1912* (Paris: Plon, 1943), 2:7.

52. Weiss, *Mémoires*, 1:174.

53. Barrès, *Dans le cloaque*, pp. 34–35. Barrès gave this description in one of a series of articles written during the proceedings of the parliamentary commission investigating the Rochette affair, a financial scandal whose connection to the Caillaux case I discuss below. As a member of the Assembly Barrès had got himself appointed to the commission, and he wrote his copy as he participated in the proceedings. Every few minutes a courier from the paper would come in to retrieve his pages.

54. Jean-Claude Allain, Caillaux's most recent and best biographer, lists all these terms in the superb concluding chapter of *Caillaux*, 1:449.

55. Poincaré, *Au service*, 4:82–84, 95.

56. This new work, mostly from the past decade or so, is elegantly summarized in Jerome Kagan, *Unstable Ideas: Temperament, Cognition, and Self* (Cambridge, Mass.: Harvard University Press, 1989), esp. ch. 3. For an excellent layman's discussion of the new research into the biochemistry of mood and mood disorders see Mark S. Gold, *The Good News about Depression* (New York: Villard Books, 1987), esp. ch. 14. See also the important work of Frederick K. Goodwin and Kay Redfield Jamison, *Manic-Depressive Illness* (New York: Oxford University Press, 1990). For an interesting journalistic account of the link between creativity and manic depression, see Gloria Hochman, "The Genius Disease," *The Philadelphia Inquirer*, 16 April 1989.

57. Transcript—*Le Figaro*, 24 July 1914.

58. Gold, *Good News*, pp. 165–89. Psychiatrists recognize two degrees of bi-polar disorders, the more severe of which is commonly known as manic depression. Caillaux most likely had the milder form.

59. For descriptions of Joseph's parents and his home life, see Caillaux, *Mes mémoires*, 1:11–89; Allain, *Caillaux*, 1:32–78; Bredin, *Caillaux*, pp. 15–29; Fabre-Luce, *Caillaux*, pp. 9–13.

60. Caillaux, *Mes mémoires*, 1:69–72, 76.

61. Ibid., 89.

62. Quoted in Allain, *Caillaux*, 1:76.

63. Caillaux, *Mes mémoires*, 1:89.

64. Quoted in Allain, *Caillaux*, 1:76.

65. Fabre-Luce, *Caillaux*, p. 38.

66. Bredin, *Caillaux*, appendix 3.

67. Caillaux, *Mes mémoires*, 1:212.

68. See Sorlin, *Waldeck-Rousseau*.

69. Fabre-Luce, *Caillaux*, p. 49.

70. With Henriette's fortune added to his own, the new prime minister more than doubled his familial holdings. On Henriette's substantial wealth, see Allain, *Caillaux*, 1:47.

71. Weiss, *Mémoires*, 1:175; Georges Suarez, *Briand* (Paris: Plon, 1938), 2:481; Binion, *Defeated Leaders*, p. 69.

72. François Piétri, "Le dernier patricien," *Encyclopédie permanente*, June 1963, p. 2023; Weiss, *Mémoires*, 1:173. See also Morceau, "Les raisons d'une audience," p. 14; Bredin, *Caillaux*, pp. 31–32.

73. Joseph Dubois, "Souvenirs sur Caillaux," *Tribune des nations*, 24 October 1947.

74. Allain, *Caillaux*, 1:122–24.

75. Jeanneney, *L'argent*, p. 115. After Caillaux's government fell over his negotiations with the Germans in the fall of 1911, Caillaux obeyed Poincaré's wish that he refrain from defending his actions in public. Caillaux later acknowledged his acquiescence to Poincaré as a grave mistake. See Caillaux, *Mes mémoires*, 3:14.

76. Quoted in Bredin, *Caillaux*, p. 156.

77. Transcript—*Le Figaro*, 22 July 1914.

78. Fabre-Luce, *Caillaux*, p. 37.

79. Ibid., p. 36.

80. Allain, *Caillaux*, 1:228–31. On the importance of indirect taxation, see Roger Magraw, *France 1815–1914* (New York: Oxford University Press, 1983), p. 365.

81. The best recent general survey of the era's republican politics is Rebérieux, *La république radicale?* See also Theodore Zeldin, *France, 1848–1945*, vol. 1 (Oxford: Clarendon Press, 1973), chs. 19–22; Claude Nicolet, *L'idée républicaine en France* (Paris: Gallimard, 1982). On the Radicals, see Serge Berstein, *Histoire du parti radical* (Paris: Presses de la Fondation nationale des sciences politiques, 1980). On efforts to achieve social reform, see Judith F. Stone, *The Search for Social Peace: Reform Legislation in France, 1890–1914* (Albany: State University of New York Press, 1985); Sanford Elwitt, *The Third Republic Defended: Bourgeois Reform in France, 1880–1914* (Baton Rouge: Louisiana State University Press, 1986). On the early efforts to enact an income tax, see Bredin, *Caillaux*, p. 45.

82. On French taxation and its history, see Jean Bouvier, *Traits généraux du système fiscal français au début du XXe siècle* (Paris: Publications de la Sorbonne, 1973); M. Frajerman and D. Winock, *Le vote de l'impôt sur le revenu* (Paris: Publications de l' A.U.D.I.R., 1973); Allain, *Caillaux*, 1:227–69; Jeanneney, *L'argent*, pt. 2, ch. 2.

83. Reactions quoted in Bredin, *Caillaux*, pp. 71–72.

84. Allain, *Caillaux*, 1:227–69, masterfully analyzes Caillaux's efforts to achieve an income tax.

85. On the extra hostility to Caillaux as a traitor to his class, see Jeanneney, *L'argent*, p. 115.

86. Bredin, *Caillaux*, p. 72.

87. Claude Pierrey, "Caillaux," *La République*, 26 March 1933.

88. Claude Digeon, *La crise allemande de la pensée française* (Paris: Presses universitaires de France, 1959); Eugen Weber, *The Nationalist Revival in France, 1905–1914* (Berkeley: University of California Press, 1968).

89. Jean-Jacques Becker, *1914: comment les Français sont entrés dans la guerre* (Paris: Presses de la Fondation nationale des sciences politiques, 1977); Keiger, *France and the Origins,* esp. pp. 74–77, 163.

90. For a fascinating and exhaustive analysis of the prewar battle over the three-year law, see Gerd Krumeich, *Armaments and Politics in France on the Eve of the First World War: The Introduction of Three-Year Conscription, 1913–1914,* trans. Stephen Conn (Dover, N.H.: Berg Publishers, 1984), pp. 87, 143–44, 174. Krumeich shows that Caillaux was careful not to oppose the three-year bill, but that even so, Poincaré desperately wanted to keep him out of government.

91. See Krumeich's powerful and convincing discussion of the significance of the new French doctrine of military offense in ibid., esp. ch. 5.

92. Quoted in ibid., p. 277 n.91.

93. Maurice Barrès, quoted in Allain, *Caillaux,* 1:467.

94. Bredin, *Caillaux,* pp. 82–83; on the Radicals in general, see Berstein, *Histoire du parti radical.*

95. The left-wing journalist Gustave Hervé, writing in *La Guerre sociale* (25–31 March 1914), declared that under present circumstances Caillaux was more important to the left than Jaurès. And rumor had it that Caillaux and Jaurès were planning a "grand ministry" devoted to peace and social justice in which the Radical leader would be prime minister and the Socialist leader foreign minister. See Charles Paix-Séailles, *Jaurès et Caillaux* (Paris: Figuière, 1914).

96. Maurice Barrès, *En regardant au fond des crevasses* (Paris: Emile-Paul Frères, 1917), p. 12.

97. Krumeich, *Armaments and Politics,* pp. 172–74.

98. This argument is taken from Krumeich (ibid.), who makes a very convincing case.

99. Keiger, *France and the Origins,* p. 142, finds the country pretty much divided in half over the law, but with only the extremes of left and right feeling very strongly about it.

100. Becker, *1914,* pp. 68–80; Keiger, *France and the Origins,* 141–42; Chastenet, *Troisième République,* 4:174: "Les récentes élections [spring 1914] ont montré que la masse française était non seulement pacifique, mais encore encline à minimiser la gravité du péril extérieur."

101. Arno J. Mayer, "Causes and Purposes of War in Europe, 1870–1956: A Research Assignment," *Journal of Modern History* 41 (1969): 291–303; Raoul Girardet, ed., *Le nationalisme français, 1871–1914* (Paris: Seuil, 1983); Digeon, *La crise allemande;* André Siegfried, *Tableau des partis en France* (Paris: Grasset, 1930).

102. Krumeich, *Armaments and Politics,* pp. 160–61.

103. Keiger, *France and the Origins,* p. 141.

104. As has been noted, Calmette presented his publication of the "Ton Jo" letter as a transgression and apologized for committing it.

105. For accounts of the press campaign against Caillaux see Allain, *Caillaux,* 1:410–24; Bredin, *Caillaux,* pp. 122–27.

106. Quoted in Bredin, *Caillaux*, p. 123.

107. Ibid.

108. The definitive work on the Agadir crisis is Jean-Claude Allain, *Agadir 1911: une crise impérialiste en Europe pour la conquête du Maroc* (Paris: Publications de la Sorbonne, 1976); see also Allain, *Caillaux*, 1:371–401.

109. Caillaux, *Mes mémoires*, 2:145, reports the exchange with Joffre, commander in chief of France's armed forces. In Joffre's own memoirs, the general confirmed the substance of this conversation: Joseph J. C. Joffre, *Mémoires du maréchal Joffre (1910–17)* (Paris: Plon, 1932), 1:15–16.

110. Keiger, *France and the Origins*, pp. 128–29.

111. Quoted in ibid., p. 35.

112. The *verts* are reproduced in Paulette Houdyer, *L'affaire Caillaux . . . ainsi finit la belle époque* (Les Sables-d'Olonne: Editions le cercle d'or, 1977), pp. 200–202.

113. Allain, *Caillaux*, 1:395–96.

114. Allain, *Caillaux*, 1:395. Allain found Lancken's dispatch exculpating Caillaux in the archives of the German foreign ministry. It was dated 31 July 1911.

115. Quoted in Keiger, *France and the Origins*, p. 139.

116. Caillaux, *Mes mémoires*, 3:108–9; Allain, *Caillaux*, 1:391; Bredin, *Caillaux*, p. 123.

117. Transcript—*Le Figaro*, 22 July 1914.

118. Keiger, *France and the Origins*, p. 140.

119. Transcript—*Le Figaro*, 23 July 1914.

120. Ibid., 22 July 1914.

121. For an excellent account of the Rochette affair see Jeanneney, *L'argent*, pt. 2, ch. 1; Allain, *Caillaux*, vol. 1, ch. 16.

122. Allain, *Caillaux*, 1:432–36.

123. Transcript—*Le Figaro*, 22 and 29 July 1914.

124. So far as I know, the German historian Gerd Krumeich was the first to make significant use of the unpublished diary as opposed to Poincaré's nine-volume published memoir, his much-rewritten version of the original diary. See Krumeich, *Armaments and Politics*, pp. 176–80. The Poincaré diaries are housed in the Bibliothèque nationale, Archives Poincaré, n.a. f. 16024–16027: notes journalières, 26 December 1912 to August 1914.

125. Instead of placing the document in the archives of the Ministry of Justice where it belonged, or submitting it to the parliamentary commission that looked into the *affaire Rochette* in 1912, Briand and then Barthou kept it for later use. See Krumeich, *Armaments and Politics*, p. 176.

126. *Le Figaro*, 10 and 12 March 1914.

127. Poincaré, *Au service*, 4:79–80; Krumeich, *Armaments and Politics*, pp. 176–77.

128. Transcript—*Le Figaro*, 22 July 1914.

129. "Jo," *L'Œuvre* 16 (16 April 1914): 591–92.

130. According to Isabelle Couturier de Chefdubois, Berthe Gueydan's

niece, Bunau-Varilla was the journalist to whom Berthe confided the original of the "Ton Jo" letter. ERJC–10, dossier 2.

131. Quoted in Krumeich, *Armaments and Politics*, p. 177.

132. Transcript—*Le Figaro*, 22 July 1914.

133. *Le Figaro*, 13 March 1914. Emphasis mine.

134. Transcript—*Le Figaro*, 22 July 1914.

135. Ibid.

136. Geneviève Tabouis, *They Called Me Cassandra* (New York: Scribner's, 1942), p. 36.

137. *Le Figaro*, 22 July 1914.

138. *Le Petit parisien*, 22 July 1914.

139. Transcript—*Le Figaro*, 22 July 1914.

140. Caillaux, *Mes mémoires*, 3:7–8.

141. Ibid., 2:241.

142. Quoted in Binion, *Defeated Leaders*, p. 80.

143. On Clemenceau, see J. Ellis, *The Early Life of Georges Clemenceau* (Lawrence: University of Kansas Press, 1980); Jean-Baptiste Duroselle, *Clemenceau* (Paris: Fayard, 1988).

CHAPTER 3

1. See the transcript of the third day in *Le Figaro*, 23 July 1914.

2. Bonnie G. Smith, *Ladies of the Leisure Class* (Princeton: Princeton University Press, 1981), ch. 6.

3. For the testimony of Labori's witnesses see the transcript—*Le Figaro*, 23 July 1914.

4. Transcript—*Le Figaro*, 22 July 1914.

5. *La Revue* 90 (March–April 1911): 587.

6. *La Petit parisien*, 18 March 1914.

7. Transcript—*Le Figaro*, 23 July 1914.

8. *Gil Blas*, 20 July 1914.

9. Transcript—*Le Figaro*, 22 July 1914.

10. Ibid.

11. Ibid.

12. Recent works by French historians touching on these issues include Yvonne Knibiehler and Catherine Fouquet, *La femme et les médicins* (Paris: Hachette, 1983); Ruth Harris, *Murder and Madness: Medicine, Law, and Society in the Fin de Siècle* (Oxford: Clarendon Press, 1989); Michelle Perrot, ed., *Une histoire des femmes est-elle possible?* (Paris: Rivages, 1984); Geneviève Gennari, *Le dossier de la femme* (Paris: Librairie académique Perrin, 1965); James McMillan, *Housewife or Harlot: The Place of Women in French Society* (Brighton: Harvester Press, 1981); Anne Martin-Fugier, *La bourgeoise: femme au temps de Paul Bourget* (Paris: Grasset, 1983). For works on the feminist movement itself, see chapter 4's notes 2, 48, and 75.

13. Charles Turgeon, *Le féminisme français* (Paris: L. Larose, 1902), 1:156–58.

14. Ibid., 1:159–63.

15. Ibid., 1:303–5. Emphasis mine.

16. Jean-Paul Nayrac, *Grandeur et misère de la femme* (Paris: A. Michelon, 1905), pp. 8, 30, 133.

17. Ibid., pp. 46–47. For other examples of similar kinds of male thinking, see Annelise Maugue, *L'identité masculine en crise* (Paris: Rivages, 1987), pp. 21–27.

18. Quoted in Nayrac, *Grandeur et misère*, p. 230.

19. Octave Mirbeau, "Propos galants sur les femmes," *Le Journal*, 1 April 1900, quoted in Maugue, *L'identité masculine*, p. 28.

20. Gennari, *Le dossier de la femme*, pp. 143–44. Jennifer Waelti-Walters, *Feminist Novelists of the Belle Epoque* (Bloomington: Indiana University Press, 1990), attempts (unsuccessfully, I think) to portray Colette Yver as a feminist; see her ch. 6.

21. Colette Yver, *Princesses de science* (Paris: Calmann-Lévy, 1907), p. 190.

22. Yver, *Princesses*, cited in Gennari, *Le dossier de la femme*, p. 143. In another of Yver's works, *Les Dames du palais* (Paris: Calmann-Lévy, 1906), the heroine is a lawyer so brilliant that she outshines her husband. The marriage suffers, and just as it is about to collapse the heroine renounces her career to become her husband's secretary. Not all of Yver's novels end so "happily." In *Les Cervelines* (The brain-women), 1908, the heroine chooses to pursue her work as an archaeologist and in doing so loses forever the man she loves.

23. Joan B. Landes, *Women and the Public Sphere in the Age of the French Revolution* (Ithaca: Cornell University Press, 1988).

24. Landes, *Women and the Public Sphere*, p. 122; Steven C. Hause, *Women's Suffrage and Social Politics in the French Third Republic* (Princeton: Princeton University Press, 1984), pp. 3–4.

25. Landes, *Women and the Public Sphere*, ch. 1.

26. Jean-Jacques Rousseau, "Letter to M. d'Alembert on the Theatre," quoted in Landes, *Women and the Public Sphere*, pp. 87–88.

27. Landes, *Women and the Public Sphere*, chs. 4 and 5.

28. Claire Goldberg Moses, *French Feminism in the Nineteenth Century* (Albany: State University of New York Press, 1984), p. 13; Hause, *Women's Suffrage*, p. 5.

29. *Feuille du salut public* quoted in Jane Abray, "Feminism and the French Revolution," *American Historical Review* 80 (1975): 50.

30. Quoted in Moses, *French Feminism*, p. 14.

31. On the concept of "republican motherhood" see Landes, *Women and the Public Sphere*, pp. 129–38. See also the lucid discussion in Bonnie G. Smith, *Changing Lives: Women in European History Since 1700* (Lexington, Mass.: D.C. Heath, 1989), pp. 103–16.

32. For an important discussion of the reception of Rousseau, though one that does not stress gender roles as much as it might, see Robert Darnton, "Readers Respond to Rousseau: The Fabrication of Romantic

Sensitivity," in *The Great Cat Massacre and Other Episodes in French Cultural History* (New York: Basic Books, 1984).

33. Quoted in Landes, *Women and the Public Sphere,* p. 144.

34. Quoted in ibid., p. 129.

35. See Smith, *Changing Lives,* p. 120.

36. See Moses, *French Feminism,* p. 245 n.16: "Le mari doit protection à sa femme, la femme obéissance à son mari."

37. Ibid.

38. For discussions of women and the Napoleonic Code, see ibid., pp. 18–20; Smith, *Changing Lives,* pp. 120–22; Zeldin, *France,* 1:343–44; Waelti-Walters, *Feminist Novelists of the Belle Epoque,* pp. 2–3.

39. Smith, *Ladies of the Leisure Class,* p. 37.

40. See Mary Poovey, *Uneven Developments: The Ideological Work of Gender in Mid-Victorian England* (Chicago: University of Chicago Press, 1988); Poovey notes that the male Victorians' desire for an antidote to economic alienation implied no criticism on their part of capitalism itself. Capitalist productivity, after all, was what made that comfortable and well-appointed home possible.

41. Ibid., pp. 10, 77–80. Though Poovey's work concerns England, much of its argument applies to France as well. For a less feminist version of this position, see Bram Dijkstra, *Idols of Perversity: Fantasies of Feminine Evil in Fin-de-Siècle Culture* (Oxford: Oxford University Press, 1986), esp. ch. 1; and Christopher Lasch, *Haven in a Heartless World* (New York: Basic Books, 1977), esp. ch. 1. Lasch maintains that men in the nineteenth century saw the family as a "haven in a heartless world," a place where they could find love and solace as an antidote to capitalism's war of all against all. See also Michelle Perrot, ed., *Histoire de la vie privée,* vol. 4, *De la Révolution à la Grande Guerre* (Paris: Seuil, 1987), esp. Catherine Hall's excellent chapter, "Sweet Home," as well as all of pt. 2, written by Perrot and Anne Martin-Fugier. For a philosophical discussion of the consequences of creating a public sphere reserved for men and a private one for women, see Jean Bethke Elshtain, *Public Man, Private Woman* (Princeton: Princeton University Press, 1981).

42. In *Ladies of the Leisure Class,* Smith structures an entire chapter (6) around the conflict of "charity versus capitalism."

43. Ibid., esp. ch. 4; Smith, *Changing Lives,* esp. pp. 183–92; McMillan, *Housewife or Harlot,* p. 32. On the care of children, see Theodore Zeldin, *France, 1848–1945* (Oxford: Clarendon Press, 1973), vol. 1, ch. 12.

44. Théodore Joran (*Le mensonge du féminisme*), quoted in Maugue, *L'identité masculine,* p. 72.

45. Quoted in Maugue, *L'identité masculine,* p. 75.

46. Linda L. Clark, *Schooling the Daughters of Marianne* (Albany: State University of New York Press, 1984), pp. 13–14. On women and public education in nineteenth-century France, see also Françoise Mayeur, *L'éducation des filles au XIXe siècle* (Paris: Hachette, 1979); Françoise Mayeur, *L'enseignement secondaire des jeunes filles sous la Troisième république* (Paris:

Presses de la Fondation nationale des sciences politiques, 1977); Jo Burr Margadant, *Madame le Professeur: Women Educators in the Third Republic* (Princeton: Princeton University Press, 1990). For other works on French public education, see Jacques Ozouf, *Nous les maîtres de l'école* (Paris: Gallimard, 1967); Mona Ozouf and Jacques Ozouf, *La classe ininterrompue: cahiers de la famille Sandre, enseignants, 1780–1860* (Paris: Hachette, 1979); Antoine Prost, *Histoire de l'enseignement en France, 1800–1967* (Paris: A. Colin, 1968).

47. Clark, *Schooling the Daughters of Marianne,* pp. 16–18. Girls' secondary schools did not prepare their students for the *baccalauréat* examination, required for all university study. Young women who sought higher education had to study for the *baccalauréat* on their own.

48. Zeldin, *France,* 1:344. Zeldin reports that of these women university students only sixty-nine received their *license,* or undergraduate degree, in 1913.

49. McMillan, *Housewife or Harlot,* pp. 56–57.

50. On the resurgence of French feminism in the last third of the nineteenth century, see Moses, *French Feminism,* ch. 9.

51. Ibid., pp. 209, 226–27; Zeldin, *France* 1:336–39.

52. Moses, *French Feminism,* pp. 229–30; Zeldin, *France,* 1:361.

53. I take up the question of how middle-class French males understood masculinity and what it was to be a man in chapter 5.

54. Poovey, *Uneven Developments,* characterizes much of the "ideological work of gender" as the construction of a static binary opposition of male and female, whose result was to maintain the privileges and prerogatives of men.

55. *Le Gaulois,* 1 January 1900.

56. Ibid. Emphasis mine.

57. Le Roux, *Un homme qui comprend les femmes* (Paris: A. Méricant, 1913), pp. 282–83. For a discussion of male fears about a new androgyny in women, see Maugue, *L'identité masculine,* pp. 85–91.

58. Le Roux, *Homme,* pp. 282–83.

59. *Action française,* 19 and 21 July 1914.

60. Transcript—*Le Figaro,* 21 July 1914.

61. Ibid.

62. *Gil Blas,* 22 July 1914.

63. *Le Petit parisien,* 17 March, 21 July 1914.

64. *Les Hommes du jour,* 25 July 1914. The notion that women were especially irrational during their menstrual periods was commonplace. See Séverin Icard, *La femme pendant la période menstruelle, essai de psychologie morbide et de médecine légale* (Paris: F. Alcan, 1890).

65. *Journal des débats,* 21 July 1914.

66. *Le Journal,* 25 March 1914.

67. *Le Miroir,* 29 March 1914. The notorious antifeminist Théodore Joran agreed with Pierre Mille that the new woman could easily become violent, and he expressed his views in his characteristically hyperbolic language. The emancipated woman, Joran wrote, acquired "a taste for carnage," for

she could no longer contain "the instincts of brutality and savagery that, in her proper state of subordination," remained suppressed. Joran (*Le suffrage des femmes*) cited in Maugue, *L'identité masculine*, p. 35.

68. Cited in Gennari, *Le dossier de la femme*, p. 135.

69. For a sense of the extent to which Pelletier departed from mainstream feminist views see Karen Offen, "Depopulation, Nationalism, and Feminism in Fin-de-siècle France," *American Historical Review* 89, no. 3 (June 1984): 673. For more extensive discussion of Pelletier's contributions to French feminism, see Marilyn J. Boxer, "When Radical and Socialist Feminism Were Joined: The Extraordinary Failure of Madeleine Pelletier," in Jane Slaughter and Robert Kern, eds., *European Women on the Left: Socialism, Feminism, and the Problems Faced by Political Women, 1880 to the Present* (Westport, Conn.: Greenwood Press, 1981); Charles Sowerwine, "Socialism, Feminism, and Violence: The Analysis of Madeleine Pelletier," in Edgar Leon Newman, ed., *Proceedings of the Western Society for French History*, 8 (Las Cruces, N.M., 1981).

70. See the commentary on *Le Figaro*'s position in *La Française*, 23 May 1914.

71. Ibid., 21 March 1914.

72. Ibid.

73. Transcript—*Le Figaro*, 21 July 1914.

74. Ibid.

75. Ibid.

76. Martin-Fugier, *Bourgeoise*, pp. 10, 182.

77. All these works were published by Flammarion in edition after edition from the 1880s on. New editions were still rolling off the presses well into the 1920s.

78. See the preface to Staffe, *The Woman in the Family*.

79. Ibid., ch. 4.

80. Caillaux family archives cited by Paulette Houdyer, *L'Affaire Caillaux . . . ainsi finit la belle époque* (Les Sables-d'Olonne: Editions le cercle d'or, 1977), p. 68.

81. See chapter 4 for Joseph's testimony comparing the feminine qualities of his two wives.

82. *Le Petit parisien*, 17 March 1914.

83. Madame Caillaux's quotations from the transcript—*Le Figaro*, 21 July 1914.

84. Cited in Martin-Fugier, *Bourgeoise*, pp. 85–86. See also Alain Corbin, *Women for Hire: Prostitution and Sexuality in France after 1850*, trans. Alan Sheridan (Cambridge, Mass.: Harvard University Press, 1990), esp. pp. 194–97; Zeldin, *France* 1:291–314.

85. Cited in Martin-Fugier, *Bourgeoise*, p. 89. For other work on sexuality and masculine fears in nineteenth-century France, see Corbin, *Women for Hire*; Corbin's contribution, "Coulisses," to the *Histoire de la vie privée*, vol. 4; and his chapter, "Le 'sexe en deuil' et l'histoire des femmes au XIXe siècle," in Michelle Perrot, ed., *Une histoire des femmes est-elle possible?* (Paris: Rivages, 1984); Robert A. Nye, "Honor, Impotence and Male Sexuality in

Nineteenth-Century French Medicine," *French Historical Studies* 16, no. 1 (Spring 1989); Angus McLaren, *Sexuality and Social Order* (New York: Holmes and Meier, 1983); Jean-Paul Aron and Roger Kempf, *La bourgeoisie, le sexe, et l'honneur* (Brussels: Editions complexe, 1984). See also Michel Foucault, *The History of Sexuality*, vol. 1, trans. Robert Hurley (New York: Pantheon, 1978); Antony Copley, *Sexual Moralities in France, 1780–1980* (New York: Routledge, 1989). On the question of sexuality and respectability in nineteenth-century Europe, see George L. Mosse, *Nationalism and Sexuality: Respectability and Abnormal Sexuality in Modern Europe* (New York: Howard Fertig, 1985). On sexuality and society in England, see Jeffrey Weeks, *Sex, Politics and Society* (New York: Longman, 1981).

86. Cited in Hubert Juin, *Le livre de Paris, 1900* (Paris: Pierre Belfond, 1977), p. 27.

87. Peter Gay, *The Bourgeois Experience*, vols. 1, 2 (New York: Oxford University Press, 1984–1986), disputes the idea that Victorian marriages were sexually repressed, basing his position on a set of intimate diaries he has found. But critics argue that Gay has not been able to show that his diarists were typical of the women and men of the era.

88. Moses, *French Feminism*, pp. 231, 278 n.5. See also Smith, *Changing Lives*, pp. 194–95; Linda Gordon, "Voluntary Motherhood: The Beginnings of Feminist Birth Control Ideas in the United States," *Feminist Studies* 1 (Winter–Spring 1973): 5–22.

89. Martin-Fugier, *Bourgeoise*, pp. 15, 80–82.

90. On adultery see Armand Lanoux, *1900: la bourgeoisie absolue* (Paris: Hachette, 1973), p. 122; Martin-Fugier, *Bourgeoise*, pp. 106–24; Alain Decaux, *Les Françaises de la belle époque* (Paris: Cercle Historia, 1975), p. 30: "Even if adultery was not practiced everywhere, it was common enough, especially among members of the bourgeoisie." For a contemporary view, see Georges Pellissier, "La femme mariée et l'adultère," *La Revue des revues* 28, no. 1 (1899): 353–68.

91. On Bourget, see Martin-Fugier, *Bourgeoise*, pp. 125–37. Martin-Fugier demonstrates the extent to which Bourget believed the sins of excess sensuality to be the woman's fault. See also Jerrold Seigel, *Bohemian Paris: Culture, Politics, and the Boundaries of Bourgeois Life, 1830–1930* (New York: Viking, 1986), pp. 70–73.

92. Louise Weiss, *Mémoires d'une européenne* (1893–1919), (Paris: Payot, 1968), 1:173.

93. Decaux, *Françaises de la belle époque*, p. 28.

94. Cited in Lanoux, *Bourgeoisie absolue*, p. 114.

95. Cited in ibid., pp. 116, 18.

96. See Gennari, *Le dossier de la femme*, p. 32.

CHAPTER 4

1. Political labels like *conservative* are by their nature imprecise. Since we are condemned to use them, we can at least broaden our definitions of the

domain of politics that envelops them; it involves much more than elections and parties, doctrines and dogmas—the traditional concerns of political historians. The realms of culture and morality are central to any understanding of politics. And for this reason we must extend our evaluation of an individual's position to views of family, gender, sexuality, education, and the like.

By my use of *conservatives* I mean those who tended to agree with the Church on moral and cultural issues, who extolled the traditional family and aimed to preserve woman's customary place in it. Intimately related to these beliefs was the conservatives' hostility to the democratic and egalitarian trappings of the Third Republic, their hatred of the revolutionary legacy of 1793. They did not necessarily oppose the republic as a form of government but rejected the "excesses" to which 1789 had been prone. Conservatives were nationalistic and more or less imbued with Germanophobia. They believed in preparing seriously for the eventuality of war. And they loathed socialism and anything that smacked of "collectivism." They could nonetheless be enlisted for projects to ameliorate working and living conditions for the poor. It was, of course, possible to be conservative on some issues and less so on others—especially when moral and cultural concerns were taken into account. But the further people were to the right of radicalism the more they fit the above definition on most counts.

Parts of this chapter first appeared as an article entitled "The Politics of Divorce in France of the Belle Epoque: The Case of Joseph and Henriette Caillaux," *American Historical Review* 93, no. 1 (February 1988): 31–55.

2. The French were obsessed with depopulation during this period, producing no fewer than eighty-two books and scores of articles on the subject between 1890 and 1914. These statistics come from Steven C. Hause, *Women's Suffrage and Social Politics in the French Third Republic* (Princeton: Princeton University Press, 1984), p. 22. See also John C. Hunter, "The Problem of the French Birth Rate on the Eve of World War I," *French Historical Studies* 2, no. 4 (Fall 1962): 490–503; Karen Offen, "Depopulation, Nationalism, and Feminism in Fin-de-siècle France," *American Historical Review* 89, no. 3 (June 1984); Robert Talmy, *Histoire du mouvement familial en France (1896–1939)* (Aubenas: Union nationale des caisses d'allocations familiales, 1962), 1:41–65. Books from the era are too numerous to list here, but the most prominent authority on the subject was Jacques Bertillon, author of *La dépopulation de la France* (Paris: Félix Alcan, 1911).

3. *Le Figaro,* 24 July 1914.

4. *Le Temps,* 25 July 1914.

5. *Journal des débats,* 25 July 1914.

6. *L'Illustration,* 1 August 1914.

7. *Les Annales politiques et littéraires,* 2 August 1914.

8. See discussion in chapter 3 and that chapter's notes 66 and 84.

9. *La Lanterne,* 24 July 1914.

10. Because Berthe Gueydan, like Henriette Caillaux, was not a public figure, no one seems to have written about her life except in connection

with the trial of Madame Caillaux. I have not been able to find a single published biographical or journalistic account of her life. Most of what can be discerned about her family background comes from the unpublished memoir written by her niece, Isabelle Couturier de Chefdubois, "Offertoire et réparation. Souvenirs et témoignages" (1966) in the Emile Roche–Joseph Caillaux Archive of the Fondation nationale des sciences politiques (hereafter ERJC–10), dossier 2.

11. Couturier de Chefdubois, "Offertoire," p. 46.

12. Bonnie G. Smith, *Ladies of the Leisure Class* (Princeton: Princeton University Press, 1981), pp. 168–76.

13. Ibid., p. 174.

14. Couturier de Chefdubois, "Offertoire," p. 48.

15. Paulette Houdyer, *L'affaire Caillaux . . . ainsi finit la belle époque* (Les Sables-d'Olonne: Editions le cercle d'or, 1977), pp. 45–46.

16. Jean-Denis Bredin, *Joseph Caillaux* (Paris: Hachette, 1980), p. 52.

17. Couturier de Chefdubois, "Offertoire," p. 49.

18. Joseph Caillaux, *Mes mémoires, Ma jeunesse orgueilleuse, 1863–1909* (Paris: Plon, 1942), 1:229.

19. Paul-Boncour wrote that Caillaux's official car was often seen "in front of those houses known for their charming women, the charming women of a happy era." Cited in Bredin, *Joseph Caillaux*, 51.

20. Caillaux, *Mes mémoires*, 1:229.

21. Journal de Magdelaine Decori (Bibliothèque nationale, n.a.f. 14768), 296; Couturier de Chefdubois, "Offertoire," p. 106.

22. Journal de Magdelaine Decori, p. 296.

23. See Houdyer, *L'affaire Caillaux*, pp. 51–53, for an excellent, if somewhat fictionalized, portrait of Berthe Gueydan.

24. *Le Petit parisien*, 24 July 1914.

25. *Le Figaro*, 24 July 1914.

26. Transcript—*Le Temps*, 24 July 1914.

27. These personal letters became part of the case's transcript. See *Le Temps*, 25 July 1914.

28. Transcript—*Le Temps*, 24 July 1914.

29. Couturier de Chefdubois, "Offertoire," p. 123.

30. For Vervoort's testimony on the fourth day, see the transcript—*Le Figaro*, 24 July 1914.

31. Ibid.

32. Transcript—*Le Temps*, 24 July 1914.

33. Ibid.

34. The refrain in a song from the era went, "Ce qu'il faut / C'est une femme douce." See Bernard Amoudru, *De Bourget à Gide: amour et famille* (Paris: Editions familiales de France, 1946), p. 42.

35. Transcript—*Le Temps*, 24 July 1914.

36. *L'Echo de Paris*, 27 July 1914. All quotes in this paragraph come from the *Echo* article except, "for something to be solid . . . institutions," which is cited in Georges Fonsegrive, *Mariage et union libre* (Paris: Plon, 1904),

p. 29. Bourget's influence as a writer was enormous; Martin-Fugier calls him "the author French women read the most." See Anne Martin-Fugier, *La bourgeoise: femme au temps de Paul Bourget* (Paris: Grasset, 1983), p. 125.

37. *L'Autorité*, 22 July 1914.

38. *La France illustreé*, 21 March 1914.

39. *Les Annales politiques et littéraires*, 29 March 1914.

40. Transcript—*Le Figaro*, 29 July 1914.

41. Alfred Naquet, *Le divorce* (Paris: E. Dentu, 1881), ch. 1.

42. Léon Richter, one of the pioneers of modern French feminism, has been credited with drafting Naquet's original divorce proposal. See Claire Goldberg Moses, *French Feminism in the Nineteenth Century* (Albany: State University of New York Press, 1984), p. 209. For discussions of France's divorce legislation of 1884, both of which appeared after this chapter was written see Roderick Phillips, *Putting Asunder: A History of Divorce in Western Society* (New York: Cambridge University Press, 1988), esp. chs. 11–12; Antony Copley, *Sexual Moralities in France, 1780–1980* (New York: Routledge, 1989), ch. 5.

43. Naquet, *Le divorce*, p. 14.

44. Jacques Desforges, "La loi Naquet," in Robert Prigent, ed., *Renouveau des idées sur la famille* (Paris: Presses universitaires de France, 1954), p. 107.

45. Quoted in Desforges, "La loi Naquet," pp. 107–8.

46. Wesley D. Camp, *Marriage and the Family in France Since the Revolution* (New York: Bookman Associates, 1961), p. 71.

47. Desforges, "La loi Naquet," p. 108.

48. For the early history of divorce in the Third Republic see Henri Le Goasquen, *Le divorce devant l'opinion, les chambres et les tribunaux* (Rennes: Bretonne, 1913). On feminism of the early Third Republic, see Laurence Klejman and Florence Rochefort, *L'égalité en marche: le féminisme sous la Troisième République* (Paris: Presses de la Fondation nationale des sciences politiques, 1989); Offen, "Depopulation"; Karen Offen, " 'First Wave' Feminism in France: New Work and Resources," *Women's Studies Quarterly* 5 (1982); and Offen's many contributions to the *Historical Dictionary of the Third French Republic* (Westport, Conn.: Greenwood Press, 1984); Patrick Kay Bidelman, *Pariahs Stand Up! The Founding of the Liberal Feminist Movement in France, 1858–1889* (Westport, Conn.: Greenwood Press, 1982); Charles Sowerwine, *Sisters or Citizens?* (Cambridge: Cambridge University Press, 1982); Maité Albistur and Daniel Armogathe, *Histoire du féminisme français* (Paris: Editions des femmes, 1977); Jean Rabaut, *Féministes à la belle époque* (Paris: Editions France-Empire, 1985); Moses, *French Feminism;* Hause, *Women's Suffrage;* and Steven C. Hause, *Hubertine Auclert: The French Suffragette* (New Haven: Yale University Press, 1987). Karen Offen's article, "The Woman Question as a Social Issue in Nineteenth-Century France: A Bibliographical Essay," *Third Republic/Troisième République* 3–4 (1977), though slightly outdated, nonetheless provides an enormously useful survey of much of this literature.

49. A characteristic, if lengthy, statement of such views can be found in Charles Turgeon, *Le féminisme français*, 2 vols. (Paris: L. Larose, 1902). Turgeon was a well-known professor of law and political economy. See Emile Faguet's critique of him in *Le féminisme* (Paris: Boivin, 1910), ch. 1. On the social and political consequences of men's rhetorical images of women, see Mary Poovey, *Uneven Developments: The Ideological Work of Gender in Mid-Victorian England* (Chicago: University of Chicago Press, 1988).

50. Other changes in women's rights within the family have already been discussed in chapter 3.

51. For the contemporary debate over what was seen as the "crisis of marriage" see Georges Art, "La crise du mariage," *La Revue bleue*, 25 September 1897; Jean Joseph-Renaud, *La faillite du mariage* and *L'union future* (Paris: Flammarion, 1899); several works by Paul Margueritte and Victor Margueritte: *Mariage et divorce* (Paris: Plon, 1900); "Enquête sur le mariage," *La Plume*, 15 April–15 June 1901; "Liberté du mariage," *La Revue socialiste*, September 1906. See also Léon Blum, *Du mariage* (Paris: Ollendorff, 1908); Paul Lapié, *La femme dans la famille* (Paris: Octave Doin, 1908). In addition, many of the *enquêtes* on divorce, analyzed below, necessarily reveal contemporary attitudes about marriage as well.

52. Offen, "Depopulation," 654.

53. Karen Offen refines and elaborates on her notion of familial feminism in "Defining Feminism: A Comparative Historical Approach," *Signs: Journal of Women in Culture and Society* 14, no. 1 (1988). Offen's important efforts to contrast what she calls "relational" feminism with "individualistic" feminism led to a pair of spirited responses from Ellen Dubois and Nancy Cott. See their commentaries and Offen's convincing answers to them in 1989 issues of *Signs*.

54. Marie Pégard, ed., *Deuxième congrès international des œuvres et institutions féminines* . . . , 4 vols. (Paris: C. Blot, 1902). See also *La Fronde*'s coverage of this event in June 1900.

55. The brothers Paul and Victor Margueritte were the tireless champions of this position and helped break open the debate with their *lettre ouverte* of 1 December 1900 to the legislature on the "imperfection of our current divorce law." See *Le Figaro*, 2 December 1900.

56. Turgeon, *Le féminisme*, 2:241. For other similar statements by conservatives see Le Goasquen, *Le divorce*, p. 189; Charles Morizot-Thibault, "La femme et le divorce," *La Réforme sociale*, 16 July 1901. Emile Faguet, who drew opposite conclusions, agreed with the conservatives' assessment of the failure of the divorce bill. See his work, *Le féminisme*, pp. 196–97.

57. Paul Margueritte and Victor Margueritte, "Mariage et divorce," *La Revue* December 1900: 449–69 and March 1901: 485–506.

58. A few of these publications are cited in note 51. See also *La Revue hebdomadaire*, *La Française*, *Le Matin*, *La Réforme sociale*, and *La Revue*.

59. Of course, Rousseau did not feel the same way about women, created, he believed, to serve men. See, for example, his novel *Emile*, trans. Barbara Foxley (New York: Dutton, 1933), pp. 324–25, 371–72.

60. All quotes in this paragraph are from Margueritte and Margueritte, "Mariage et divorce," pp. 485–98.

61. Quotes in this paragraph are from ibid., pp. 453, 468.

62. Judith F. Stone, *The Search for Social Peace: Reform Legislation in France, 1890–1914* (Albany: State University of New York Press, 1985), pp. 28–31.

63. Léon Bourgeois, quoted in Theodore Zeldin, *France, 1848–1945* (Oxford: Clarendon Press, 1973), 1:657.

64. In addition to Stone's excellent discussion of solidarism, see Sanford Elwitt, *The Third Republic Defended: Bourgeois Reform in France, 1880–1914* (Baton Rouge: Louisiana State University Press, 1986), esp. ch. 5; Zeldin, *France*, vol. 1, ch. 21; J. E. S. Hayward, "The Official Philosophy of the French Third Republic: Léon Bourgeois and Solidarism," *International Review of Social History* 6 (1961). For solidarist treatises from contemporaries, see Léon Bourgeois, *La solidarité* (Paris: A. Colin, 1896); Celestin Bouglé, *Le solidarisme* (Paris: Giard et Brière, 1907).

65. Jean Joseph-Renaud, *La faillite du mariage*, p. 41.

66. *La Plume*, 1 May 1901. M. Saint-Pol-Roux.

67. "La liberté du mariage," *La Revue socialiste*, September 1906.

68. Martin-Fugier explains that divorce stigmatized women because men tended to consider them as "marked" or possessed forever by their first husbands. See *Bourgeoise*, pp. 95–99. For statistical evidence on the male advantage with respect to remarriage, see Camp, *Marriage and the Family*, pp. 47–53. On women and work, see Louise A. Tilly and Joan W. Scott, *Women, Work, and the Family* (New York: Holt, Rinehart and Winston, 1978).

69. The male marriage rate turned upward during the Belle Epoque; save for the war years, it subsequently remained well above the nineteenth-century average. See Camp, *Marriage and the Family*, p. 37. See also Barbara Ehrenreich, who finds a more extensive masculine revolt in our own era, *The Hearts of Men: American Dreams and the Flight from Commitment* (Garden City, N.Y.: Anchor Press, 1983).

70. Quoted in Henri Coulon and René de Chavagnes, *Le mariage et le divorce de demain* (Paris: Flammarion, 1909), p. 135.

71. Margueritte and Margueritte, "Mariage et divorce," pp. 485, 497.

72. Martin-Fugier, *Bourgeoise*, pp. 10–14, 267–91.

73. On women and the civil code, see Jean Derruppé, "L'évolution du droit français de la famille du début du siècle à la guerre de 1939," in Robert Prigent, ed., *Renouveau des idées sur la famille* (Paris: Presses universitaires de France, 1954), pp. 149–60; James F. McMillan, *Housewife or Harlot: The Place of Women in French Society, 1870–1940* (Brighton: Harvester Press, 1981), pp. 25–28; Moses, *French Feminism*, pp. 229–30. For statistics on the male-female ratio of requests for divorce see Jacques Desforges, *Le divorce en France: étude démographique* (Paris: Editions familiales de France, 1947), pp. 39–40.

74. *La Française*, 30 November 1912. As noted in chapter 3, feminists and

their allies did succeed during the first decade of the twentieth century in enhancing women's marital rights.

75. Speech by Marguerite Durand, 28 February 1903, cited in Fonsegrive, *Mariage et union libre*, pp. 183–84. Not all feminists agreed, of course, with mainstream leaders like Durand and Misme. Bradamante, a journalist who contributed to *La Fronde*, supported any and all attempts to liberalize divorce, even those that might harm women in the short run. The Marguerittes cited her comments in "Mariage et divorce," p. 501. Catholic feminists such as Marie Maugeret opposed divorce altogether, while certain Protestant members of the movement expressed serious reservations. On Maugeret and Catholic feminism, see Hause, *Women's Suffrage*, pp. 64–67, 81–87; Jean Rabaut, *Histoire des féminismes français* (Paris: Editions Stock, 1978), pp. 238–39. On Protestantism and feminism, see Hause, *Women's Suffrage*, pp. 37–39, 255–59.

76. *La Française*, 30 November 1912. It should be noted that not only women expressed such reservations. The socialist historian Georges Renard feared excessive liberalization would "degenerate into the kind of freedom that enables men and women to change partners whenever their capriciousness moved them." And René Viviani, still a socialist at this point, worried that divorce at the request of one party would give undue advantage to men, whose superior financial position and employability would allow them to remarry much more easily than women. These socialist views can be found in Margueritte and Margueritte, "Mariage et divorce," pp. 495, 500.

77. The standard work on the new nationalism of the prewar years remains Eugen Weber, *The Nationalist Revival in France, 1905–1914* (Berkeley: University of California Press, 1968). See also Raoul Girardet, ed., *Le nationalisme français, 1871–1914* (Paris: Seuil, 1983), ch. 5; Jean-Jacques Becker, *1914: comment les Français sont entrés dans la guerre* (Paris: Presses de la Fondation nationale des sciences politiques, 1977), ch. 1.

78. Maurice Maindron in *La Plume*, 15 April 1901; E. Carry, *Famille et divorce* (Paris: Librairie Bloud, 1908); F. A. Vuillermet, *Le suicide d'une race* (Paris: P. Lethielleux, 1911).

79. Arvède Barine (*Le Figaro*, 2 December 1902) cited in Fonsegrive, *Mariage et union libre*, p. 169; *Fémina*, 15 October 1904; Turgeon, *Le féminisme*, 2:466.

80. Jacques Peltier, *Le divorce et la puissance paternelle* (Paris: A. Pédone, 1908).

81. Turgeon, *Le féminisme*, 2:366. I discuss other changes to the Napoleonic Code that reduced paternal authority in chapter 3.

82. Turgeon presented many of these figures in ibid., esp. 2:240–42. More complete numbers can be found in Desforges, *Le divorce*, chs. 1–4, esp. p. 54. See also Camp, *Marriage and the Family*, p. 80.

83. Desforges, *Le divorce*, pp. 172–73; Hause, *Women's Suffrage*, p. 22; Hunter, "The Problem of the French Birth Rate," p. 491.

84. See for example Louis Delzons, *La famille française* (Paris: A. Colin,

1913); Vuillermet, *Le suicide d'une race;* Henry Clément, *La dépopulation en France* (Paris: Librairie Bloud, 1910).

85. Conservatives produced some dramatic statistics to support this claim. In 1900, 44 percent of all divorced people had no children. See Fonsegrive, *Mariage et union libre,* p. 219.

86. Frédéric de France, "La question du divorce," *La Revue,* 1 March 1903, p. 528.

87. Ibid., pp. 529–39.

88. Emile Durkheim, "Le divorce par consentement mutuel," *La Revue bleue,* 5 May 1906, pp. 550–52.

89. Ibid., p. 551. See also Emile Durkheim, *Le suicide: étude de sociologie* (Paris: F. Alcan, 1897), pp. 298–300.

90. Durkheim, "Le divorce," pp. 552–53.

91. In his 1913 law thesis, "Le divorce devant l'opinion," Le Goasquen commented: "That a women's magazine largely devoted to fashion has raised the question of divorce, confirms, it seems to us, the depth and persistence of the nation's interest in this problem" (p. 209).

92. Bourget's position won by fifty-two votes. See Paul Abram, *L'évolution du mariage* (Paris: Bibliothèque internationale d'édition, 1908), p. 140.

93. The central characters in works by writers like Bourget and the Marguerittes were often women, no doubt to appeal to their mostly female readership. These social-issue novels written for women deserve much more study than they have received, but for a brilliant example of what can be done see Martin-Fugier, *Bourgeoise,* esp. pts. 2 and 4. Bourget turned *Un Divorce* into a play four years later and produced it with considerable success.

94. *Fémina,* 15 October 1904.

95. "The worth of the family is the worth of the nation." Quoted in *La Réforme sociale,* 1 April 1901, p. 404. On Cheysson, a key figure in the Belle Epoque's debate over family and society, see Elwitt, *The Third Republic Defended,* ch. 2.

96. In addition to the *enquêtes* already cited, see two law theses: Alfred Valensi, *L'application de la loi du divorce en France* (Montpellier: Messiet et Jeanjean, 1905); and Henri Rousseau, *La vulgarisation du divorce* (Poitiers: Blais et Roy, 1903); see also the religious tirade by Paul Bellée, *Du divorce au mariage* (Paris: A. Roblot, 1913). The era witnessed the pro-divorce plays of Paul Hervieu, *Les Tenailles* and *La Loi de l'homme;* the pro-family sociology of *La Réforme sociale;* and countless works of journalism such as Hugues Le Roux's *Le bilan du divorce* (Paris: Calmann Levy, 1909) and Coulon and Chavagnes's *Le mariage et le divorce de demain.*

97. Statistics for the circulation of Paris newspapers in 1910 and 1912 can be found in Claude Bellanger, ed., *Histoire générale de la presse française* (Paris: Presses universitaires de France, 1972), 3:296.

98. *Le Matin* reported this figure in its issue of 18 February 1908.

99. On the *fait divers* see Michelle Perrot, "Fait divers et histoire au XIXe siècle," *Annales: Economies, sociétés, civilisations* 38, no. 4 (1983): 911–19;

Roland Barthes, "La structure du fait divers," in *Essais critiques* (Paris: Seuil, 1964), pp. 188–98; Romi, *Histoire des faits divers* (Milan: Editions du Pont-Royal, 1962); an exhibition catalogue of the Musée national des arts et traditions populaires, "Le fait divers" (Paris, 1982).

100. *Le Matin*, 9 February 1908.

101. Ibid., 10 February 1908.

102. Ibid., 18 February 1908.

103. Ibid., 22 February 1908. Le Roux seems to have abandoned the individualist perspective that had shaped the survey itself. It should be noted in addition that *Le Matin*, surprisingly progressive on some issues, stood fast against demands for women's suffrage.

104. Amélie Gayraud, *Les jeunes filles d'aujourd'hui* (Paris: G. Oudin, 1914), pp. 48–50.

CHAPTER 5

1. On honor and society see Bertram Wyatt-Brown, *Southern Honor: Ethics and Behavior in the Old South* (New York: Oxford University Press, 1982), p. 14; Julian Pitt-Rivers, "Honor," in David L. Sills, ed., *International Encyclopedia of the Social Sciences* (New York: Macmillan, 1968) 6:503–11; Julian Pitt-Rivers, *The Fate of Shechem: or, the Politics of Sex* (Cambridge: Cambridge University Press, 1977); V. G. Kiernan, *The Duel in European History: Honour and the Reign of Aristocracy* (New York: Oxford University Press, 1988); Kenneth S. Greenberg, "The Nose, the Lie, and the Duel in the Antebellum South," *American Historical Review* 95, no. 1 (February 1990); François Billaçois, *The Duel. Its Rise and Fall in Early Modern France*, trans. Trista Selous (New Haven: Yale University Press, 1990).

2. In his famous analysis of American democracy, Tocqueville argued that status anxiety was an inescapable feature of democratic society, for the ever-present possibility of upward and downward mobility rendered all individuals insecure in their social standing. From this analysis it follows that a hybrid aristocratic-democratic order in which hierarchy remained absolutely central could engender even more status anxiety than in a more egalitarian culture such as that of the United States. See Alexis de Tocqueville, *Democracy in America*, trans. Henry Reeve (New York: Modern Library, 1981).

3. See chapter 3's discussion of editorial comment in *Le Gaulois* and surveys in *Le Matin*.

4. Wyatt-Brown, *Southern Honor*, p. 172.

5. Transcript—*Le Figaro*, 26 July 1914.

6. *Le Figaro*, 25 July 1914. Confidential government reports of this incident are housed in the Archives nationales (hereafter AN), BB[6] 11 616. Personnel director of the Paris Court of Appeals to the Premier Président of the Paris Court of Appeals, 30 July 1914. Judge Albanel maintained that the exclamation had been "Monsieur, vous nous déshonorez; vous êtes un misérable" (Monsieur, you dishonor us; you are a scoundrel), whereas

Dagoury claimed he had said, "Monsieur, vous nous déshonorez; c'est misérable" (Monsieur, you dishonor us; this is wretched).

7. AN BB⁶ 11 616. Personnel director to Premier Président, 30 July 1914.

8. AN BB⁶ 11 616. Albanel to Premier Président, 25 July 1914.

9. The subject catalogue of the Bibliothèque nationale for 1892 to 1924 contains well over one hundred entries under the headings "Duel" and "Honor." It is interesting that for the following period, 1925 to 1937, there were only a handful under the two categories.

10. Gabriel Tarde, *Etudes pénales et sociales*, pt. 1, *Le duel* (Paris: Masson, 1892), p. 77.

11. Tarde, *Etudes pénales*, p. 75.

12. Micheline Cuénin, *Le duel sous l'ancien régime* (Paris: Presses de la Renaissance, 1982), esp. pp. 307–8.

13. Eugen Weber, *France: Fin de Siècle* (Cambridge, Mass.: Harvard University Press, 1986), p. 219, reports several instances in which juries acquitted duelists who had killed their opponents.

14. *Les lois du duel* (Paris: Manzi, Joyant, 1906). The meeting with Bruneau de Laborie was reported in *Le Figaro* on 26 July 1914 and in most of the other major newspapers a day later. On Emile Bruneau de Laborie, see Pierre d'Hugues, *Bruneau de Laborie: homme d'épée, chasseur de grands fauves* (Paris: Société d'éditions géographiques, maritimes et coloniales, 1939).

15. The anthropologist Julian Pitt-Rivers explains that in societies imbued with a culture of honor, judicial solutions to the claims of honor are seldom adequate. "To go to the law for redress," writes Pitt-Rivers, "is to confess publicly that you have been wronged and the demonstration of your vulnerability places your honor in jeopardy, a jeopardy from which the 'satisfaction' of legal compensation at the hands of a secular authority hardly redeems it." See Pitt-Rivers, *The Fate of Shechem*, p. 9.

16. *Le Figaro*, 26 July 1914.

17. *Le Matin*, 26 July 1914.

18. AN BB⁶ 11 616. Dagoury to Premier Président, 29 July 1914. Emphasis mine.

19. Kiernan, *Duel*, pp. 199, 261: "France was the country of western Europe where it [the duel] was most energetically alive." See also Robert Baldick, *The Duel: A History of Dueling* (London: C. N. Potter, 1965), p. 93: In France, "as the nineteenth century wore on . . . political duels became more frequent in the civilian population."

20. Hubert Juin, *Le livre de Paris, 1900* (Paris: Pierre Belfond, 1977), pp. 52–53; Arthur Conte, *Le 1er janvier 1900* (Paris: Plon, 1975), pp. 333–34.

21. Maupassant's stories featuring the duel include "Un lâche," "Un duel," and "L'héritage." See Kiernan, *Duel*, p. 268.

22. In addition to Bruneau de Laborie, *Les lois du duel*, see Georges Bibesco and Féry d'Esclands, *Conseils pour les duels* (Paris: Lemerre, 1900).

23. Ferréus (pseud. of Edouard Dujardin), *L'annuaire du duel* (Paris: Perrin, 1891).

24. Tarde, *Etudes pénales*, pp. 31–34. Here Tarde tabulates and analyzes the information Ferréus recorded in *L'annuaire du duel*.

25. The cost of a duel was estimated by Victor Méric, "A propos d'un duel," *Les hommes du jour*, 25 December 1909. Working-class budgets can be found in Jacques Chastenet, *Histoire de la Troisième République* (Paris: Hachette, 1955), 3:337–38.

26. Quoted in Kiernan, *Duel*, p. 266.

27. On Cassagnac's duels see Ferréus, *L'annuaire du duel*; on Drumont see Claude Bellanger, ed., *Histoire générale de la presse française* (Paris: Presses universitaires de France, 1972), 3:344; for Méric, see his article, "A propos d'un duel."

28. *Le cri de Paris*, 10 May 1914; Kiernan, *Duel*, pp. 266–69; Joseph Caillaux, *Mes mémoires* (Paris: Plon, 1947), 3:147.

29. For a short biography of Prévost-Paradol, see René Mazedier, *Histoire de la presse parisienne* (Paris: Editions du pavois, 1945), pp. 125–30.

30. Lucien Anatole Prévost-Paradol, *La France nouvelle* (Paris: Michel Lévy, 1868), pp. 357, 358.

31. Emile Faguet, *La démission de la morale* (Paris: Société française d'imprimerie et de l'Académie française, 1910), pp. 307, 316, 303–4, 321. Emphasis in original.

32. Faguet, *Démission*, p. 321.

33. See the entry for Faguet in the *Dictionnaire biographique de la France*.

34. André-Jean Tudesq, *Les grands notables en France (1840–1849)*, 2 vols. (Paris: Presses universitaires de France, 1964). It is a tradition of French historiography to argue that the revolution of 1830 ushered in a "bourgeois monarchy" that ruled France in the interests of a rising commercial and industrial middle class. See, for example, Jean Lhomme, *La grande bourgeoisie au pouvoir, 1830–1880* (Paris: Presses universitaires de France, 1960); Charles Morazé, *Les bourgeois conquérants* (Paris: A. Colin, 1957); Christopher H. Johnson, "The Revolution of 1830 in French Economic History," in John M. Merriman, ed., *1830 in France* (New York: Franklin Watts, 1975). It is notable, however, that many of the historians in this tradition admit that the bourgeoisie did not rule in its own name but only indirectly through a "liberal" monarchy supposedly sympathetic to middle-class economic interests. The admission is significant in itself, but it still overlooks the overwhelming extent to which the July Monarchy's (1830–1848) parliament and high civil service was composed of members of the landed notability, not a classic bourgeoisie. On this latter point see David H. Pinkney, *The French Revolution of 1830* (Princeton: Princeton University Press, 1972); Patrick-Bernard Higonnet, "La composition de la chambre des députés de 1827 à 1831," *Revue historique* 239 (1968); Patrick-Bernard Higonnet and Trevor B. Higonnet, "Class, Corruption, and Politics in the French Chamber of Deputies, 1846–48," *French Historical Studies* 5, no. 2 (Fall 1967).

35. In Karl Marx's classic account, *The Eighteenth Brumaire of Louis Bonaparte* (New York: International Publishers, 1972), the bourgeoisie realizes

that it can hope to maintain social power only by abdicating its own class rule in favor of Louis-Napoleon Bonaparte. For a particularly incisive discussion of class and politics in Marx's writings on 1848, see Jerrold Seigel, *Marx's Fate: The Shape of a Life* (Princeton: Princeton University Press, 1978), ch. 7.

36. See David Gordon, *Merchants and Capitalists: Industrialization and Provincial Politics in Mid-Nineteenth-Century France* (Tuscaloosa: University of Alabama Press, 1985); Sanford Elwitt, *The Making of the Third Republic* (Baton Rouge: Louisiana State University Press, 1974).

37. On the social and political character of the early Third Republic, see Jean-Marie Mayeur, *Les débuts de la Troisième République (1871–1898)* (Paris: Seuil, 1973). In *Making of the Third Republic,* Elwitt considers the advent of the Third Republic something of a bourgeois revolution, one that swept farmers and petty producers along with it. But he largely overlooks the extent to which peasants and artisans, already republicanized between 1848 and 1851, embraced the Third Republic on their own terms. There is an enormous debate on the politicization of peasants during the Second Republic and its implications for the Third Republic. For surveys of the literature, see Philippe Vigier, "Un quart de siècle de recherches historiques sur la province," *Annales historiques de la Révolution française* 47 (1975); Ted W. Margadant, "Tradition and Modernity in Rural France During the Nineteenth Century," *Journal of Modern History* 41, no. 4 (December 1984); Eugen Weber, "Comment la Politique Vint aux Paysans: a Second Look at Peasant Politicization," *American Historical Review* 87 (1982); Edward Berenson, "Politics and the French Peasantry: the Debate Continues," *Social History* 12, no. 2 (May 1987).

38. On the aristocratic right of the early Third Republic, see Robert R. Locke, *French Legitimists and the Politics of Moral Order in the Early Third Republic* (Princeton: Princeton University Press, 1974).

39. On the aristocratic *ralliement* to the Third Republic, see Debora L. Silverman, *Art Nouveau in Fin-de-Siècle France* (Berkeley: University of California Press, 1989), ch. 2; Pierre Sorlin, *Waldeck-Rousseau* (Paris: A. Colin, 1966), p. 362; David Shapiro, "The *Ralliement* in the Politics of the 1890s," in *The Right in France, 1890–1919,* St. Antony's Papers no. 13 (Oxford: Oxford University Press, 1962).

40. M. Lemire, *Proposition de loi relative au duel* (Paris: Molteroz et Martinet, 1906), p. 2.

41. For the persistence of upper-class rule in Europe, see Arno J. Mayer, *The Persistence of the Old Regime* (New York: Pantheon, 1981); Martin J. Wiener, *English Culture and the Decline of the Industrial Spirit, 1850–1980* (New York: Cambridge University Press, 1981).

42. On the *grandes écoles* see Theodore Zeldin, *France, 1848–1945* (Oxford: Clarendon Press, 1977), 2:333–41.

43. The school's librarian, Lucien Herr, became notorious for converting Jean Jaurès and many other *normaliens* to his humanitarian socialist politics. See Harvey Goldberg, *The Life of Jean Jaurès* (Madison: University of Wiscon-

sin Press, 1962), pp. 62–63; Daniel Lindenberg, *Lucien Herr, le socialisme et son destin* (Paris: Calmann-Lévy, 1977).

44. On the bourgeois attraction to aristocratic styles and ideals see Mayer, *Persistence*, pp. 13–14, 104–6. See also Zeldin, *France*, 1:11–22.

45. Proust's *Remembrance of Things Past* provides an indispensable portrait of the Belle Epoque's Parisian *haut monde*. For other accounts, see Jacques Chastenet, *La belle époque* (Paris: Fayard, 1951), pp. 11–12; Cornelia Otis Skinner, *Elegant Wits and Grand Horizontals* (Boston: Houghton Mifflin, 1962), esp. ch. 3; Armand Lanoux, *1900: la bourgeoisie absolue* (Paris: Hachette, 1973), pt. 1.

46. Chastenet, *Belle époque*, pp. 12–25. Some commentators have compared the social snobbery of New York in the 1980s with the high-society life of the Belle Epoque's faubourg Saint-Germain. See Debora L. Silverman, *Selling Culture: Bloomingdale's, Diana Vreeland, and the New Aristocracy of Taste in Reagan's America* (New York: Pantheon, 1986); Tom Wolfe, *The Bonfire of the Vanities* (New York: Farrar Straus Giroux, 1987).

47. Bellanger, *Histoire générale* 3:322–23; Chastenet, *Belle époque*, p. 26.

48. Tarde, *Etudes pénales*, p. 61.

49. For an interesting—and all too rare—historical account of masculinity in the modern West, see Peter Stearns, *Be a Man! Males in Modern Society* (New York: Holmes and Meier, 1979). See also the extremely important work by Annelise Maugue, *L'identité masculine en crise* (Paris: Rivages, 1987), esp. pp. 69–77.

50. Barrès, Zola, and Faguet (*Le féminisme*) quoted in Maugue, *L'identité masculine*, p. 73.

51. L. Jeudon, *La morale de l'honneur* (Paris: Félix Alcan, 1911), pp. 73, 79. Emphasis in original.

52. Ibid., pp. 95–99, 120.

53. Ibid., p. 124.

54. Tarde, *Etudes pénales*, p. 61.

55. Alfred von Bogulawski (*Die Ehre und das Duell*, 1896) quoted in Robert de Herte, "Le duel et l'éthique de l'honneur," *Etudes et recherches* 2 (1983): 6.

56. Emmanuel Lasserre, *Les délinquants passionnels et le criminaliste Impollomeni* (Paris: Félix Alcan, 1908), p. 98.

57. Méric, "A propos d'un duel."

58. *Le Gaulois*, 1 January 1900.

59. F. A. Vuillermet, *Soyez des hommes: à la conquête de la virilité* (Paris: P. Lethielleux, 1909), pp. 12, 248, 251.

60. G. Letainturier-Fradin, *L'honneur et le duel* (Paris: Flammarion, 1897), pp. 55, 62. On the growing interest in sports during the Belle Epoque, see Weber, *France: Fin de Siècle*, pp. 217–33; Robert A. Nye, *Crime, Madness, and Politics in Modern France* (Princeton: Princeton University Press, 1984), ch. 9.

61. Tarde, *Etudes pénales*, p. 69.

62. Anonymous, *Deux vieilles questions: 1. La question du duel, 2. La question juive* (Paris: Berger-Levrault, 1905). It was not that dueling had

vanished from military mores in this period, only a "combative virility." Duels between soldiers were a normal part of military service; enlisted men, as well as officers, could be reprimanded for refusing to fight one. Writing in *L'Eveil démocratique* (17 February 1907), Marc Sangnier told of an army corporal whose captain and colonel had both made it clear that his military career would be finished if he refused to duel.

63. Déroulède quoted in Jean-Denis Bredin, *L'affaire* (Paris: Julliard, 1983), p. 26.

64. Quoted in Paul Bénichou, *Les mages romantiques* (Paris: Gallimard, 1988), p. 182. I have profited enormously from Bénichou's penetrating discussion of Vigny's morality of honor. It is interesting that this historian, writing in 1988, does not quote the words "pudeur virile," while those who discussed Vigny during the Belle Epoque featured them. See Jeudon, *Morale*, p. 133; G. LeBidois, *L'honneur au miroir de nos lettres* (Paris: Garnier, 1919), p. 344. LeBidois's work appears to have been written mostly in 1914.

65. Jeudon, *Morale*, pp. 117–19.

66. Ibid., p. 173.

67. See chapter 3's discussion of morality and the separation of spheres.

68. For evidence of Jeudon's pro-Dreyfus position, see *Morale*, pp. 124–25.

69. Bruneau de Laborie, *Les lois du duel*, pp. 14–15, 24.

70. Ibid., p. 23.

71. See Sanford Elwitt, *The Third Republic Defended* (Baton Rouge: Louisiana State University Press, 1986). Despite the "conservative" interest in social reform that Elwitt has uncovered, France was notorious for its inability and unwillingness to take even the hesitant steps toward welfare capitalism evident in the United States, Germany, and England.

72. Debora L. Silverman, "The Paris Exhibition of 1889: Architecture and the Crisis of Individualism," *Oppositions* 8 (Spring 1977); and *Art Nouveau*, esp. chs. 1 and 15.

73. Quoted in Silverman, *Art Nouveau*, pp. 4, 5–7.

74. Ibid., p. 293.

75. On Haussmann's efforts to transform a quasi-medieval city of 1850 into a modern commercial capital of the fin de siècle, see David H. Pinkney, *Napoleon III and the Rebuilding of Paris* (Princeton: Princeton University Press, 1972); Jeanne Gaillard, *Paris, la ville 1852–1870* (Lille-Paris: Honoré Champion, 1977); Philip G. Nord, *Paris Shopkeepers and the Politics of Resentment* (Princeton: Princeton University Press, 1986), esp. ch. 3; T. J. Clark, *The Painting of Modern Life* (New York: Knopf, 1984), esp. ch. 1; Norma Evenson, *Paris: A Century of Change, 1878–1978* (New Haven: Yale University Press, 1979), esp. ch. 2.

76. Silverman, *Art Nouveau*, ch. 4.

77. On the reaction against Haussmannization, see Clark, *Painting*, ch. 1.

78. For reactions from middle-class male republicans, see Silverman, *Art Nouveau*, ch. 4.

79. Le comte Estève, *Le duel devant les idées modernes* (Paris: Société française d'imprimerie et de librairie, 1908), pp. 208–9.

80. Faguet, *Démission*, p. 316.

81. Bruneau de Laborie, *Les lois du duel*, pp. 19, 16.

82. On the view of the Belle Epoque as a culture of hermaphrodites, see the discussion in chapter 3 of Le Roux's survey and Hugues Le Roux, *Un homme qui comprend les femmes* (Paris: A. Méricant, 1913), pp. 269–86.

83. *Le Petit parisien*, 25 March 1914. Emphasis mine.

84. Ibid., 26 March 1914.

85. Transcript—*Le Temps*, 21 July 1914.

86. Chastenet, *Belle époque*, p. 137.

87. Transcript—*Le Figaro*, 21 July 1914.

88. *Le Matin*, 20 July 1914.

89. *La Lanterne*, 23 July 1914.

90. *La Guerre sociale*, 16–24 March 1914.

91. Transcript—*Le Figaro*, 22 July 1914.

92. Ibid., 23 July 1914.

93. This anecdote is reported, unfortunately without attribution, in Paulette Houdyer, *L'affaire Caillaux . . . ainsi finit la belle époque* (Les Sables-d'Olonne: Editions le cercle d'or, 1977), p. 104.

94. *Le Figaro*, 20 July 1914.

95. Caillaux, *Mes mémoires*, 3:113.

96. Transcript—*Le Figaro*, 22 July 1914.

97. On civic republicanism see J. G. A. Pocock, *The Machiavellian Moment: Florentine Political Thought and the Atlantic Republican Tradition* (Princeton: Princeton University Press, 1975). In his memoirs, Caillaux presented himself not as a politician but as a servant of the nation's finances. Caillaux, *Mes mémoires*, 2:40.

98. Jules Delahaye quoted in *Un livre noir: diplomatie d'avant guerre d'après les documents des archives russes* (Paris: Librairie du travail, 1923), 2:253; article by Lucien Descaves, *Le Journal*, 25 March 1914.

99. As it was, the contrast between the assassination of Calmette and the duel with d'Allières provoked journalistic sarcasm. Following Joseph's duel, which took place just a few weeks after Henriette's attack, the morning papers exclaimed, "Elle tire mieux que lui" (She shoots better than he does).

100. Transcript—*Le Figaro*, 25 July 1914.

101. Transcript—*Le Temps*, 29 July 1914.

102. Transcript—*Le Figaro*, 28 July 1914.

103. Ibid.

104. *Le Figaro*, 28 July 1914.

105. Charles Péguy, *Note conjointe sur M. Descartes et la philosophie cartésienne*, in *Œuvres complètes* (Paris: Editions de la Nouvelle revue française, 1924), 9:147.

106. Herte, "Le duel et l'éthique," p. 4.

107. Péguy, *Note conjointe*, 9:152, 154, 158, 155.

108. Ibid., p. 158.

CHAPTER 6

1. The letters are reproduced in the transcript—*Le Figaro*, 26 July 1914.

2. Claude Bellanger, ed., *Histoire générale de la presse française* (Paris: Presses universitaires de France, 1972), 3:297.

3. Foucault's writings on the subject were collected and translated into English in a volume edited by Colin Gordon: Michel Foucault, *Power/Knowledge: Selected Interviews and Other Writings, 1972–77* (New York: Pantheon, 1980); see also Mark Poster, *Foucault, Marxism, and History* (New York: Basil Blackwell, 1984).

4. Michel Foucault, *Birth of the Clinic*, trans. Alan Sheridan (New York: Pantheon, 1973); *Discipline and Punish*, trans. Alan Sheridan (New York: Pantheon, 1977); *Les machines à guérir (aux origines de l'hôpital moderne)* (Paris: Institut de l'environnement, 1976).

5. Michel Foucault, *The History of Sexuality*, vol. 1, trans. Robert Hurley (New York: Pantheon, 1978).

6. For *enquêtes* on the jury system, see chapter 1; on divorce, see chapter 4; on women and feminism see chapter 3 and the *enquête* sponsored in 1913 by *L'Opinion* and published by Amélie Gayraud, *Les jeunes filles d'aujourd'hui* (Paris: G. Oudin, 1914). The famous Agathon survey that revealed young and elite French men as deeply nationalistic had itself been published by *L'Opinion* in 1912. The *Petit parisien* sponsored a referendum on capital punishment in 1907, and the *Journal* surveyed opinion on the question of women's suffrage in the spring of 1914.

7. On the popular literature of the era, see Anne-Marie Thiesse, *Le roman du quotidien* (Paris: Le chemin vert, 1984); Patrick Dumont, *Etude de mentalité: la petite bourgeoisie vue à travers les contes quotidiens du journal (1894–1895)* (Paris: Aux lettres modernes, 1973).

8. Michael B. Palmer, *Des petits journaux aux grandes agences: naissance du journalisme moderne* (Paris: Aubier, 1983), p. 26.

9. Ibid., p. 27.

10. The *Petit parisien's* survey on capital punishment found 1,083,000 votes in favor and 327,000 against.

11. Bellanger, *Histoire générale*, 3:257; Madeleine Rebérioux, *La république radicale? 1898–1914* (Paris: Seuil, 1975), p. 146; Pierre Sorlin, *Waldeck-Rousseau* (Paris: A. Colin, 1966); Pierre Sorlin, *La Croix et les juifs (1880–1899)* (Paris: Grasset, 1967); Jeannine Vergès-Leroux, *Scandale financier et antisémitisme catholique: le krach de l'Union générale* (Paris: Le Centurion, 1969).

12. In *Les Thibault*, Martin du Gard's hero, the intellectual socialist Jacques Thibault, regularly refers to the press as the bulwark of capitalism. For the anti-Semitic view, see Paul Soleilhac, *Le grand levier, ou de la presse et de son influence politique et sociale à notre époque* (Paris: Blériot, 1906). The preface to this work is by the notorious anti-Semite Edouard Drumont.

13. The list of diatribes against the press as an all-powerful source of evil is endless in this period. See for example: Georges Maze-Sencier, *Le role*

social et moral de la presse (Paris: P. Lethielleux, 1911); Augustin Lémann, *Un fléau plus redoutable que la guerre, la peste, la famine* (Paris: Vitte, 1908).

14. Séverin Icard, "De la contagion du crime et du suicide par la presse," *La nouvelle revue*, 15 April 1902, p. 5. Icard was a man of considerable standing in the medical community, a laureate of the Académie des sciences and a member of the prestigious Institut de France.

15. Quoted in Jacques Pigelet, *Organisation intérieure de la presse périodique française* (Orleans: P. Pigelet, 1909), p. 132.

16. Icard, "Contagion," p. 9. Emphasis in original. This view enjoyed considerable longevity, in France and elsewhere. Marshall McLuhan quotes a Minneapolis police chief who was overjoyed that his city had been without a newspaper for several months in 1962. "Sure I miss the news," he declared, "but so far as my job goes I hope the papers never come back. There is less crime around without a newspaper to pass around the ideas." Marshall McLuhan, *Understanding Media* (New York: Signet, 1964), p. 183.

17. Hippolyte Bernheim, *De la suggestion dans l'état hypnotique et dans l'état de veille* (Paris: Octave Doin, 1884). Bernheim's collaborator, Jules Liégeois, extended Bernheim's views directly into the realm of criminology in his *De la suggestion et du somnambulisme dans leurs rapports avec la jurisprudence* (Paris: Octave Doin, 1889). The eminent psychologist Pierre Janet provided an excellent overview of the literature on suggestion in *L'automatisme psychologique* (Paris: Félix Alcan, 1889), ch. 3. See also Emile Laurent, *Les suggestions criminelles* (Paris: Société d'éditions scientifiques, 1891). For excellent discussions of Bernheim and the questions he raised see Debora L. Silverman, *Art Nouveau in Fin-de-Siècle France* (Berkeley: University of California Press, 1989), pp. 83–88; Ruth Harris, "Murder under hypnosis in the case of Gabrielle Bompard: psychiatry in the courtroom in Belle Epoque Paris," in W. F. Bynum, Roy Porter, and Michael Shepherd, eds., *The Anatomy of Madness* (London: Tavistock Publications, 1985), pp. 207–10 and passim; Susanna Barrows, *Distorting Mirrors: Visions of the Crowd in Late Nineteenth-Century France* (New Haven: Yale University Press, 1981), pp. 119–25.

18. The case of Gabrielle Bompard, analyzed by Ruth Harris in "Murder under hypnosis" is the most prominent among them.

19. Transcript—*Le Figaro*, 21 July 1914.

20. Icard, "Contagion," pp. 12, 13.

21. Henry du Roure, *La presse d'aujourd'hui et la presse de demain* (Paris: Au Sillon, 1908), pp. 14–15. On Marc Sangnier's Sillon, a movement fascinating in itself, see Paul Cohen, "Heroes and Dilettantes: The Action française, Le Sillon, and the Generation of 1905–14," *French Historical Studies* 15, no. 4 (Fall 1988).

22. Roure, *Presse d'aujourd'hui*, p. 15.

23. See the penetrating discussion of Bergson's *Essai sur les données immédiates de la conscience* (1889) in Silverman, *Art Nouveau*, pp. 89–90.

24. Roure, *Presse d'aujourd'hui*, p. 16.

25. See Jacques Kayser, *Le quotidien français* (Paris: A. Colin, 1963);

Madeleine Varin d'Ainvelle, *La presse en France: genèse et évolution de ses fonctions psycho-sociales* (Paris: Presses universitaires de France, 1965), p. 208.

26. In *La presse en France*, pp. 209–10, Varin d'Ainvelle quotes Kayser's phrase, "la fait diversification de la politique." See also Jean Stoetzel, "Fonctions de la presse: à côté de l'information," *Etudes de presse* 3 (15 July 1951).

27. *Le Temps*, for example, produced a supplement containing the trial transcript for the duration of the case.

28. Jean-Jacques Becker, *1914: comment les Français sont entrés dans la guerre* (Paris: Presses de la Fondation nationale des sciences politiques, 1977), pp. 131–36. The papers he analyzed are *Le Temps*, *L'Humanité*, *L'Echo de Paris*, and *Le Petit parisien* from Paris, and *L'Est républicain* and *Le Petit dauphinois* from the provinces.

29. The exception is Monday 27 July, when there was no news of the trial to report since the court had not been in session on Sunday.

30. Bellanger, *Histoire générale*, 3:122.

31. *La Presse*, 21 July 1914.

32. *La Croix*, 26 July 1914.

33. Biographical information on Calmette is surprisingly slim. The main sources are an entry in the *Dictionnaire biographique de la France* and a polemical *hommage* to Calmette written shortly after his death by a leading journalist for *Le Figaro*. See Raymond Recouly, *Gaston Calmette: une campagne politique, ses raisons—ses résultats* (Paris: Plon, 1914). Some discussion of Calmette's family can be found in a book devoted to his brother Albert, famous for a series of medical discoveries. See Noël Bernard, *La vie et l'œuvre de Albert Calmette* (Paris: Albin Michel, 1961).

34. Recouly, *Gaston Calmette*, p. 7.

35. The story of *Le Figaro*'s political and financial troubles and of Calmette's ascension to its leadership is reported in Bellanger, *Histoire générale*, 3:347–51.

36. Circulation figures for all the major Paris papers can be found in Archives nationales F^7 12842.

37. Quoted in Bellanger, *Histoire générale*, 3:350.

38. Arthur Conte, *Le 1er janvier 1900* (Paris: Plon, 1975), p. 332.

39. Ibid.

40. Recouly, *Gaston Calmette*, p. 8.

41. Raymond Poincaré, *Au service de la France: neuf années de souvenirs* (Paris: Plon, 1927), 4:30.

42. Quoted in Jean-Claude Allain, *Joseph Caillaux* (Paris: Imprimerie nationale, 1978), 1:423.

43. Caillaux, in his intervention on the trial's third day, quoted from an article Calmette had written to this effect. Transcript—*Le Figaro*, 23 July 1914.

44. Alain Decaux, "L'honneur de Mme Caillaux," in the Emile Roche–

Joseph Caillaux Archive of the Fondation nationale des sciences politiques (hereafter ERJC–10), dossier 2.

45. Recouly, *Calmette*, p. 4.

46. Bellanger, *Histoire générale*, 3:348–50.

47. Archives in Berne, Switzerland (E 2001 [D] a I). Report of the Swiss ambassador in Paris, 17 March 1914.

48. *Le Figaro*, 29 July 1914; Charles-Maurice Chenu, *Le procès de Madame Caillaux* (Paris: Fayard, 1960), p. 188.

49. See discussion of Poincaré's military policy and its accompanying domestic politics in chapter 2; the relevant notes are 90 and 91.

50. For an excellent general account of the French press in the early nineteenth century, see Claude Bellanger, ed., *Histoire générale de la presse française*, vol. 2 (Paris: Presses universitaires de France, 1969); for a discussion of working people's access to the political press, see Edward Berenson, *Populist Religion and Left-Wing Politics in France, 1830–1852* (Princeton: Princeton University Press, 1984), chs. 5–7.

51. On Emile de Girardin, see René Mazedier, *Histoire de la presse parisienne* (Paris: Editions du pavois, 1945), pp. 84–102; Bellanger, *Histoire générale*, 2:114–20; Joanna Richardson, "Emile de Girardin, 1806–1881: The Popular Press in France," *History Today* 26 (1976): 813; David H. Pinkney, *The Decisive Years in France, 1840–1847* (Princeton: Princeton University Press, 1986), pp. 121–22; Theodore Zeldin, *France, 1848–1945* (Oxford: Clarendon Press, 1977), 2:494–97.

52. Perhaps the only reliable gauge of literacy rates—though it unfortunately excludes women—that extends from the early nineteenth century on is the information gathered each year from France's class of potential draftees. In 1832, a year before primary education became compulsory, some 53 percent of young men eligible for the military draft were illiterate. By 1872 the figure had dropped to a mere 8.5 percent, and by 1914 to under 4 percent. See Bellanger, *Histoire générale*, 3:142. Most historians of the subject believe that women's literacy rates lagged behind men's until the early twentieth century, when women joined men in nearly universal literacy. See François Furet and Jacques Ozouf, *Lire et écrire* (Paris: Editions de minuit, 1977).

53. Palmer, *Petits journaux*, pp. 23–24.

54. No full-fledged study of *Le Petit journal* exists, but a number of scholars have devoted some important pages to its history. See Roger Bellet, *Presse et journalisme sous le Second Empire* (Paris: A. Colin, 1967); Michael B. Palmer, "*Le Petit journal* et les débuts de la Troisième République," *Presse et politique* 1 (1973); Palmer, *Petits journaux*, pp. 23–40; Mazedier, *Presse parisienne*, pp. 131–39; Bellanger, *Histoire générale*, 3:220–22. For other works on the press of the Third Republic, see Raymond Manevy, *La presse de la IIIe République* (Paris: Joseph Foret, 1955); Raymond Manevy, *L'évolution des formules de présentation de la presse quotidienne* (Paris: Editions Estienne, 1958), ch. 2; L. Gabriel-Robinet, *Journaux et journalistes* (Paris: Hachette, 1962), chs. 5–8.

55. For one sou's percentage of a worker's wage, see Palmer, *Petits journaux*, p. 270 n.3. The newspaper's price in relative terms during the Belle Epoque and in 1980 is given in Thiesse, *Le roman*, p. 17.

56. Micheline Dupuy, *Le Petit parisien* (Paris: Plon, 1989), p. 30.

57. Bellanger, *Histoire générale*, 3:301.

58. See Geneviève Bollème, *Les almanacs populaires aux XVIIe et XVIIIe siècles* (Paris: Mouton, 1971); Geneviève Bollème, *La bibliothèque bleue: littérature populaire en France du XVIIe au XIXe siècle* (Paris: Julliard, 1971); see Eugen Weber, *Peasants into Frenchmen* (Stanford: Stanford University Press, 1976), p. 464 and passim, for a discussion of this popular literature and of the *Petit journal*'s success in perfecting the techniques of the older *canards* or lowbrow newssheets.

59. *Le Petit journal* (8 June 1866) cited in Palmer, *Petits journaux*, p. 24.

60. Urbain Desvaux (*Les lecteurs du journal à un sou*, 1868) cited in ibid., pp. 33–34.

61. Ibid., p. 26.

62. Ibid., p. 31. For an excellent discussion of the Troppmann affair see Michelle Perrot, "L'affaire Troppmann," *L'Histoire*, 30 January 1981. See also Michelle Perrot, "Fait divers et histoire au XIXe siècle," *Annales: Economies, sociétés, civilisations* 38, no. 4 (1983): 914.

63. James Moran, *Printing Presses: History and Development from the Fifteenth Century to Modern Times* (Berkeley: University of California Press, 1973), p. 125.

64. Bellanger, *Histoire générale*, 3:82–83.

65. Ibid., pp. 84–94.

66. Ibid., p. 72; Pigelet, *Organisation intérieure*, p. 95.

67. Berenson, *Populist Religion*, ch. 5.

68. Bellanger, *Histoire générale* 3:297–98.

69. Francine Amaury, *Histoire du plus grand quotidien de la IIIe République: Le Petit parisien, 1876–1944* (Paris: Presses universitaires de France, 1972), 1:374; Pigelet, *Organisation intérieure*, p. 91.

70. Bellanger, *Histoire générale*, 3: 302; Amaury, *Histoire du plus grand quotidien*, 1:472.

71. For copies of the *Petit parisien* in which the contest was advertised, see Amaury, *Histoire du plus grand quotidien*.

72. Circulation figures in Bellanger, *Histoire générale*, 3:297.

73. Varin d'Ainvelle, *La presse en France*, p. 221.

74. Quoted in Bellanger, *Histoire générale*, 3:263.

75. For Guesde's quote, see Arthur Raffalovitch, *L'abominable vénalité de la presse* (Paris: Librairie du travail, 1931), p. xi. In *Histoire générale*, 3:268 Bellanger lists Panama payments, and circulation figures on pp. 195, 235, 353.

76. Bellanger, *Histoire générale*, 3:271.

77. Cited in ibid., p. 272.

78. Caillaux also insinuated that Calmette had begun to violate French national interests as far back as 1902 when he became *Le Figaro*'s direc-

tor. The Radical leader testified that Calmette had conspired with his father-in-law, Georges Prestat, to attract new capital for the paper not from French investors but from German banks. Already, Caillaux suggested, Calmette had made himself beholden to tainted foreign money. See transcript—*Le Figaro,* 28 July 1914.

79. Allain, *Caillaux,* 1:438–39.
80. Transcript—*Le Figaro,* 22 July 1914.
81. Ibid.
82. Ibid.
83. Ibid., 28 July 1914.
84. Ibid.

EPILOGUE

1. Transcript—*Le Figaro,* 29 July 1914.
2. Ibid., 30 July 1914.
3. Ibid.
4. Geneviève Tabouis, *They Called Me Cassandra* (New York: Scribner's, 1942), p. 36.
5. Decisions in the *Cour d'assises* were made by majority vote of the twelve jurors. Unanimity was not required. For the jury's vote, see Benjamin F. Martin, *The Hypocrisy of Justice in the Belle Epoch* (Baton Rouge: Louisiana State University Press, 1984), p. 206.
6. See the reports in *Le Figaro, Le Temps,* and other papers on 29 July 1914.
7. Jean-Denis Bredin, *Joseph Caillaux* (Paris: Hachette, 1980), p. 145; Jean-Claude Allain, *Joseph Caillaux* (Paris: Imprimerie nationale, 1978), 1:443. The murderous intentions of Villain are confirmed by Jean-Antoine Calvet, *Visages d'un demi-siècle* (Paris: Grasset, 1958), p. 59.
8. So maintains his biographer Allain, *Caillaux,* 1:443.
9. Maurice Barrès (*Mes cahiers,* 1939) quoted in Bredin, *Caillaux,* p. 173.
10. Joseph Caillaux, *Mes mémoires, Clairvoyance et force d'âme dans les épreuves, 1912–1930* (Paris: Plon, 1947), 3:152. It is true that this information comes from Joseph Caillaux himself, but historians have tended to believe in its accuracy because Poincaré never contradicted it. See Bredin, *Caillaux,* p. 137.
11. *Action française* (6 October 1920) quoted in Bredin, *Caillaux,* pp. 171–72.
12. Rudolph Binion, *Defeated Leaders: The Political Fate of Caillaux, Jouvenel, and Tardieu* (New York: Columbia University Press, 1960), p. 108.
13. Isabelle Couturier de Chefdubois, "Offertoire et réparation. Souvenirs et témoignages" (1966) in the Emile Roche–Joseph Caillaux Archive of the Fondation nationale des sciences politiques (hereafter ERJC–10), dossier 2, p. 132.
14. On Caillaux's later career, see Bredin, *Caillaux,* chs. 26–45; Allain,

Caillaux, vol. 2; Alfred Fabre-Luce, *Caillaux* (Paris: Gallimard, 1933), pp. 121–273; Binion, *Defeated Leaders*, pp. 71–116.

15. Barthou's death was tragic; he succumbed to an assassin's bullet in 1934.

16. Allain, *Caillaux*, 2:26.

17. Fabre-Luce, *Caillaux*, p. 192.

18. See the evidence for Joseph Caillaux's extramarital affairs in the 1920s in ERJC–10, dossier 2, Rose Deschamps-Deshayes to Emile Roche.

19. Henriette Caillaux, *Dalou (1832–1912): l'homme—l'œuvre* (Paris: Delagrave, 1935). ERJC–9, dossier 1; Allain, *Caillaux*, 2:515.

20. ERJC–9, dossier 1, Emile Roche to Georges Duhamel, 29 November 1935.

21. Quoted in Allain, *Caillaux*, 2:480. Upper case as in original.

22. Couturier de Chefdubois, "Offertoire," p. 49.

23. Berthe Gueydan, *Les rois de la République*, 2 vols. (Paris: Perrin, 1925).

Index

Compositor:	Keystone Typesetting, Inc.
Text:	10/13 Palatino
Display:	Palatino
Printer:	Maple-Vail Book Mfg. Group
Binder:	Maple-Vail Book Mfg. Group